THE GREATEST ESCAPE

THE GREATEST ESCAPE

NEIL CHURCHES

WITH EDMUND GOLDRICK

MACMILLAN

First published 2022 by Macmillan
an imprint of Pan Macmillan
The Smithson, 6 Briset Street, London EC1M 5NR
EU representative: Macmillan Publishers Ireland Ltd, 1st Floor,
The Liffey Trust Centre, 117–126 Sheriff Street Upper,
Dublin 1, D01 YC43
Associated companies throughout the world
www.panmacmillan.com

ISBNs: 978-1-5290-6033-1 and 978-1-5290-6034-8

1 3 5 7 9 8 6 4 2

A CIP catalogue record for this book is available from the British Library.

Map artwork by Neil Churches

Typeset in Janson Text LT Std by Jouve (UK), Milton Keynes
Printed and bound by CPI Group (UK) Ltd, Croydon, CR0 4YY

Visit **www.panmacmillan.com** to read more about all our books
and to buy them. You will also find features, author interviews and
news of any author events, and you can sign up for e-newsletters
so that you're always first to hear about our new releases.

For Lucy

A note on Slovenian pronunciation

The Slovenian language uses the Latin alphabet. There are some differences from English in pronunciation.

C is pronounced ts
  ('Latsko' is written 'Lacko')

Č is pronounced ch
  ('Cholnik' is written 'Čolnik' and 'Semich' is written 'Semič')

Š is pronounced sh
  ('Shentilj' is written 'Šentilj')

Ž is pronounced zh
  ('Ozhbalt' is written 'Ožbalt')

Contents

Prologue   1

PART ONE

1. **Setting the Stage**   9
2. **Becoming a Soldier**   22
3. **Greece**   27

PART TWO

4. **Debacle**   35
5. **Stragglers**   40
6. **Rowing to Crete**   47
7. **Captive**   52
8. **The Corinth Cage**   57
9. **Surviving to Thessaloniki**   62
10. **The Train to Maribor**   68
11. **Occupation**   72
12. **All-You-Can-Eat Potatoes**   80
13. **Farmhand**   86

CONTENTS

14. **Resistance** 95

15. **Thoughts of Escape** 101

16. **The Extermination Camp** 105

17. **Vengeance** 111

PART THREE

18. **The Crow** 119

19. **El-Alamein, Stalingrad, and Slovenia** 125

20. **In the Papers** 129

21. **The First Spies** 134

22. **The Combine** 139

23. **The Greatest Show in Maribor** 144

24. **The March of the 14th Division** 152

25. **Bombs and Recreation** 159

26. **Thieves and Traitors** 165

27. **Looking for the Connection** 172

28. **The Escape Network** 177

29. **A Partisan Agent** 185

30. **The Battle of Savinja Valley** 193

PART FOUR

31. **Getting Away** 199

32. **Meeting the Partisans** 203

33. **Dutch Courage** 207

34. **The Raid at Ožbalt** 214

35. **Into the Mountains** 222

CONTENTS

36. **Across the Sava** 237

37. **The Chance to Become a Spy** 250

38. **Base 212** 256

39. **The Journey Home** 265

40. **Greater Escapes?** 274

41. **The War's End** 281

Epilogue 286

Appendix 299

Notes 305

Bibliography 337

Acknowledgements 353

Image Credits 355

Prologue

Sydney, Australia, in late spring. Standing at the door is a tall stranger, asking for my father. It's 1972, a Saturday afternoon; Dad is playing golf. Mum is out the back, gardening. It's left to me to tear myself away from Tolkien and answer the door. I am fourteen. A man is waiting there, dressed to the nines: a grey silk suit, sky blue tie, tailored shirt, and Italian shoes. His grey hair and moustache are perfectly groomed, his nails manicured.

I've met many well-dressed salesmen by now; our house is often full of them, drinking, smoking, dancing, telling unlikely stories, paying court to my father. This man is not like that. The stranger is quiet, with an edge of nervousness.

'I am calling to see Mr Ralph Churches.' His accent is middle European.

Mr Churches is playing golf, I explain – might be out for a while.

'I wish to wait for him.'

I'm now beyond my pay grade. I bolt through the house and down the stairs to the garden. 'Mum, there's this guy with an accent looking for Dad. He wants to wait until Dad gets back.'

From then on, it is Mum's show: the polite enquiries and rituals of welcome – the weather, coffee, or tea? – while the stranger perches on the edge of his chair, ready to spring up. Fascinated, I hang around. This is far more interesting than Frodo moaning through Mordor.

Half an hour later, we hear Dad's car turn into the drive. He must have won, as he is singing to himself in German. The key turns in the door; the stranger is on his feet. Unsettled, he is feeling all his pockets, as though he has lost something. Mum goes to the door and has a quiet word with Dad. By the time Dad enters the living room, the stranger has relaxed again. In his hand, he holds a small black-and-white photograph showing a column of men climbing a hill. The stranger reaches out his other hand. The handshake is firm, his eyes intense.

'Ralph, it's Čolo. I've been looking for you for over twenty-five years.'

Dad processes, brightens, then roars with delight. A bear hug turns into a shuffling dance. Mum brings out three glasses of *slivovica*. Čolo gives the photo to Ralph, my dad.

'That's me on the left, Švejk, Franjo, then you and Les.'

The party that follows lasts two days, Dad insisting that Čolo stays with us. It is during these two days of revels that I hear the ridiculous news. My boisterous, sarcastic father is a secret hero.

The story comes out in fits and starts. The photo: Dad has seen it before; Mum has seen it before. It shows a young version of Dad, wearing a slouch hat, in a pine forest. There are at least fifty men strung out down a hill behind him. Dad won't give a straight answer to any of my questions, but Čolo and Mum become a double act to line up the bones of the past. Dad fleshes out a detail here and there. A lot of it sails straight over my fourteen-year-old head. I knew that Dad had been in the army during the war. That was the limit of my knowledge.

That day I learned that the Germans captured him in Greece. Why he had been in Greece was a mystery to me. He was held as a prisoner of war in a camp in what I knew as Yugoslavia. With his gift for mimicry, he taught himself German and was elected camp leader, negotiating on behalf of his fellow prisoners. He escaped, and in some woods came upon Partisans who were fighting against the Germans. He persuaded them to come back with him and liberate his camp. Then, a real adventure began. The photograph Čolo brought had been taken during the escape.

The whole episode was an official secret, and Dad was under orders not to talk about it. Čolo was one of the Partisans who had helped Dad: he *was* free to talk.

Now the last six months made sense! Over the previous winter Dad and Mum had taken their first long-haul trip together. He took three months' long-service leave for a tour: Greece, Yugoslavia, Germany, France, and the UK. I'd stayed behind with Dad's eldest surviving sister Claire.

Before his apprehension, villagers in Greece had helped Dad evade capture by the Germans, so on their grand tour Dad and Mum had thrown a thank-you party in every Greek village that had sheltered him. The Yugoslav consul in Sydney had given Dad introductions to officials in Yugoslavia, which enabled Dad to be reunited with the Partisans who had helped him all those years ago. The food, wine, stories, and dancing had gone on for days.

In the three months since they'd returned, the family diet had changed. Mum now made salads with feta cheese and olives; she cooked garlic lamb. We had bottles of imported mineral water at the table; Dad was barbecuing *ćevapi*, rich Balkan minced sausages.

During all these reunions one person had been missing. Even though he was a Partisan war hero, Čolo had fallen foul of the post-war regime in Yugoslavia and fled via Austria, settling in Melbourne in 1947. There he had established a thriving market garden and nursery and become a wealthy man. In 1972, by now an affluent Australian citizen, he'd decided he could now go back and visit his family. There he'd renewed many friendships, which had eventually led to an extraordinary conversation with his old comrades.

'I've been looking all over Australia for Ralph Churches, but I'm damned if I can find him . . .'

There was an outburst of laughter.

'Why are you laughing?'

'Ralph and his wife were here a week ago! Here's his address!'

So Čolo came to our front door, and I left Middle Earth.

In 1977 my parents returned to Yugoslavia for another round of parties. Then, in 1985, Yugoslav television wanted to make a documentary about the escape story. With Australia's SBS TV they developed the story, and then they approached Dad. Sorry, he told them: he was still bound by the Official Secrets Act. Eventually, after some negotiation between SBS and the Australian Army, Dad was allowed a special release to talk about his experiences. Later, I began to nag Dad to write his story down for his family, and the memoir he wrote became a book, *A Hundred Miles as the Crow Flies*. Dad made some enquiries of the Australian and UK authorities to clarify some details, but although he was now free to speak, officialdom would not, which he found incredibly frustrating.

Now some official records have opened a little, and more of the story can be written. Given Dad's capacity for elaboration,

I expected to be correcting his narrative. However, extraordinary research by Edmund Goldrick through the UK National Archives, and those of Slovenia, Australia, and New Zealand, shows I was wrong to doubt Dad. Edmund and I have pieced together evidence of a wild adventure, even though some details are still classified – Dad was true to his word to protect official secrets to the end. His yarn made Tolkien's words pale for a fourteen-year-old boy in 1972. How a bloke from the Australian bush charmed his way out of prison, and then went back for his mates.

PART ONE

1

Setting the Stage

Ralph Churches worked hard to put his farming childhood behind him. He did not talk of it much and he was not interested in nostalgic visits to where he began life. He enjoyed camping expeditions in the Australian wilderness but avoided anything agricultural that wasn't a vineyard. Most Australians of his generation were urban and dreamed of life 'in the bush', but Ralph knew 'the bush' well and wanted to put himself as far as he could from it. He took pride in being a multilingual sophisticated European bourgeois. He created that identity through one escape after another, the first being from his roots.

In the 1850s, my great-grandfather Samuel Churches emigrated from the Somerset Levels in England. He chased his fortune in the Australian gold rushes and found it supplying provisions to the miners. Having become prosperous, he settled in the plains north of Adelaide, South Australia, where he built a significant business of four grocery and butcher shops. His eldest son James was the foreman and expected to inherit, but Sam had other ideas, and on his death in 1900 the business and property were split between his four sons. None of Sam's sons could match their father's success; each sold up and moved on.

James was the last to go. The outbreak of war in 1914 pushed his business in the small town of Mallala, north of Adelaide, to the wall. By 1915, James and his wife Emily found themselves nearly bankrupt, and turned to bush farming to scratch out an existence, selling up and moving to the arid scrubby plains of the Murray Mallee. It was a rather drastic move, from Mallala to a half-cleared Mallee farm near Kulkami. Ralph was born in Lameroo hospital in November 1917, the youngest of four boys and four girls, and before he was seven the family had moved twice more, each time to a smaller farm. The Churches scratched a living from livestock pasture until enough land could be cleared of stubborn mallee roots to sow grain. They ended up on half-cleared land near South Parilla, which was nothing more than a general store and a scatter of buildings, though James soon organized his oldest sons to carve a perfect bitumen tennis court out of the scrub.

They may have been a low-income family, but the Churches' homestead was now a social hub for the region. James was the local champion, even in his late fifties the mainstay of the local football and cricket teams, as well as the pub's chief raconteur and arbiter of sport. Emily, a forceful personality, keenly felt the family's loss of income and status since leaving Mallala and was determined that her children should do well in life. She encouraged all her children, but Ralph was her favourite. He was also treated by his two elder sisters Rita and Clare, seventeen and fifteen years older than he, as their favourite pet, which was a source of resentment for the other children. Ralph was anxious and shy, with a significant stammer that he learned to master. Throughout his life it would emerge at points of high stress or fatigue. Emily instilled in him a thirst to improve his lot and had him learning to read long before he went to school.

Map I. South Australia

Ralph had started school in September 1923 at Kulkami, a few kilometres from where they lived, but when the family moved to South Parilla there was a hitch. Allenby School was eighteen kilometres away. It took over an hour to travel there by pony trap and on the way Ralph's brothers were merciless: he was not Ralph; he was 'The Runt'. Verbal and physical humiliations were habitual. They encouraged their two younger sisters to join in, and the journey to and from school became a daily torture. To survive the family pressure Ralph pushed himself to upstage everyone in everything: school, sport, and style. Ralph alone had combed hair and a blazer in his primary school photo. Teased about it, he didn't care; he would be better than them.

The family were Anglican churchgoers, but tolerant in their religious faith and 'showed respect to any bloke with his collar turned back to front'.[1] The different clergy who moved around the area would call by once a month or so to the little galvanized-iron building that served as a school, church, and dance hall. Someone different turned up every week to take the services. As Emily was the only keyboard player for miles, she pedalled the little harmonium and played the hymns for the congregation. Ralph stood beside his mother turning the sheet music, which she had taught him to read. Ralph became an accomplished singer through accompanying her. Music, reading, and religion were his foundations.

At the age of seven, Ralph found himself on a stock drive with his brothers, walking from the town of Keith to the new farm at South Parilla. His only shoes were for school – the family couldn't afford a second pair – so he drove sheep, for a whole week, 130 kilometres, in bare feet. That was when Ralph decided a life on the farm was not for him.

He began to plan. In the early mornings and evenings, he would roam the paddocks carrying two hessian sacks. In one he would put wool that had been caught on branches and barbed wire; in the other, animal bones. It gave him a pretext to escape his brothers as much as he could and be alone with his thoughts. When the bags were full, he would walk to the Parilla railway siding, where each bag earned him a shilling from the local stock agent: the train would carry the sacks to Adelaide, where the bones became fertilizer, the wool became felt. His escape fund had begun.

By now Ralph's eldest sister Rita had married. Her husband, Jack Bowden, was a farmer near Kainton, 400 kilometres away. Rita had survived rheumatic fever in her early teens, which had left her heart damaged, and she and Jack needed some help with childminding their new daughter, so she offered to have Ralph move to York Peninsula with them. The local schoolteacher had an excellent reputation and Ralph could complete his primary education free of his tormentors. The surrounding countryside was more fertile; life was pleasant. It was 1927; he had two good years, flourishing at school and making friends.

Late October 1929 gave Ralph an unpleasant early twelfth birthday present. Wall Street crashed. His parents' farm at Mallee was already struggling and they needed his help there. His mother presented him with a stark choice: he had to win a scholarship to Adelaide High School or return to the family farm as an unpaid labourer. Thirty pounds a year for two years was on offer annually to six rural boys, and Ralph made sure he won a scholarship. It covered board and lodging but not the cost of textbooks or stationery. His family couldn't pay for his books, but his escape fund did: the years of gathering bones and wool meant Ralph had enough.

His mother arranged to board him with a friend from her youth. Her house was near South Terrace, in the poor heart of Adelaide, and from there, for two years, he went to Adelaide High School. The world he entered was not one of dazzling city lights. Fewer than 40,000 people lived in Adelaide at the time, and the nearest large settlement was over 600 kilometres away, in Victoria.[2] The Great Depression had hit Australia hard, more than any developed country besides Germany, and of all Australia's cities Adelaide was worst affected. Two years into the crisis, one in three Adelaide residents had no work and no income.[3] Many lived in crude shelters dug out of a rubbish tip along the Torrens River.[4] Ralph knew genteel poverty well, but not this kind of utter destitution. On the farm, if they were short of food, they could shoot a rabbit.

But Adelaide High School proved an oasis amid the poverty. The youngest and smallest in his class, bullied once more, this time as the country bumpkin, Ralph learned to hide his Mallee upbringing. He even changed his name: he was still Ralph to his family, but at school he was now Rory. Rory was always better groomed than his peers, his uniform always immaculate. He got good reports, was placed in the top stream, played well in all the sporting teams as opening batsman, ruckman, striker, and earned for himself a grudging respect.

Then, of course, the two years ran out, and all he had was an Intermediate Certificate. He wanted to matriculate; he might yet get to university. But there was no more money, and there were no further scholarships. A high-school family took him for a year as a non-paying guest in exchange for him informally tutoring their son. Rory managed to get his Leaving Certificate, which should have offered him matriculation, but his results weren't up to the standard required for someone of his social status. At the time it was notoriously difficult for a member of the working class to enter a university – most university admissions were granted to private grammar school boys from the 'Old Adelaide Families' (known to the rest of the city as the OAFs). After a Mallee Christmas he returned to Adelaide, where he had persuaded another family to have a live-in tutor for a year while

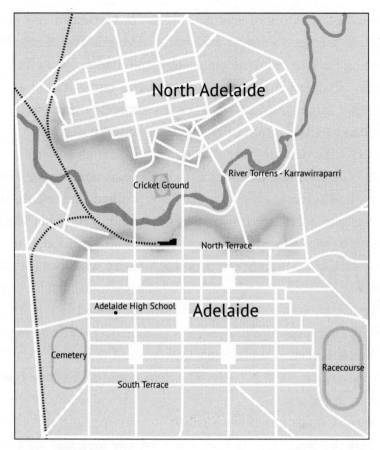

Map 2. Adelaide, 1930

he repeated his matriculation studies. He was in time to watch the 'Bodyline' cricket Test match and witness the near riot when Bert Oldfield copped a fractured skull. Rory read more than the sports pages, and when Hitler came to power in Germany in January 1933, Ralph wrote to his mother saying what bad news it was, but nobody else saw it that way.

This time 'Rory' got a high credit in history, but it still didn't help him much. This was now late 1933, and the depth of the economic crisis; there was no way he could afford university even if he secured admission. Ralph loved his family, but the idea of going back to the farm and doing unpaid work filled him with dread. He spent the Christmas holidays writing letters to any firm that might need a clerk – eighty-three of them, each with two handwritten copies of character references.

Finally, he struck a bargain with a family friend in North Adelaide called Frank. An electrical engineer struggling for work, Frank had taken to shoe repairs. Rory proposed door-knocking for business in return for 20 per cent of any sales. He rode his bicycle to the mansions of North Adelaide. He knocked on the front door of the first house he tried. A butler answered the door in tails.

'Yes?'

Rory began his pitch.

'Not here, boy – trades' entrance, around the side.'

Rory went around the side. The door opened, the same butler, now in shirtsleeves.

'Righto, mate, what's your story?'

He gave Rory a trial with some of the servants' footwear, then the family's. Soon the butler had become an ally, teaching Rory the manners of the well-to-do. With encouragement, Ralph learned to soften his Mallee twang: when required, he could switch to Old Adelaide posh. On a good day, putting on his school tie and 'Old Adelaide', Rory would get shoes from several families. Within six weeks, he was making three pounds a week, an astonishing sum in 1935 for an unqualified seventeen-year-old.

Then Ralph's father, now past sixty, decided that he was too old for heavy farm work, and so James and Emily sold the farm and retired to the city. In his mother's eyes, shoe sales lacked prestige, so Emily persuaded Ralph to apply for a job at the State Bank. Rural Australians had a high regard for bank workers at that time: bank clerks handled money, possessed good arithmetic skills, and were considered trustworthy. However, of all the banks, the State Bank was the poorest. Rory got the job, but took an eye-watering two-thirds drop in income. The party in Adelaide was over. For the last two months of 1935, Ralph stayed with his parents in the new suburb of Flinders Park while completing the bank's clerical training.

In January 1936 the State Bank transferred Ralph to its branch in Renmark on the Murray River. In a new town, he introduced himself as Rory once more. He developed a taste for beer, spirits if he was flush, wine if he couldn't afford beer. Rory had very little in the way of brass in his pocket: by the time he'd paid twenty-five shillings a week board out of his weekly wage of thirty-two shillings, it was hard going.

He was there for twelve months until a road trip with colleagues to see the cricket in Adelaide went wrong: on the return journey their soft-top car skidded and rolled off a causeway near Blanchetown. Everyone escaped with minor injuries, except Rory: Ralph was in Waikerie hospital for six weeks with significant head injuries. Discharged, disoriented, and confused, he couldn't go back to work. Ralph recuperated with his parents without pay for two months, and that ended Rory.

In May 1936 he was fit to return to the bank and was sent to Wudinna on the Eyre Peninsula, boarding a boat to Port Lincoln, then a day-long train ride to the west. Though it was on the frontier of viable agricultural territory, Wudinna had once been prosperous, serving as a fuelling stop for planes between

Perth and Adelaide. But now the flights didn't need a pit stop, and the town was hard-up.

Ralph was quick to make friends and drinking buddies, most of all with Ted Wreford and Tom Patrick. Tom was a young Methodist minister who had arrived in Wudinna, his first posting, on a motorcycle with his luggage in the sidecar. He did his parish rounds on his motorbike. Ted Wreford was the junior clerk for the rival bank across the street, and he and Ralph would spend hours cycling together at weekends. Both Ralph and Ted had trouble paying their boarding house rent on their small salaries; Tom had a large manse to himself, so he invited Ted and Ralph to move in, and the manse became an unlikely lads' house. Ralph took over the amateur dramatic society, opened for the Wudinna cricket team, was ruckman for the Aussie rules football team in winter, and represented the town in the inter-club tennis league. He even persuaded Tom and Ted to dig a swimming hole for the town with him.

In September 1937, Ralph was bowling leg-spin for Wudinna's cricket team at Cootra, a dusty collection of farms eighty kilometres south-east of Wudinna with a parched oval and a matting wicket. Two tall and attractive young women were doing the scoring, and while he was fielding Ralph teased them about Cootra's paltry total. They turned out to be sisters. The taller of them was called Olive, born in 1919, the year of peace, into a family of nine children and, like many other girls, sick of rural life. Like Ralph, she was the only one of her family to attend high school, also at Adelaide High. When it was Cootra's turn to bowl Olive became so frustrated by the lack of progress that she took to the field as a fast bowler herself – and annihilated half of Wudinna's batting order. Only Ralph could withstand her assault. He was smitten.

Tom had a circuit to follow, taking church services to isolated communities every Sunday. These tiny towns had no choirs, so Ralph suggested to Tom that he needed an extra voice to lead the singing, and soon found himself slumped, hungover, in the side-car early every Sunday morning as Tom rode through big-sky country towards one of these remote churches. Once a month, that circuit took him to Cootra, where Olive's mother Muriel, like Ralph's, was the organist and leading parishioner.

The two young men got to know Olive and her family well. Her father, Jasper, was dour, hard, blind in one eye, and prosperous, the absolute opposite of Ralph's father James. Jasper and his three sons were all enormous – even the youngest, 'Shorty', was six feet tall. It baffled Olive's parents that their daughter took a liking to this junior clerk, but over the next two years they met in dance halls, on tennis courts, at dusty ovals, and every month Tom made sure to have long conversations at the church door with every single member of the parish so that Olive and Ralph had time to talk down the road. But Ralph and Olive – or Ronte, the family nickname she preferred to be called – knew that marriage was not an affordable option on a junior bank clerk's pay. They were going to have to plan for the long term.

Meanwhile life went on. Ralph organized the local dramatics society into the Wudinna Vaudevillians Revue and booked the hall in Streaky Bay, the big town 150 kilometres away. He knew Ronte's family would come to see it. The show they put on, with twenty songs, sketches, and playlets, was the hit of the Agricultural Show weekend.

Ralph would rage about the danger of Hitler and the Nazis to anyone who would listen, be it his bank colleagues, Ronte's family, the cricket team, or the regulars at the Wudinna pub. In late 1938 the Czechoslovakian crisis came and went: the area of Czechoslovakia primarily inhabited by ethnic Germans, Sudetenland, was handed over to the Reich. Ralph felt ashamed of the Western democracies and their appeasement of Hitler. A year later, on a Sunday evening in the manse, Ralph, Ted, and Tom heard Neville Chamberlain on the radio declaring war on Germany. The radio then immediately broadcast Australian Prime Minister Robert Menzies announcing, 'Fellow Australians, it is my melancholy duty to inform you officially that in consequence of a persistence by Germany in her invasion of Poland, Great Britain has declared war upon her and that, as a result, Australia is also at war.' There was no patriotic rush to enlist. Few of the early Australian Imperial Force (AIF) dispatched to Europe were idealists. Most were sick of unemployment or dull work at low pay.* The force was purely volunteers, intended specifically for overseas service, and its members had to be at least turning twenty-one.

Then came 1940. Germany's armies were smashing through Denmark, Norway, Belgium, the Netherlands, and France. All eyes in Wudinna were on Ralph. He hated violence, having experienced more than his fair share at his brothers' and schoolmates' hands, but he'd banged on about Hitler for a long time, and he now believed people thought he ought to sign up and were saying, 'He's not married . . . he's been going on about doing something for long enough . . .'

A mixture of idealism and peer pressure saw Ralph enlist, along with tens of thousands of others shocked by the Allied

---

* The Second AIF's pay was notoriously poor. An unmarried private made less than the dole, but he did get food and shelter.

collapse in Europe. Ralph's head injuries should have disquali-
fied him but the alcoholic local doctor, another friend, ignored
the injuries and gave him a clean bill of health. He also gave
Ralph the keys to his car: 'Go out to Cootra on Sunday and say
goodbye to that girl of yours.'[5]

Ralph told Ronte and her family that he was enlisting, and that
it wouldn't be fair on her to wait for his return. There could be
no immediate future for them if he went off to Europe. It didn't
work out quite like that. Ralph and Ronte both burst into tears,
and somehow a break-up became a marriage proposal. Ralph
signed his enlistment papers on 29 May 1940, just as the UK
began the evacuation from Dunkirk. Tom sorted a fast marriage
licence and, ten days later, both families travelled to Adelaide for
a June wedding in a shoebox church. It was the last time Ralph's
family were all together.

2

Becoming a Soldier

Ralph made his oath to the King and collected his uniform on 24 June. He'd joined the 2/43rd Battalion of the AIF, but when he learned Ted and Tom were in the 2/48th he succeeded in getting a transfer. With a few months' training they progressed from marching practice with broom handles for rifles in the Adelaide Showgrounds to bayonet practice in the local park. Weekend visits to Ronte were like gold dust, but Ralph had only a short stint as a footslogger. He had far more education than most enlisted men, and battalion staff picked Ralph out and sent him to train as a mapmaker. Private Churches became the map specialist for A Company, 2/48th Battalion, and so a very junior member of military intelligence. Other privates, with less education, but taller heads and broader shoulders, were being raised to sergeant, and then commissioned as officers, with more pay.

Every soldier got six days pre-embarkation leave, and when he received the call, Ralph spent a few days at a seaside guest-house with Ronte, then went by train to Rita's farm, which he had promised to visit before he left the country. Rita had been a second mother to him, protecting Ralph from his brothers and the world beyond. Her heart had become much weaker in the past few years. When it was time to leave, Ralph said, 'Well, I'll see you when I come back, darling.'

'Oh, Ralph,' she said. 'I don't think so.'[1]

Ronte took the impending departure of her husband quite philosophically. Ralph's parents had retired and moved to Adelaide, so Ronte found work at a munitions factory there and moved in with them. 'In truth, I didn't know Ralph when we got married,' she admitted later. 'He seemed nice – but he was my ticket off the farm.'[2] Ralph had married a kindred spirit.

He said his last farewell and marched in the parade to Port Adelaide. On Sunday 17 November 1940, they boarded the *Stratheden*, a luxury liner that had been gutted to be a troopship. Ralph was well down below the waterline in hammocks, but if he didn't like the hammock, he could sleep up on deck in the open air. The *Stratheden* pulled out in the early hours of the next day and steamed to Fremantle. They remained there for six days due to a German merchant raider scare in the Indian Ocean. Then they headed north-west until they reached port at Colombo. Ralph had a day's leave: a ride in a rickshaw, and a curry – food hotter than he'd ever tasted before. No matter how much he had read, he was still a boy from the Mallee. Everything about Ceylon (modern-day Sri Lanka) was exotic to Ralph, yet (apart from the heat) his barracks, Galle Face Green, was very British. On the next leg of the journey Ralph had a first taste of what might lie ahead. During the nights, as they crossed the Arabian Sea, some unpleasant sergeants disappeared overboard – a story he told later in life, still shocked at some of his comrades' behaviour.

Arriving at the Red Sea strait of Bab-el-Mandeb, Ralph had his next sight of land; he could see the coastline on either side of the ship: Somaliland to one side, Yemen the other. The

Stratheden sailed right up to the northern entrance of the Suez Canal, El-Qantara, and there they disembarked and got on a train that took them to Dimra in Palestine. There, practical combat training began.

Ralph's war then separated from the mates he had made the previous July. He was transferred on temporary secondment to Corps Headquarters just outside Alexandria in Egypt, and never returned to his battalion. Now he was a clerk for the Allies' North Africa campaign to push the Italians back west along the Mediterranean coastline. His job was to correct the existing military maps of the Western Desert, Egypt, and the two provinces

Map 3. The Mediterranean, 1941

of Libya the Allies had advanced in to. It was a long way from parading with broom handles at the Adelaide Showgrounds.

After a few weeks at Corps HQ, he was sent to Marsa Matruh, a dowdy Egyptian port halfway along the coast between Alexandria and Tobruk, which was now the British headquarters. Here Ralph became a driver. In civilian life his boss, the Captain, was a licensed surveyor in Sydney; Ralph described him as the wildest man he ever met.* The days became just the two of them, in a small Chevrolet half-truck, driving the stony desert on surveying missions, usually on goat tracks, far from the coast, camping under the African stars. Often Ralph didn't know whether he was behind the enemy line or not.

The recent British advance had captured over 200,000 Italian prisoners of war. They didn't want to fight, and many spoke excellent English as a result of living in the USA before the war. This gave Ralph his first experience of a phenomenon he would call 'the eternal Yank': wherever you were in the world, there would be someone speaking English with an American accent. He got talking to a group of prisoners who were being kept occupied digging a trench in the desert, then filling it in again. 'Well, look,' an Italian captain said to him, 'if you want to scrap over all this rock and rubble here, be my guest. But you know, I've got Mum and the kids back home, and we're not interested. I mean, we know you are civilized people and we'll get back after the war, but we're not fighting. It's Mussolini's idea.'³ Ralph knew many of his mates thought of the Italians as cowards. He

---

* No amount of research has established a name for this wild captain. Ralph did not, or would not, recall his name.

didn't; he was sure it would be different if they were fighting for the defence of their homeland.

At this time, Ralph drove immense distances in Northern Africa: out into the desert with the Captain, then back to HQ to pass on their mapping intelligence. He would never know accurate details, but at HQ he could track his old battalion and find out what his mates were doing and roughly where they were. They were advancing in their training but had not been moved to the front line yet. Knowing these vague details enabled him still to feel connected to them and wonder what they were going through.

Then the orders changed. Ralph and the Captain were to finish all calculation and mapping details and leave. Ralph packed and drove the long stretch back to the docks of Alexandria, where Brits, Kiwis, Aussies, Cypriots, and Palestinians were loading into ships. There were so many rumours. Was it Syria, Cyprus, Crete? Most troops agreed Greece was the destination.

3

Greece

Corps Headquarters and the AIF 6th Division were indeed going to Greece. They would be part of Operation Lustre: a plan to move around 58,000 troops from Egypt to Greece in March and April 1941.

The Greeks were fighting the Italians, who had invaded at the end of October 1940. The Italian attack was Mussolini's way of asserting his independence when Hitler failed to consult him before German troops entered Romania. It had the potential to satisfy Mussolini's unfulfilled ambition to dominate the Balkans.[1] But in heavy rains the Italian advance had bogged down after only a week, and by late November Greece had begun a counter-offensive. Britain occupied the island of Crete to allow Greek forces there to leave and move to the front further north, but this only made Hitler worry that the RAF would be within range to strike at the precious oilfields Germany had just occupied in Romania.[2] From their cracking of German codes the British knew that the German High Command was planning a spring invasion of Greece. By mid-January 1941 Churchill, under the impression that if the British were in Greece, Turkey would join them, had ordered the British Middle East Commander-in-Chief Archie Wavell to send what forces he could.[3]

The British had learned from their mistakes in France, where messy chains of command had sabotaged operations. Now all Allied forces in Greece would be under a single commander-in-chief. That man was to be General Papagos, who was already in command of the Greek Army. It seemed a sensible choice: pick the man who already knew the fight. Churchill believed the campaign would be popular in neutral America. The Greek counter-offensive was front-page news for *The New York Times* on six days in one week of November 1940. Britain was also coming to the aid of the Greeks when the Lend-Lease Act, vital to reducing Britain's crippling supply issues, was about to face the US Senate.

From 4 March, a series of convoys at regular three-day intervals moved from Alexandria to Athens, with Royal Navy and Royal Australian Navy warships providing an escort. This deployment included the British 1st Armoured Brigade, the New Zealand 2nd Division,* and the Australian 6th Division. On 26 March 1941, British, Australian, and New Zealander logistics staff, with Ralph, the Captain, and the Chevy truck among them, crammed aboard six hulking transport ships and left on the high tide after dark. Most of the combat troops had gone in the preceding weeks.[4] Logistical staff usually went ahead of a force, not after it; Ralph thought it was odd, but he buried these doubts for now.

Ralph's ship was full to bursting, the cabins crowded and noisy – he was hardly able to breathe, let alone move. Standing on deck provided fresh air but was often as crowded as inside. He found himself among elements of the 6th Division, a

---

* At this point still called 'the New Zealand Division' of the 2nd New Zealand Expeditionary Force.

battle-seasoned group from New South Wales and Victoria. Its soldiers had a harder edge to their humour and conversation. Ralph was now grateful for the two months he had been able to spend with the Captain: they had prepared him for these big-city blokes from Sydney and Melbourne. He and thousands of others had to sweat, chat, and stew for three days. There was a mixture of excitement and fear in the convoy: excitement that 'Lusterforce' would fight alongside the Greeks, legendary after their victories over the Italians; fear that the undefeated *Wehrmacht* (German armed forces) would destroy them.

The Greek and Italian lines had stabilized in Albania to the north-west, and it was expected that Germany would attack from the north-east via Bulgaria. The British wanted Papagos to withdraw some of his forces and establish a short defensive line further south, near Mount Olympus. There the Greco-British force could hold if the Germans smashed through the border defences.[5] However, the prestige of besting Mussolini had swollen Papagos's head. He committed, irrationally, to defending that prestige instead of Greece. Papagos wrote, '[We] decided that in the event of a German intervention . . . the Greek Army should not jeopardize its position as victor in the fight against the Italians.'[6] Though the British thought they had an agreement, only a token Greek force would end up joining them at Mount Olympus.

Ralph's ship was in danger. An Italian fleet had gone to sea to destroy the convoy and stop the British intervention before it began. On 28 March 1941, their third night at sea, there was little moonlight as Ralph and hundreds of others stood on deck. It was so dark that they could see distant flashes of shell fire that were deciding their fate. They had no details, but they knew a great battle was underway. At 22.20, after a long pursuit, the Royal Navy's Admiral Cunningham and his fleet found part of the Italian fleet and had opened fire at close range.[7] A savage four-minute barrage sank five ships and damaged another two in what became known as the Battle of Cape Matapan. The Italians retreated. 2,300 Italian sailors were dead, and over 1,000 more were rescued, to become prisoners of war.[8]

The following day, 29 March, Ralph arrived in Athens, where the convoy received the exciting news that an Italian fleet had been defeated. Spirits soared as the soldiers formed ranks and marched through Athens to camp, cheered by joyous Athenians.

Here in Athens Ralph saw his first German soldiers. Greece and Germany were still at peace, so German guards stood outside the German Embassy in full dress uniform. It felt bizarre. It must seem crazy to them too, he thought. Everyone knew the situation would change in a matter of days.

Although every minute was precious, Ralph's first order was to take a few days' leave. During that time, he got to explore the Acropolis and the Agora, like many of the other men on leave. He found a few who were as interested in history as he was – even the Captain crossed his path in the ruins. He purchased an English–Greek dictionary and tried to talk with the locals. Before long, Ralph came face to face with Greece's crippling poverty, seeing malnourished children everywhere in Athens, and respectably dressed women loitering around the Australian camp scavenging the soldiers' food scraps.[9] For Ralph it brought back memories of the shanty town along the Torrens in Adelaide ten years before.

Meat was impossible to get, but the exchange rate meant even the poorest Allied soldier ate like a king. Basking in the spring sun, they gorged on oiled vegetables and rice, washing them down with a coffee substitute made from roast acorns, or with alcohol. The Australians at advanced positions made a nuisance of themselves with drunkenness[10] – the British called them 'Blamey's Bludgers', a reference to the Australian commander, Lieutenant General Thomas Blamey.[11]

Map 4. Greece, 1941

At the beginning of April, his leave was over. Ralph was reunited with the Captain and the pair journeyed north to the village of Gerania, the Australian HQ and the best spot from which to communicate with Lusterforce HQ to the south and the New Zealand HQ to the east. The Gerania HQ, situated on the western slope of Mount Olympus, also had direct command of Australian combat troops further north. The locals were hospitable, but the village was poor, and the HQ itself was less than impressive. It was in a damp, mosquito-infested forest and was described as 'a collection of wretched hovels, and its inhabitants had a bad record of malaria . . . the houses were infested with vermin and the yards with savage dogs'.[12] Day and night, Ralph was eaten alive by mosquitos.

Ralph, the Captain, and the Chevy resumed their work, mapping the landscape near Mount Olympus. It was beautiful: the countryside shimmered green and gold after the spring rains. Olympus was still capped with snow, the first Ralph had ever seen. Tales of the Greek Army's courage against the Italians were legendary but, worryingly, since leaving Athens Ralph and the Captain had not seen a single Greek soldier. Where were the Greeks? They weren't coming.

PART TWO

4

Debacle

On 6 April 1941 Germany crossed the Bulgarian border and invaded Greece. Lusterforce was at Olympus, while the Greek Army was on the frontier with Bulgaria, or fighting the Italians in Albania. The Allied defence was a disaster. The Germans smashed through the 70,000 Greeks on the Bulgarian border and simply bypassed the holdouts. In no time, German tanks were in Thessaloniki.[1] Once the German infantry had caught up with the armour, their assault on Olympus would begin. With an attack imminent, Ralph's mapping work ceased, and he became message runner at General Blamey's Australian HQ. Lusterforce prepared to make its stand on Olympus, with or without help from Papagos.

Ralph was present at the formation of the Second Australian and New Zealand Army Corps (ANZAC). The hope was that the troops would rally to the name, which recalled Australian and New Zealand resilience in the Gallipoli campaign of 1915. The appellation 'gives all ranks the greatest uplift', declared Blamey. 'The task ahead, though difficult, is not nearly as desperate as that which our fathers faced twenty-six years ago. We go together with stout hearts and certainty of success.'[2] The announcement was greeted with a certain amount of eye-rolling.

This was not a new combined Australian–New Zealander force: it was just Australian HQ with a new title. It 'could never be more than a name', the New Zealand staff noted, 'when all the personnel on the headquarters were Australian'.[3]

Ralph and his fellow Anzacs prepared for the German assault, but it never came. The Germans did not attack Olympus; they smashed into the rear of the Greek Army on the Albanian front instead.[4] Outflanked, Lusterforce had no choice but to retreat to Thermopylae, where it hoped to make a stand before evacuating from Greece.

On 15 April the retreat began. Ralph boarded an Anzac HQ truck on a cold, foggy morning that then filled with rain. At least the fog shielded them from air attack. Morale was low; all the side roads turned to slush so the entire force had to merge onto the main highway south. Fleeing Greek civilians and soldiers completely crammed the road, on foot or on skeletal, dying horses, in wagons or battered cars.[5] As the clouds cleared, the *Luftwaffe* (German air force) tried to trap Lusterforce by bombing a bridge ahead of it. The attacks missed, but a British ammunition truck caught fire and exploded just past the bridge, leaving a crater metres deep. The convoy was held up for hours in the spring sun. Finally, Royal Engineers filled the hole and got the convoy moving again.[6]

After this, instead of mounting large assaults, the Germans ran relays of the column. A single plane would fly in low and fast from the rear and run the whole length. Many soldiers leapt from their vehicles and fled to the fields. The German planes passed by most of the column, saving their ammunition for any truck at the front: if they could immobilize that, everything behind would be stuck again, until troops could push the wreckage aside. As one plane finished its run, another would begin the process anew.[7] By such means the Germans hoped to delay Lusterforce, preventing it from creating defensive positions.

Despite the Germans' tactics, however, on 19 April Lusterforce reached Thermopylae. Ralph went with Anzac HQ to a new base at the town of Livadia.[8] At Thermopylae, Lusterforce dug defences and waited. The only way this would work was if the Greek Army to the west could delay the Germans.

By now the Greeks were cut off, with little fight left in them. On 20 April the Greek Army's field commanders mutinied and asked the Germans for an armistice. The terms were that Greek soldiers handed in their weapons and returned home, though officers would keep their sidearms. Greek forces still fighting the Italians would continue for a few hours, for the 'prestige'.[9] The Germans had cut the Greek Army to pieces: the supply lines were gone, the Italians were marching in from Albania, and the longer the Greeks waited to surrender, the more soldiers would die, the more civilians would be bombed. Even so, the principal concern was honour in beating the Italians – the sentiment that had led Papagos to abandon Lusterforce at Olympus. But Greece's allies were now in mortal danger. For Allied commanders, hopes of a heroic stand at Thermopylae ended. After the mutiny, the only option was urgent evacuation.

General Blamey held a midnight conference with Royal Navy officers to discuss details. The navy told him that a daylight evacuation would be too dangerous: the British had too few planes to stop the Luftwaffe from attacking Allied shipping.[10] Evacuating from Athens was impossible – its port had been devastated by an ammunition explosion – so evacuation would begin on the night of 24 April from beaches across the Greek south coast. Just as at Dunkirk nearly twelve months before, it would be slow: without deep-water ports, infantry would have to be ferried out to the ships in smaller craft. All heavy equipment would have to be destroyed and left behind. During a hazardous evacuation, strong leadership and good communications would be critical, with plans undoubtedly changing by the minute. At 07.00 on 22 April, Anzac HQ issued the order to evacuate.[11]

Lusterforce withdrew from Thermopylae. Engineers engaged in tactical destruction while rearguards held off the Germans.[12] Behind the front line, Ralph ran evacuation orders to field commanders and rejoined HQ on the 23rd. Anzac HQ established its last base at the town of Mandra on the road from Athens to the south coast. Thoroughly frustrated by now with the whole business, Ralph determined to do his part to get everyone home.

That evening a courier arrived with a message for Blamey: he was to report to Athens. When he arrived there at midnight his superiors directed him to return to Egypt immediately with his senior staff. He protested in anger that he needed to oversee the evacuation.[13] It was a dangerous blunder on the part of the high command: now over 60,000 troops were being deprived of their primary commander in the field. Blamey was told he could take five senior officers and confidants. For the last spot, the General wrote the name of his own son, Major Thomas Blamey Jr, an artillery officer already seconded to HQ.[14] By prioritizing his only surviving son, General Blamey opened himself to great criticism. But he was only human.

In Ralph's recollection he was the one to deliver Blamey Jr by car to the sea plane.* At 02.00 on 24 April, the Blameys left Greece by flying boat. Ralph returned to Mandra, dog-tired. He'd been awake for over twenty-four hours.

---

* He never committed this detail to writing, nor was any documentation found during research.

5

Stragglers

Ralph woke late, to find headquarters gone. All that remained were a few non-commissioned officers (NCOs), papers, and furniture. The unfortunate few who remained had drawn the short straw. They gathered every scrap of paper that might be useful to the enemy and burned it. Ralph saved and pocketed a map of Greece. The burning done, they exchanged nervous looks before a sergeant major ordered them on their way. They wouldn't catch up with the rest of HQ, but their order was to get to the evacuation point at Nafplion. Ralph Churches was now a straggler without a unit; his time at Anzac HQ was over. That night, 24 April, most HQ staff boarded ships and evacuated.[1] Behind them lay a country in chaos, Blamey gone, Papagos resigned. Anzac HQ had left in such a hurry they forgot to inform their Kiwi counterparts in the New Zealand 2nd Division.[2]

The 2nd Division commander, Brigadier-General Freyberg, had similar orders to Blamey, though they came by cable, not in person. Freyberg asked who was to take over from him. Unhappy with the vague response, Freyberg disobeyed his orders and stayed.[3] He was now the senior field commander, and his HQ kept the evacuation together. The same day as Anzac HQ departed, he had to issue revised orders for new beaches and new times. Priority would go to intact fighting units. Rearguards would remain in place to hold off the Germans.[4]

For Ralph, reaching Nafplion would be a slog. Between Mandra and the south coast port lay the enormous Corinth Canal, with a single bridge over it. Ralph's map showed it was over sixty kilometres to Corinth and another fifty to Nafplion. Separated now from the rest of Lusterforce, his only companions were a few NCOs. Behind Ralph, the last car out of HQ rumbled down the road with an orderly at the wheel, and a major in the passenger seat; it was an open-top with running boards mounted on the sides. It pulled over and the Major told them to jump on, so Ralph and his companions clambered aboard.

The car meandered along bombed-out roads, slowing to manoeuvre around recent craters. The drone of an aircraft engine became audible: a German fighter was swooping towards the vehicle. Someone shouted, 'Bail!' The Major and the orderly opened their doors and threw themselves on the ground. The standing passengers leapt off into the nearest crater – still hot, it scorched their hands. The drone became a roar, and guns opened fire, spraying bullets across the crater's edge. Dirt showered over Ralph. As he pressed himself down into the earth the heat burned through the entire front of his uniform. Into his mind came the memory of gunning down rabbits in the Mallee: now he knew how it felt to be a bunny. The plane peeled off and did not return. Ralph and the others climbed out of the hole and brushed off the dirt. Everyone was okay; so was the car. They all climbed back aboard and drove on.

Halfway to the Corinth Canal the car halted at a supply dump. The Major needed to destroy the supplies to avoid them falling into the invaders' hands. He told his passengers to take anything

41

they could carry and go on their way. They stuffed their pockets and haversacks with food and water and headed off on foot. That night they slept out in the open. One of the NCOs had grabbed a fire starter, so it was roasted tinned beef for dinner. Like the others, Ralph found himself being woken by the pain of burned skin and blisters from the spell in the crater.

Once on the road again, they met another straggler from HQ. He was a private, and in considerable pain. Ralph thought that his neat moustache seemed as French as his name, Gaston Renard. Apparently, he was from the intelligence section of HQ, so Ralph was curious how he'd got there and how he'd got injured. Renard told them his mission was secret, and that his wound was an old one from the London Blitz that had flared up again. He was trying to evacuate but could hardly walk and asked for their help so he could complete his mission. Ralph felt sympathy for a fellow straggler but his colleagues thought he would slow them down and they departed, leaving Ralph and Renard by the road. Ralph's greatcoat was weighed down with ration tins, he was tender from blisters and now had Renard in his care.

Ralph didn't know (and never discovered) that his companion was not on any secret mission. In fact, Renard had gone absent without official leave (AWOL) months after arriving in Britain. A naturalist from Queensland, he was an early volunteer, but soon found that war was not for him. At some point in his absence, he had acquired a severe leg injury. He was court-martialled and imprisoned, then released early to serve in Greece. When the evacuation orders had arrived on 22 April, Renard had not moved with HQ from Livadia to Mandra, claiming that he had visited Greece in peacetime and could find his own way. He'd walked off the job, AWOL once again.[5]

Ralph may have felt charitable, but Renard crippled his marching time – without him Ralph could have made it past the Corinth Canal by nightfall with ease. Instead, for a second night, he found himself camping in the open. He shared his rations, and they ate tinned beef straight from the can. Early morning on 26 April the pair hobbled their way towards the bridge.

Their luck had now run out. From behind came the roar of a hundred planes – fighters and transports. To Ralph, it seemed as though the whole Luftwaffe had come to get him. At 07.25, an entire regiment of *Fallschirmjäger* (German parachutists) fell from the sky. The 2nd Fallschirmjäger was attacking the Corinth Canal.[6] Ralph and Gaston stood in stunned silence. On the other side of the canal, they could hear Allied forces opening fire. By the sound of things, the Allies didn't have enough guns.

Ralph heaved Renard back the way they'd come, to a wooded hill. They were for it now: if the Germans took the canal, the two of them would be cut off. Most of Lusterforce was already across, and Ralph and Renard couldn't turn around. Their best bet was to wait until night and cross under the cover of darkness. The Germans might not take the bridge, but if they did, there was the chance that it would be chaotic enough for the pair of them to slip by. Ralph and Renard hunkered down in the shade and waited for the day to pass.

The outnumbered Fallschirmjäger took the Corinth Bridge with ease, getting the better of disorganized Allied troops. Once they'd secured the bridge, the Fallschirmjäger sat tight. They had thousands of prisoners. An intact bridge and German tanks on the way meant Lusterforce would never be able to evacuate in time. The Germans found and removed the demolition charges the British had laid before they could detonate them, and they set the bombs aside in a pile on the bridge – a stunning blunder. A stray shot hit the pile, there was an almighty bang and a great plume of smoke, and the bridge was wrecked.[7]

Now Ralph did have chaos on his side. As night fell, he and Renard made their play. The Germans were in control, but there were more Allied prisoners than Germans, and many of them walked away behind the Germans' backs. It was also a new moon, a night so dark that patrols would be near blind. Ralph and Renard crept their way to the coast and along the shore to the canal's edge. On the water Ralph could make out a white shape: a dinghy. He loaded Renard aboard.[8] Ralph didn't have much experience rowing, much less silent rowing, and it was nerve-wracking. All it would take was a German patrol to poke their head over the canal to see the white shape, and if the enemy erred on the side of caution, they'd start shooting.

No Germans came, though, and on arriving at the southern bank the Australians headed south. By sunrise they'd made enough progress to justify a pause. There was no sign of any Germans. Ralph had got away with it.

As well as being a dead weight, Renard wasn't talkative, and overall made a poor travelling companion. Luckily, they stumbled on a British signals unit, so at least they had company for breakfast. The signalmen seemed beaten and lost, and it perplexed Ralph that the officer took meals separate from his men – when the food was coming straight from the can, Ralph expected divisions of class and rank not to matter.[9]

Breakfast over, the signalmen left Ralph and Renard behind; they had no desire to be slowed down. Ralph was coming to resent his companion. Tired and frustrated, the pair continued south. It was unlikely any Allied vehicles would pass their way with Corinth in enemy hands, yet Ralph still expected some semblance of order. He thought the roads would be lined with checkpoints and military police. They weren't. [10] The two men would have never made it to a beach by nightfall had it not been for a ride on a Greek horse cart heading to Nafplion.

Before they arrived, a friendly Greek travelling in the other direction gave them fresh intelligence. Ships had come to Nafplion last night, but now men were moving east to the fishing village of Tolo. Ralph consulted his map: Tolo wasn't far away and made sense as a secondary site if Nafplion was a problem. Ralph and Renard got off the cart; Ralph thanked their driver and the passing Greek. He and Renard now made their approach to Tolo on foot. As the road became congested with Allied soldiers also heading to Tolo, Ralph felt a sense of relief. For the first time in days his spirits lifted, and he felt confident of rescue. The sun was beginning to set, and the last light faded as they entered the small, charming village.

Square whitewashed houses lay crammed between a beach and a steep hill. Beyond the shore lay an island, and beyond that, endless sea. In better times, this would have been an excellent spot for a romantic weekend. From the edge of town, more Allied soldiers emerged: they'd been hiding from the Luftwaffe during daylight.[11] Exhausted, Ralph and Renard lay down on the beach and joined over 1,000 others waiting for the navy. It turned out there had also been ships at Tolo last night, but things hadn't gone well. Two Australian ships had come: the destroyer HMAS *Stuart* and the cruiser HMAS *Perth*. Landing craft designed for tanks had come to collect the men. As the water was so shallow, they had run aground, and hundreds of men had had to strip off and wade in to push them free. When sunrise approached *Stuart* and *Perth* were still nowhere near full. The ships withdrew to avoid air attack, leaving many still stranded on shore.

The whole thing had been avoidable; a naval officer had begged the evacuating army to move to a location with deeper water, but the army officers had insisted the operation remain here.[12] They had a plan to solve the problem: the officers had pooled money to charter caiques – Greek sailing boats – to ferry their men out to the ships. In the end they succeeded in acquiring just a single craft.[13] Ralph and the others now stood waiting patiently on Tolo beach. Last night's arrival time for *Stuart*, 22.00, had passed: no ships. Then 23.00, then midnight. As 03.00 came and went, anxiety turned to despair. The previous night had been the last for evacuations from Tolo and Nafplion; Freyberg had ordered everyone left to head further south for another evacuation at Monemvasia.[14] The orders hadn't reached Tolo and 1,500 men waited all night on Tolo beach, but the navy wasn't coming.

Daybreak brought chaos and approaching Germans; no one was in clear command. A Royal Artillery officer reported that his superior had agreed to surrender, but this provoked protests that it was beyond his authority. Cut off and without leadership, the order of the day was every man for himself. The single caique chartered took on 150 men and sailed away. Others lay down and waited for capture. Some fled into the hills; a few stayed in the vain hope that the navy would return.[15]

6

Rowing to Crete

Ralph didn't have the legs for more hiking but, having dragged Renard all this way, he was not going to give up now. He headed to a shop and spoke to its owner, a tobacco merchant and part-time coastguard. He explained his predicament: he was stuck and wanted a boat to make for Crete. Even with nothing to offer, Ralph was persuasive and the merchant said he would make enquiries. On his return he led Ralph and Renard to the southern end of the beach, where they were confronted by a five-metre-long wooden rowing boat with three oars. It had no motor or sails and wasn't what Ralph had been hoping for, but he reckoned from his map that they could make it to Crete in a week and a half. Given the state Renard was in, Ralph would have to do all the rowing.

Ralph thanked the merchant and took possession. He must have looked as if he knew what he was doing; three men came down the beach towards him. One was a New Zealand sapper, doubtless having missed the evacuation after slowing down the German advance. The other two were Australians, one of them a driver, the other a lieutenant by the name of Jim Forrest of 2/1st Battalion. Hailing from Sydney's wealthy Elizabeth Bay, he looked every part the officer. The Lieutenant reached his hand out to Ralph and asked if the three of them could join the boat. Ralph replied that five was better than two and explained his plan to row down the coast and then on to Crete. With that, the five Anzacs pushed the boat out to sea and waved goodbye to the merchant.

Jim took a pair of oars and began rowing south-west across the bay. Ralph took the third oar as a rudder and sat at the stern. Overhead came the sound of engines: the Luftwaffe had arrived. They weren't strafing the beaches, thank God, but there was no chance of evacuation now. The five men decided to take off their uniforms, hoping to get mistaken for fishermen, and sat in the boat stripped down to white singlets and boxers.

Jim rowed on; he was authoritative and calm under pressure. When the craft reached the west end of the bay, he took some blankets and shirts and improvised a crude sail, which he hoisted on the third oar.[1] It turned out that Jim had been sailing most weekends since he was a boy. A north wind was at their backs just in time, and they set out on the long voyage to Crete. Behind them, Tolo fell. A British and Australian rearguard held while Ralph and hundreds of others fled, but they eventually had to surrender in mid-afternoon on 28 April.[2]

Far down the coast, the last evacuations began at Monemvasia and went smoothly. In the early hours of the following day, Freyberg was on the last transport off. His efforts and refusal to leave earlier helped save thousands of lives. Meanwhile, as Lusterforce was ceasing to exist, the five men aboard the wooden boat rowed all night. They planned to move only at night; before dawn they'd find a likely cove to pull into and sleep by day. What they would do for food and water, Ralph didn't know – they had a little, enough for a few days at most. They rowed in shifts, except Renard. The boat made good time on the first night and as planned pulled into a cove before first light. They lay down to rest, a couple on the shore and a couple in the boat, after posting Renard as the watch.

He nudged them awake a couple of hours later. Three Greeks were heading down towards the cove. Two were elderly, weather-beaten types, the third a man in his late twenties – an eternal Yank. He asked if they were English. Being Anzacs increased the warmth of the Greeks' greeting.

What were they trying to do?

Hoping to sail to Crete.

'Hopeless', was the firm opinion: the Germans were already swarming down the Peloponnese. Their patrol boats would make the coastal journey impossible.

Was there any alternative apart from surrender to the Germans?

The men offered shelter until they could be evacuated by submarine.

The Anzacs were sceptical, not expecting that a submarine would be risked on their account. How would they even go about hiding?

The Greeks said they would dress the Anzacs as Greek soldiers, giving them the identities of local young men who had fallen on the Albanian front, then pass them off as shell-shocked casualties. It was a generous offer. The problem for Ralph was, if he was captured, his family would at least be notified through the Red Cross. If he went on the run, the report would be 'Missing in action'. He wouldn't do that to Ronte. The other Aussies agreed: they'd press on. The Kiwi sapper, however, decided to take up the Greeks' offer. It surprised Ralph and the others, though no one was going to deny a man his decision over his own fate.

What happened to the Kiwi, Ralph would never know. Some soldiers returned home after months on the run. Some joined Greek partisans and resistance groups and fought on. A few integrated into their hiding places, married, settled, and never returned home.[3]

Before night the eternal Yank returned with food and water and wished them well. On the second night of rowing, the wind was against them, and the sail came down. Following their plan, the four again pulled into a likely spot before dawn. Greek hospitality arrived again that day. And the next, and the next, and the next. They worried that if the Greeks could spot them, so could the Germans, but it was a risk they had to take as they needed food and water. Jim even acquired some canvas to rig a better sail.

The crew's experiences with Greek civilians were repeated up and down the country. While the Greek Army still fought, relations with the British expeditionary force had been jittery. Various stand-offs between Lusterforce soldiers and Greek soldiers and civilians over transport priority had been solved at gunpoint.[4] Lusterforce supplies and soldiers' belongings had a habit of disappearing. The situation got so bad that at one point General Blamey threatened to kill a Greek civilian he suspected of stealing his coat.[5] Now, faced with Allied soldiers in need, Greek civilians displayed nothing but charity, despite their own poverty, without regard for their own safety. '[Everywhere] we were kissed,' wrote an Australian sapper who crossed by boat to Turkey, 'wept over, given bread, cheese, and wine, and provided a guide within the space of half an hour.'[6] Without Greek help, Ralph's boat journey could not have even started, let alone continued.

After a week of rowing, the crew knew that only the German base at Monemvasia lay between them and the open sea. They would row past the town in the night, pull into a cove at the tip of Greece, and cross to Crete.

For the seventh night, the Aussies hauled along the Ionian coast. But after passing Monemvasia they heard the roar of a motorboat. They withdrew the oars, lowered the sail, and lay quiet. The boat's engine cut out close to their vessel. The moon was out, but clouds had covered its glow, enough to hide them. 'Vee know you dere,' a voice shouted. 'Mister Englishmens. Soon vee comes for you.'[7]

Silence hung between the vessels.

Then the German engine started again, and the boat chugged away. The Aussies' hearts were racing as they put the oars out and sail up, and they rowed like madmen to get as far away as possible. Before dawn they reached Cape Maleas, the southern tip of the Greek mainland. They pulled the boat up in a likely spot, but there was no sentry that night. The crew were shattered and fell asleep nestled in pairs for warmth. Ralph and Jim lay wrapped up in the boat; Renard and the driver slept on a flat patch on the rocks.

7

Captive

'Oop, oop, oop. Ahnds oop.' It was 06.00, and they woke to two young Germans pointing guns at them. Bleary-eyed, Ralph rose and complied, standing in the boat with his arms raised. He could make out another two dozen Germans on the shore and two patrol boats.[1] The Australians had had the misfortune to lay up to rest at the meeting point for German patrols.

Despite the commotion, Jim was still fast asleep. Ralph gave him a whack with his boot: *Wake up* – the Germans are here! 'They're not Germans, they're Greek police,' Jim mumbled, and rolled back to sleep. Ralph and the Germans looked at each other, perplexed. Ralph nudged him again, Jim groaned, and then stood up.[2]

They lay demoralized on the shore. The German soldiers patted them down and robbed them. They took everything: binoculars, wristwatches, writing cases, dispatch folders, mess kits – they even took Ralph's New Testament and leather-bound photos of Ronte and his family. The Australians protested that this was illegal under the Geneva Convention regarding prisoners of war, but they were in no position to negotiate. Ralph at least succeeded in getting the photos and New Testament returned, and they would continue to be a great comfort in the years to come. Apart from his clothes, all he now possessed were the pictures and a mapping pencil his captors hadn't found. While the German patrol boats prepared to leave, the *Hauptmann* (Captain) tried to reassure his new charges: their internment would be short. Soon the Germans would triumph, and everyone could go home. There was no reason that their stay should be unpleasant, 'so long as you makes nudding stupid'.[3] They got on one of the German patrol boats and found another four captured Australians on board. To try to soften the blow a little, the German crew broke out some schnapps to share around the prisoners, and the boat then headed back up the coast to Monemvasia. From there it was a truck to the town of Molaoi, to be locked in the top floor of a schoolhouse with a dozen other prisoners. Renard moved as far away as possible, wanting nothing more to do with Ralph; Ralph preferred the company of the other Australians anyway.

A pair were leaning back on the small school chairs as though they were back in class. Henry Walter Steilberg and Gerrard Pollock had made themselves comfortable. Ralph introduced himself. Wal was an inspiring presence, a six-foot-two Sydney-sider used to manual labour.[4] Gerry was a natural comedian hailing from the port of Newcastle. Jim Forrest, though, had gone quiet: he'd taken capture badly. Ralph felt terrible for the Lieutenant; Jim was a good man and a great leader. He didn't deserve to have his war end like this.

Two German guards entered, both English-speakers. One was an eternal Yank, and an honest one. He'd come back to Germany in July of 1939, he explained, to convince his parents to help run a restaurant in Chicago. The war had started, and he'd been conscripted into the army, and made a translator.[5] The other Germans regarded him with suspicion, he said. The other English-speaker only wanted to boast that nothing could stop the glory of Germany.

'What about the Russians?' someone asked.

'What about them?' the guard replied, puzzled. 'Are they not our great friends and allies?' He was in for a shock in a few weeks' time.

Ralph's stay at the school was mostly uneventful. The food was adequate, and the guards were urging the prisoners to eat more. An officer from the SS (the paramilitary wing of the Nazi Party) who was passing through decided to show how to extract intelligence from the captives. He barked because the room did not spring to attention for him. Rather than conduct separate interviews in private, the Nazi interviewed everyone at once. He had obviously never interrogated Australians before. Now the Aussies were in the mood for some fun. Each question was met with a barrage of excited heckles and replies. He eventually stormed off in a hail of jeering and cynical flippancies.

After a few days, the prisoners were moved from the school via another truck. Because he was an officer, Jim Forrest went separately from the enlisted men. He turned to Ralph before departing, and they shook hands. Loaded on board, Ralph, Wal, Gerry, the silent Renard, and a few other prisoners began the long drive to Corinth. They were nodding off by the time the city came into sight. Ralph stood up and peered over the side. They were at *Frontstalag* (Front Camp) Corinth, a temporary holding camp for prisoners of war. An old Greek Army barracks, it had a few buildings and a square of bare earth fenced with barbed wire. There were almost 12,000 men crammed within its confines.

Prisoners taken at Kalamata (now known to Lusterforce soldiers as 'Calamity Bay') filled the camp. The chaos at Tolo and Nafplion had been bad, the Allied soldiers lost to captivity numbering a few thousand. Events at Kalamata on the night of 28 April were worse. The town lay on Greece's south-western edge, and all those who had not been able to evacuate earlier had fled there – more than 8,000 in all: support staff, stragglers, mule drivers, and the entire Cypriot and Palestinian Labour Corps.[6] It was no army. Only a few men had firearms: 400 Brits, 800 New Zealanders, and 70 Australians.[7] There was no suggestion that evacuation wasn't going to happen – 8,000 had been rescued from the same site two days before, with the navy sending in eight warships, led by *Perth*.[8]

But the Germans now knew of the site. Most were too far away to intervene, but two motorized companies of the 5th Panzer Division, a few hundred men, made a bold attempt to spoil the evacuation. At 17.00, the Germans had broken through the British-held perimeter and ram-raided into Kalamata. The quay fell, along with half the town, and the British naval liaison officer had been captured. Everyone on the beach knew that if the Germans held the town the navy wouldn't risk coming. If the Allies were going to get out, they had to remove the enemy. The New Zealanders had launched a savage counter-attack with a few Australians.[9]

HMS *Hero*, a destroyer, had gone ahead of the flotilla to check the situation, and its crew had sighted gunfire in the town and received a message from the beach: 'Germans in the town.' *Hero* had relayed this to *Perth* while putting an officer ashore to assess the chances of evacuation. The New Zealanders had fought street to street to press the counter-attack, outnumbering the

Germans,[10] but though the Allies had won the Battle of Kalamata and *Hero* had radioed all-clear, a glitch meant the message didn't reach *Perth* for forty minutes, by which point *Perth*'s captain, too spooked by the prospect of losing his ships and their crews, had decided not to turn back.[11] *Hero* had taken on board those few it could, and the following night three destroyers did pick up a few hundred stragglers,[12] but the rest were left to the Germans, who had begun to arrive in force. So now nearly 12,000 Allied troops were crammed into the tiny Frontstalag Corinth. One was Driver Leslie Laws of the Royal Engineers, who Ralph would meet almost twelve months later.

8

The Corinth Cage

Australians and New Zealanders had provided the combat troops for Lusterforce, and most of them had been evacuated. The majority of the prisoners in Frontstalag Corinth were British, Cypriot, and Palestinian – drivers, engineers, logisticians, clerical troops, and labourers. There were also 4,000 Italian prisoners in the camp. Originally captured by the Greeks, they had been released when the country fell and had promptly begun looting the town, so, allies or not, the Germans had thrown them back in prison.[1]

Conditions were dire. There was no shade or shelter. Many had lost their greatcoats and blankets. Ralph had kept both, so during the cold nights he shared his with Gerry and Wal. Rations consisted of weevil-ridden lentils and Greek Army biscuits which were so hard many soldiers broke teeth (or dentures) on them, before they learned to soak them in water – usually in a steel helmet-turned-cauldron – to create a sort of communal porridge.[2]

Part of the reason for their plight was Greece was already in famine. Imports had vanished, and Bulgaria had occupied the primary bread-producing region in the north-east. Soon the Germans in Athens had sent a grim warning to Berlin: it must ship grain to Greece immediately to prevent mass starvation.[3]

There were no washing facilities, but the Germans permitted daily beach trips. The chance to wash was welcome, but as days grew to weeks the four-kilometre round trip proved too much for men on starvation rations. Malnutrition was leading to increasing numbers of instances of 'black-outs': any exertion would lead to unconsciousness.[4] There were a few washbasins of water to keep the 12,000 men hydrated.[5] A single ditch running two-thirds the width of the camp was the camp toilet; some satirical soul had made signs dividing the trench by rank. Cases of malaria and dysentery rose fast. Coping with dysentery at the trough was an intense exercise, with men blacking out over the pit; the lucky ones fell forwards. Many of the guards were young and recent conscripts, and youth, incompetence, bad luck, or bad timing meant they had been assigned to second line units following rapid advances, and played little part in German victories. Resentful, they took it out on the prisoners by brutalizing them in random assaults. Some guards would patrol the latrine ditch and kick squatting men in the chest.[6] German combat troops won Hitler's affection with great victories; these guards looked for it by kicking starving men into a latrine.

There would have been more deaths had it not been for the heroic efforts of one woman, Ariadne Massautti, the seventy-year-old Greek Red Cross administrator who was head of the Corinth POW hospital. As soon as the 2nd Fallschirmjäger seized Corinth, she had gone in search of a German medical officer and convinced him to send troops to locate any doctors among the Allied prisoners. With half a dozen prisoner-doctors, she treated the wounded and sick, while occupying Corinth's best hotel – to the chagrin of the German officers.[7]

Prisoners who were fit for work had to load bombs onto

Luftwaffe planes, which was a severe breach of the Geneva Convention.[8] The dire conditions broke many friendships, but drew Ralph, Gerry, and Wal together. Surviving captivity meant a new morality emerged. 'Corinth had taught me there was only one law,' recalled prisoner Barney Roberts, 'the law of the German gun. Hunger bred in many a single-minded sense of self-preservation which seemed to thrive on distrust and larceny.'[9] This instinct of self-preservation inspired violence by prisoners as well as guards. There were no safeguarding protocols, and with British Empire prisoners in the majority, the Italians were now vulnerable. Some prisoners went into the Italian section every night in search of a victim who would be given a beating, and any valuables snatched. Enough violence administered, and enough booty looted, the attackers would withdraw until the next night.[10] Ralph was disgusted by his comrades. He'd experienced plenty of beatings during his youth, and been robbed himself just days before, and he was determined to survive in a better fashion.

Trading at a local market was permitted for anyone who still had money or goods to barter – the Greek farmers sold a modest range of dried fruits. But almost no one had any money left; only the Palestinians, wise enough to know that robbery would follow capture, had somehow stashed their cash.[11] Ralph had his pen and hoped it would fetch a reasonable price, but going to market, he knew, would invite the attention of the guards on duty. That was not always a bad thing, as one of them often intervened when a prisoner was not getting a fair price, usually to haggle on their behalf.[12]

Ralph was not so lucky. While he was attempting to bargain, a passing guard clubbed him on the side of the head with a single ferocious blow with a rifle butt. Ralph's ear filled with blood. When the guard lost interest, Gerry and Wal hauled Ralph up. He would be nearly deaf in his left ear for the rest of his life.

Discouraged from trading, other prisoners found creative ways to stave off famine. A few Brits fashioned schoolyard slingshots to hunt sparrows – the camp record was sixteen in a day. One group managed to capture and carve up an unfortunate stray dog.[13] Faced with a breakdown in normality, many prisoners became more religious. Ralph was among them. Two captured chaplains began to lead church services, which proved very popular. 'When you are starved, of necessity filthy, lousy, and ragged,' Ralph wrote, 'when nothing else seems worth hanging on for, an inner faith in something, in something independent of either yourself or earthly tyrants, gives a comfort which alone makes the struggle seem worthwhile.'[14] From the camp the prisoners also saw part of the invasion of Crete when German planes filled with Fallschirmjäger flew overhead on 20 May. Gerry, Ralph, and Wal stood counting: sixty-seven out, forty-seven back – the Germans took heavy losses. The Allied force, led by Freyberg, was low on supplies, and lower on morale. They struggled with the island's defence. The Germans broke through; another evacuation followed.[15]

At Corinth, meanwhile, conditions worsened. Advancing through Crete, the Germans began finding the mutilated bodies of Fallschirmjäger, and held the British responsible. First the camp authorities cut rations, then they said they would kill five prisoners for every German that showed up disfigured.[16] The corpses were not in fact the work of Allied soldiers, but Cretan civilians. The islanders did not like being invaded and, when Germans landed in their villages, individual citizens and militias attacked. Many German paratroopers were unable to disentangle their parachutes from trees, olive groves, and houses, or retrieve their weapons fast enough to avoid being met with Cretan pitchforks, hoes, clubs, and kitchen knives, and mauled to death.[17] In Corinth, the Germans dropped the matter and restored rations once they learned the truth, and instead murdered many Cretans for their defiance. The Allied defeat in Crete would bring another 12,000 prisoners to the Greek camps, after Ralph and his fellows had been sent on to the Reich.[18]

9

Surviving to Thessaloniki

On 5 June the Germans began clearing out Corinth. The end goal was to send all prisoners to Germany or elsewhere in the Reich – by the Geneva Convention all POW camps had to be within the territory of the capturing country. First, all 8,000 Allied prisoners had to be shifted to another transit camp in the port city of Thessaloniki.

The move was in batches of several hundred, beginning with a twelve-kilometre march across Corinth. At Isthmia they boarded a train.[1] Ralph had stuck with Gerry and Wal, and they crammed into a carriage with dozens of others. Many took the chance of a clean floor to catch some sleep. For some this turned out to be a fatal mistake: the train stopped at every station – the passengers weren't sure why – and when the carriage doors opened at one, a prisoner sleeping against it tumbled out. The nearest guard then put a bullet through the fallen prisoner's head. A small Greek boy came running across the platform: he grasped the dead man's hand and began to cry. As the train pulled away those still on it were left with this shocking image.[2] The train halted in Athens before shuddering north into the night. At Bralos, north of Thermopylae, Allied sappers had done such a good job of damaging the rail bridge that the train could go no further.[3] The starving prisoners had to walk thirty kilometres over the Bralos Pass to join the next train at Lamia.

The guards set a cracking pace, wanting to cover as much ground as possible before the heat rose, but by dawn even the guards themselves were worn out. The sun brought with it beautiful views, but oppressive temperatures. On their right were sheer cliff faces. On their left was an expanse of green scorched shrublands with a few mountain peaks beyond. Anyone sane would avoid marching this terrain in direct sun. Everyone's boots were splitting; a few sailors from ships that had been sunk had no footwear at all, and their feet turned to a bloody pulp. There was no rest, no stopping, and they hadn't had a bathroom stop since leaving Corinth, but to stop would risk collapse, being left behind, and death. No one would be able to pick you up if you fell. 'They won't let you stop,' wrote one prisoner, 'so you [piss] down the leg of your trousers. Is it yours you can smell? It's a relief to let it go at last.'[4] For Gerry, Ralph, and Wal, only Gerry's indefatigable humour kept them going. For a moment, the trio occupied a fantasy world. 'Strewth!' Gerry declared. 'This ain't heat, though. I remember going camping out back o' beyond in '38. It was so bloody hot it was scorching the rabbits' fur.'

'God, Poll,' replied Wal, 'what would you give for a bottle of Toohey's now?'

'Hell, you don't drink that stuff, do you, Hans?' Gerry interjected. 'I drink Tooth's! Now that's a beer!'

'You haven't got a beer in New South Wales. Come to Adelaide and try some West End,' Ralph suggested.

'Shall we go to Adelaide and have a West End with old Churchie?'[5] Wal said it with such conviction that they walked into an imaginary Adelaide pub and shared a drink.

The fantasy was distracting enough for them to reach the rest stop intact. After they descended the pass, a halt was called at a mountain stream, and a bread ration distributed – enough to keep everyone going a little longer. The last stage of the march took them across a flat sun-scorched plain to Lamia Station. Another overcrowded train awaited, but there the endless generosity of Greek civilians made itself felt again. At every later station, despite growing shortages, crowds of local women gathered with food. Some were Greek Red Cross, others were just ordinary civilians.[6] The guards would usually form a barrier to stop aid from reaching the train, so the Greeks lobbed cabbages and boiled eggs over the guards' heads. The selflessness of the Greeks continued to astonish; the prisoners would remember the defiant bravery of these women forever. Finally, after more than a day of travel, the train reached Thessaloniki, an ancient, bustling commercial hub of the Greek, Roman, Byzantine, and Ottoman Empires.

The cruel ordeal of the prisoners' journey was not yet over. The Germans now made a great show of parading the starved prisoners through town in a three-kilometre shuffle up the hill from the railway station to the Greek Army barracks named after Pavlos Melas, a Greek revolutionary hero. Crowds came to offer aid to the prisoners with food and cigarettes, and some locals were assaulted and thrown in with those they had tried to help.

Many in the crowd were members of the city's great Jewish community, some of whom were descended from families who had fled the Spanish Inquisition. The Nazis would destroy almost the entire population, and their culture with it. Throughout the German occupation and the Holocaust the

Jews of Thessaloniki showed the defiance and courage that they demonstrated on the streets of their city. 'These few survivors from the Jewish colony of Salonica,' wrote the Auschwitz survivor Primo Levi, 'with their two languages, Spanish and Greek, and their numerous activities, are repositories of a concrete, mundane, conscious wisdom, in which the traditions of all the Mediterranean civilisations blend together.'[7] The sight of the starved men must have been a cruel foreshadowing. All the way here, thousands had given what little they had to help. The coming famine would kill as many as 450,000 Greeks from a population of 7,400,000.[8]

Sunburned, thirsty, lousy, malnourished, and in considerable pain, Ralph, Gerry, and Wal soon entered the barracks now renamed *Durchgangslager*, or *Dulag* (Transit Camp), 183. The Germans issued the prisoners with 'new' clothes – rags pilfered from the Greeks, and wooden-soled clogs to replace split boots.[9] Many of the prisoners cast off or supplemented their uniforms to reduce the stench of their clothes. Ralph kept his greatcoat and slouch hat: they were almost all he had left to outwardly identify him as some sort of soldier. Unlike at Corinth, there was shelter at this camp: some red-brick buildings, and a few wooden shacks. Thousands crammed inside the wire fences, but anyone hoping for better conditions was disappointed – shelter turned out to be worse than sleeping in the open. Though there were no beds as such, bed bugs infested the buildings. The prisoners were already crawling with fleas and lice, but now there were so many bugs one could scoop them up by the handful – rolling over in the night would crush dozens of them. Their tiny corpses soon added to the appalling smell from the endemic dysentery and general filth.

Hardly any slept well in Dulag 183, and the few capable of work when they arrived weren't fit for long. Able-bodied men were sent to the city port and were forced to load munitions; no longer needed in Greece, these shells were intended to soften up Germany's next conquest.[10] Food was still appalling: a daily ration was, at most, three-quarters of a biscuit, 110 grams of bread, a pint of watery soup and two cups of tea.[11] Disease continued to run wild, with just five POW doctors and thirty orderlies for the whole camp.[12] Gerry, Ralph, and Wal embraced all the actions best suited for survival, except violence, excelling in barter, stealth, and theft. There was no Greek market in Dulag 183 but the guards ran a black market and prised out the prisoners' last valuables. For his mechanical pencil, Ralph raised the sum of two bread loaves and 100 Greek drachmae. Sixty drachmae bought 100 cigarettes; the other forty he stashed. Wal, despite his stature, proved an adept thief. He talked himself into cooking detail and purloined bread loaves from the German stores.[13] The three shared all their gains to keep themselves alive.

In this hell on earth, the first escape attempts began. They did not go well. An Australian tried to scale the fence and was gunned down. A wiser group found an entrance to a sewage tunnel and climbed in. Guards spotted them and waited at the other end. The camp knew it had all gone wrong when they heard the gunshots. The leading man's limp body went tumbling down the shaft, while those behind fled back the way they had come. Many never got out of the tunnel at all, suffocating down there.[14] Escape attempts seemed doomed to fail.

After a week in Thessaloniki, Ralph heard the shocking news of Operation Barbarossa: Germany had invaded the Soviet

Union. Wild rumours spread. There was a tremendous Soviet offensive into Romania. Yugoslavia and then Greece would soon be liberated. Turkey had joined the war and was advancing to Thessaloniki.[15] It was, of course, all nonsense, but rumours persisted.

10

The Train to Maribor

A few days later they were told they were moving again, to Germany. Thirty minutes to pack up was the order. It took two minutes: no one owned anything. The prisoners stood on parade in the camp square waiting. Then the move was called off – now it was going to happen in the morning. Wal used the time to steal another loaf – if this was going to be anything like the last journey, the trio would need all the food they could find. Morning came, and when provisions were distributed everyone knew they would move today. Each man was given three biscuits, half a loaf of bread, a tin of meat and a water flask: more food than anyone had seen in two months. They were told it would have to last for two days. Many devoured it all immediately, making themselves sick. The wiser men took nibbles and saved the rest.

Gerry, Ralph, and Wal marched out with the first group. At Thessaloniki railway station they saw the bizarre spectacle of a German naval band. The musicians' immaculate white and navy uniforms and shining brass and chrome were a stark contrast to the prisoners' filthy khakis, beards, and messy hair. As the platform filled, the band began to play German marching songs. Those prisoners with some fight left in them tried to sabotage the display with songs of their own. A lone voice cried out,

'There's a garden . . . what a garden! Only happy flowers bloom there.' As tired prisoners joined in to sing 'Beer Barrel Polka' the German band faltered. 'Roll out the barrel, we'll have a barrel of fun. Roll out the barrel, we've got the blues on the run . . .'

Realization dawned on the German band leader – the tune was a hit across Europe, albeit under different names. He turned to his band and shouted, '"Ro-sa-mun-de"! *Eins, zwei, eins, zwei!*' All at once, the Kriegsmarine band transformed into a polka act and the brass section hopped to the gay cheers of the prisoners. The chorus grew louder as the guards shepherded the prisoners onto the rolling stock. When 'Beer Barrel Polka/Rosamunde' ended, terrific applause broke out.[*][1]

Music was an effective distraction from the imminent privation: more than fifty prisoners were packed into a single carriage. Written in French on the side was '*40 Hommes ou 8 Chevaux*' – 40 Men or 8 Horses.[2] The compartments were bare, save for a single bucket. Ventilation consisted of two small, slatted windows, and the men with more foresight positioned themselves next to those fragments of fresh air.[3] When the band ceased its second song, the passengers cried 'Rosamunde!' and the music struck up again, until the train was full and departed northwards. There only was enough room for everyone to sit if knees were pressed to chests. To give each other some chance of rest, the men took turns standing and sitting.

With so many crammed inside, the train became an oven during the hot summer days. All the water was gone in a matter

---

* The song also appears at the end of a railway journey in Primo Levi's Auschwitz account. There a band used it during inductions of new victims to the camp.

of hours. That first night, escape attempts began again. Several men in Ralph's compartment hacked a hole in the floorboards with pocket knives. When the train reached a slow enough speed, the men lowered themselves through the hole.[4] No one else followed; no one else had the strength. Those who remained suffered the repercussions of the escape in the morning. The guards boarded up the escape hole and, with the passengers begging for water, also boarded over the ventilation slats. Water for knives was the deal: the guards said they would only let the prisoners drink if all hidden weapons were surrendered. Pocket knives and razors came tumbling out of the door. In exchange for the loot, two buckets of water were passed in.[5]

The locomotive groaned on and the train crossed into Yugoslavia. It was day two, but still a very long way to go to the Reich. The train passed first through Niš (in modern-day Serbia), then on to Belgrade. At Belgrade, the Yugoslav Red Cross stood, offering bread, cake, and buckets of lemonade. It would've made a fine picnic. The carriage doors opened, and the prisoners waited. Up the platform, a German captain began to run the length of the train. Screaming at the Red Cross workers, he kicked the buckets over to stop the prisoners from taking them. But Ralph's carriage was right at the back. In her Sunday best, a Belgrade woman managed to thrust lemonade in before the captain's boot could reach it.[6] Later trains had better luck. Some German officers allowed food to get to the prisoners, but there wasn't enough to go around.[7]

Sarajevo was day three. The toilet bucket had long since overflowed. Besides, the carriages were too crammed for it to be practical for men to move to the lavatory. Most urinated through gaps in the floorboards. Others would excrete into the meat tins once they had eaten the contents. Much would spill. Shirts were torn up to mop the filth and the rags were then passed along and shoved out of the window or through a suitable crack.[8]

Dawn of the fourth day. Through a gap in the planks Ralph could see the word 'Zagreb' (in modern-day Croatia). They were close to Germany now; he hoped they weren't headed to Berlin, several more days' travel. The train followed the Sava river upstream, then turned north to follow the smaller Savinja river. It finally came to a stop in the afternoon. The front half detached and continued further north, to the Austrian town of Wolfsberg, while the back half, including Ralph's carriage, stayed put. The doors opened, the afternoon light stinging the passengers' eyes. '*Alle raus!*' shouted the guards.

Wal was first to disembark. 'Come on, Poll, Churchie. Let's get out of this stinking bloody mess.'[9] Behind Wal on the platform was a sign that read 'Marburg an der Drau'. Until a few months previous it had gone by its Slovenian name: Maribor.

11

Occupation

Ralph was now at camp Stalag XVIIID in Slovenia (before the German invasion, part of Yugoslavia). The Slovenians were a Slavic people settled in the south-east corner of the Alps; for centuries they had been under Habsburg rule as part of the Holy Roman and Austrian Empires. Following the First World War most had found themselves assigned by the Treaty of Versailles to a new country, the Kingdom of Slovenes, Croats and Serbs, known from 1929 as the Kingdom of Yugoslavia. The Slovenians bordered Austria (annexed by Nazi Germany in 1938), Italy, Hungary, and what is today Croatia. There were also other ethnic groups in Slovenia: Germans, Italians, Hungarians, and Roma. Many Slovenians in the west found themselves in Italy, under fascism. The multi-ethnic city of Trieste, and the surrounding Primorska region – dominated by Slovenians – were annexed by Italy as its reward for switching sides in the First World War. There were also Slovenians living alongside Austrians over the northern border. By early 1941 the situation for Yugoslavia was also grim, surrounded by the Axis powers, Germany, Italy, Hungary, and Bulgaria, who all coveted Yugoslav territory. The Prince Regent Pavle, the Yugoslav leader, was no admirer of Hitler but he needed a way to keep his people safe.

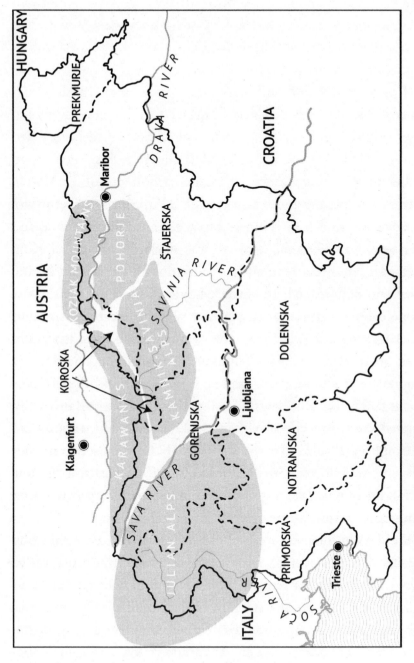

Map 5. Slovenia regions and mountains

He brokered a compromise with Hitler: Yugoslavia would join the Axis but not go to war nor assist in other wars; it would be a neutrality pact in all but name. On 25 March 1941, Yugoslavia signed the Tripartite Pact and joined the Axis.[1]

Prince Pavle had underestimated his people. In the First World War, Germany, Austria-Hungary, and Bulgaria had waged war against Serbia, and one in five of all Serbs had been killed by the enemy, starvation, or disease.[2] To ally with the Axis, even in name only, was treachery.[3] In the early hours of 27 March, Belgrade rose in rebellion, and Prince Pavle's government was overthrown in a coup. He was replaced by a military junta, and his seventeen-year-old nephew was declared of age as King Petar II. For a moment, all was calm. But Hitler did not let the slight go unpunished, and ordered Yugoslavia be invaded at the same time as Greece. It began with a Luftwaffe bombardment of Belgrade on 6 April. The city's population had swollen in the lead-up to Palm Sunday. Thousands perished, and Axis forces poured over almost every border. King Petar and the government fled to Britain, Belgrade fell without a fight, and in a week almost the entire Yugoslav Army had disintegrated. Yugoslavia's unconditional surrender was signed on 17 April 1941, eleven days after its war began.[4] 360,000 soldiers, mostly Serbs, were now prisoners of war. The rest of the million-strong army were either allowed to return home or evaded capture.[5]

Leaders in Slovenia were not idle at this time. After the coup against Pavle, Slovenia's largest political party, the conservative Slovenian People's Party (SLS), attempted to defect, offering to rule a Slovenian puppet state on Hitler's behalf.[6] The offer was ignored, and Slovenia was dismembered: everything from the river Sava northwards went to Germany; the south, including

Ljubljana, went to Italy.*[7] Now 800,000 more people, mostly Slovenians, were under Hitler's thrall. Hitler's directive, issued from a Maribor balcony on 26 April 1941, was, 'Make this land German for me again.'[8]

What this meant was theft and violence. The provinces of Gorenjska and Štajerska were absorbed into their neighbouring Reich regions. The SS established itself, going from house to house, business to business, looting. They stole money, furniture, carpets, clothing, cars, radios, and all weapons and ammunition.[9]

The violence appeared to be driven by greed, but other motives were in play. Reichsführer-SS Heinrich Himmler was writing plans for the future of Europe. *Generalplan Ost* ('The Master Plan for the East') laid down that the non-Germanic peoples east of Germany, foremost the Jewish, Roma, Slavic, and Baltic peoples, should be murdered or worked to death as slaves. When they had perished, German settlers would begin colonization.[10]

Slovenians were declared by the Nazis as not Slavic after all.† They would be Germans, a complete fantasy.[11] Until the Treaty of Versailles of 1919, Slovenia had been ruled by the Austrian Habsburgs for centuries, but now there were only a few thousand ethnic Germans in the north, concentrated in the town of Maribor. The entire population of German-occupied Slovenia had to join Nazi Party affiliates. There was almost no Jewish community, but 357 patients at a psychiatric hospital

---

* The north-east region of Prekmurje was annexed by Hungary. The Sava was not the exact border – Germany took a buffer zone a few kilometres south of the river.

† They were dubbed 'Wends'. Ironically just an old German world for Slav.

were shipped to the Hartheim Euthanasia Centre, where they were murdered with poison gas.[12]

Towns and streets had their signs stripped and were given new names. Town squares became Adolf Hitler Platz, as in most other German towns. Libraries, bookshops, and homes were raided for books written in Slovenian; over two million were burnt.[13] The Bishop of Maribor was ordered to cease all sermons in Slovenian. He refused and almost the entire clergy was arrested for his defiance, cloistered not far from Ralph.[14] Himmler then ordered the deportation of one-third of the whole population, to rid himself of 'hostile' elements and to make way for German colonists. First, the jailed priests and all Slovenian teachers would be deported. Then, anyone who had fled Italian Fascism after the last war. Finally, the entire population along the new southern border would go.[15]

Deportations began in June 1941. Within two months, 10,000 had been packed onto trains and sent to the new fascist puppet state in Croatia, or to occupied Serbia. Thousands more fled with their loved ones. Most would not stay in the place to which they had been sent; instead, they escaped to Ljubljana, which was under Italian control.

The de facto Slovenian capital and the rest of southern Slovenia had become the 'Ljubljana Province' of Italy, and Italian occupation was initially charitable. The province was bilingual, everyone kept their jobs, men were not conscripted, and a blind eye was turned to refugees fleeing the Nazis. The SLS were even invited to form a consultative body to the Italian governors. It was not that the Fascists had discovered kindness; Mussolini was annoyed that Hitler had spread his influence through the Balkans, and Il Duce planned to upstage the Führer by showing

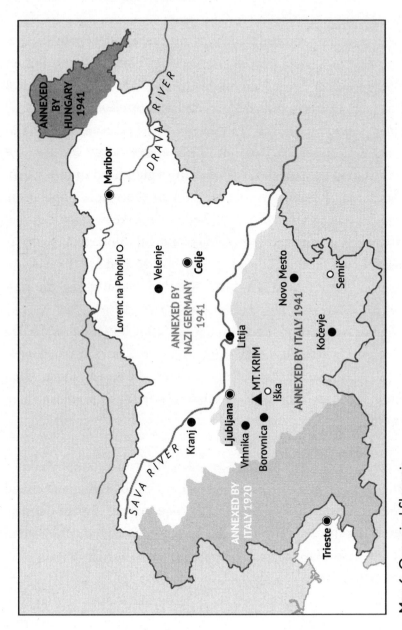

Map 6. Occupied Slovenia

benevolence.[16] Few bought this charade: Italian Fascists had been inflicting similar horrors on Slovenians since the 1920s.

Underground resistance groups formed immediately in Slovenia. The two most prominent were the SLS, which gathered its able-bodied (male) membership into the *Slovenska legija* (Slovenian Legion), and what would become known as the *Osvobodilna fronta*, or the *OF* (Liberation Front).[17] Founded by the outlawed Communist Party of Slovenia, this was a coalition of trade unionists, nationalists, left-wing Catholics, and women's rights activists. Both groups gathered weapons, and bided their time.

Passive resistance to the occupation ended on 22 June 1941, when Nazi Germany invaded the Soviet Union. If Moscow fell, what hope was there that Nazi rule would end in tiny Slovenia? America was neutral, and the British had proved incapable of beating the Germans on land. In the view of the OF, the only way Slovenia would survive was if it fought the occupiers and won. The OF rebel army was known as the Slovenian Partisans.* An underground newspaper announced their formation:

> The establishment of [the Slovenian Partisans] means a new step towards freedom, a new step towards liberation and the unification of all Slovenians, and a new step in the era when the Slovenian nation will be the lord of its own land. The rage of the occupiers against the struggling Slovenian nation is

---

* Officially the National Liberation Army and Partisan Detachments of Slovenia (*NOV in POS*)

intensifying . . . It is clear to Slovenians today that a relentless reckoning is needed with both German and Italian oppressors . . . Death to fascism, freedom to the people![18]

These Partisans would decide the fate of not only their own country, but many hundreds of Allied POWs. A number of POWs would even fight, and die, as Partisans.

12

All-You-Can-Eat Potatoes

The newly arrived POWs knew none of this. They didn't even know what a Slovenian was. All they knew was that they were in a city that looked German. It also sounded German, thanks to the Nazis' decree that only German be spoken in public. Their first contact with the new reality was the Stalag XVIIID processing centre, the *Zollschuppenlager* (customs shed camp), which had been set up in the old inspection point for railway freight on the Yugoslav–Austrian border, another grim, bug-infested building with a small yard ringed with barbed wire. The prisoners would sleep on the floor of the customs shed.

The camp authorities made a good impression with an arrival meal – soup with actual meat! Wal seemed to have an iron stomach, even after the journey, and managed three servings.[1] The prisoners were then gathered for parade. XVIIID's commandant was Colonel Ulbrich of the 891st *Landesschützen* Battalion. 'Welcome to our Fatherland!' he began, with a German soldier translating his words into English. 'If you are good, you will be well looked after. If you are wicked, you will be punished. If you try to escape, you will be shot!'[2] The prisoners hoped that last bit was a bluff, but the speech put them in no mood to cooperate. Camp bureaucrats went along the lines, taking names and details. Many prisoners sabotaged the count by slipping back to give a second, false identity.[3]

A routine was soon established. Colonel Ulbrich paraded the prisoners every morning until processing was complete. The guards would goosestep into position and load rifles on command. Thanks to a guard dubbed 'Horseface', this was usually a slapstick comedy. Horseface would never get it right. His goosesteps would be out of time; he'd fumble his ammunition or jam the bolt. One morning when ordered to load, Horseface stood motionless. His superior bellowed, 'Why haven't you loaded?'

'Sir, I did it before I arrived,' Horseface replied.[4] The crowd burst out laughing, and poor Horseface was sent off for a reprimand. After a few days, processing was completed to Ulbrich's satisfaction, and each man received an aluminium tag with his prisoner of war number. Ralph's was 5204. Then they were deloused, which was a major morale boost. Powdered down before a hot shower, most were clean for the first time in months. Their clothes were steamed clean (and free of bugs) too.

Afterwards, the POWs were transferred next door: Stalag XVIIID proper, an unremarkable collection of buildings centred on an old Austro-Hungarian cavalry barracks. XVIIID's population was in flux. Preceding Ralph's group were thousands of French, Belgian, and Yugoslav prisoners; then a few hundred mostly Australian prisoners taken in northern Greece had arrived. By the end of July, Stalag XVIIID held over 4,000 British Empire prisoners.[5] It was not a permanent prison but a staging post for cheap labour. The inmates would be transferred to smaller camps, near places of work.

Under the Geneva Convention, officers were to have segregated camps and not be put to work, but the imprisoning power could make use of enlisted men.[6] Almost the entire young male German population was in the armed forces and, since the Nazis rejected the British and Soviet model of women as heavy industry workers, the Reich looked to its prisoners for a workforce.

Processing POWs into *Arbeitskommando* (labour battalions and sub camps) took time. In the meantime there was little for inmates to do: no recreational facilities, no books, no letters from home. After the initial feast the food was awful, rations consisting of two ladles of cabbage or potato soup a day. Twice a week, a loaf of bread would be given to share between five. To drink was mint tea or *ersatzkaffee* (replacement coffee), which was ground roast barley or acorns designed to mimic the taste of coffee.[7] Taken together, it was enough to sustain the men, but not restore their battered health. Food was the subject of most conversations; so many had starved almost to the point of death in Greece and on the train.

Many kindly locals tried to ease the prisoners' suffering. Well-dressed local men and women would approach the gate and ask to give food or cigarettes, which was a grave risk for a small mercy.[8] Some prisoners started to become aware that they were in a land under occupation. Next to XVIIID was the 'Slavic Section', where Slovenians targeted by the German *Geheime Staatspolizei* or *Gestapo* (secret state police) filled the compound. Some threw a 'V for victory' sign from behind their bars when they caught the eye of a British prisoner. They had it even worse than the POWs. Some would be released. Others were shot, or sent to concentration camps.[9]

There were no boisterous men in Stalag XVIIID, and for some the meagre diet and a hot shower were not enough to keep their sanity. They survived in body but died in spirit. In those first months, some prison wraiths roamed the camp. They didn't wash, eat, or talk much. They were long since separated from friends, so no one knew their names. Instead they had gained nicknames: Ghosty, Conduit, Creeping Jesus.[10] One was suffering from pneumonia, but by the time the guards came to take him to the hospital, he was delirious and believed he was being snatched from his mother's arms, and screamed out for her. The man died a few days later.[11] Few of these men survived long. After the war, few chose to remember those poor souls had even existed.

Others had their mental strength tested by ghastly work assignments. One group of prisoners had to grave-rob. Marched to Maribor Cemetery, they were set to disinterring the dead. Then German soldiers plundered the bodies of wedding rings, necklaces, and tooth fillings.[12] With such options, if someone came recruiting for an ordinary work assignment, there were always volunteers. Wal, Ralph, and Gerry volunteered for an Arbeitskommando of 150 men, working at the village of Ruše for a firm contracted to build a road west along the river Drava. Conditions were poor, and the work was gruelling. Their accommodation was a rotting barn filled with bugs and lice, and in exchange for all their hard work they were promised 'all the potatoes you can eat'. Spuds came by the wagon load, but their employers underestimated demand: the prisoners devoured every potato and asked for more. When none came, they stripped orchards of fruit and pillaged corn from the fields.[13]

Ralph did not share this plunder. He had dysentery, which had followed him since Corinth. Then he was struck down by a recurrence of malaria and spent weeks from July into August in the camp hospital. The doctors here, Captain Michelides and

Map 7. Maribor region

Major George Thomson, the only officers in XVIIID, saved
Ralph and countless others.[14] Rested and beginning to recover,
Ralph returned to work a few weeks later, bringing with him all
the 'griff', the latest dubious camp tales – the Soviet Air Force
had bombed Graz, the British Army had landed in France but
had been thrown back into the sea again, the Red Cross had

begun sending aid to the camps . . . Only the last rumour was not believed.[15]

Ralph returned to work just as the road job was ending. The employers had had enough of them; not only had the prisoners eaten everything, but they had also achieved little – British Empire prisoners had an excellent talent for sabotage. The company begged for prisoners of other nationalities.

Back at Maribor, the crew learned that one bit of griff was true. Red Cross parcels had arrived! The allocation was one parcel between two men every week; later, this became one per man per week. They contained luxuries: tinned beef, sausage, sardines, cheese, sugar, dried fruit, margarine, tea! Most valuable of all were chocolate, soap, and coffee, a holy trinity already in short supply in Europe that fetched a fat profit on the black market.[16]

Better yet came the first contact with home. Their next of kin now had news of the prisoners' survival, so a postcard was issued to every man for immediate dispatch.[17] The prisoners were ecstatic, celebrating, as Ralph put it, 'the world's mightiest mercy organization, which recognized no barrier of race or creed in bringing aid and comfort to those who need it'.[18] The gratitude was so intense that many men became lifelong supporters of the Red Cross. At least one, Donald Luckett, was so moved that he arranged for much of his salary to be donated to the Red Cross during his captivity.[19]

13

Farmhand

Ralph, Gerry, and Wal were picked out for work as farmhands. On Sunday 10 August they went to Maribor railway station with nine other men, a mix of Scots, English, and New Zealanders. There they were joined by a German-speaking Welshman, Peter Anderson.[1] Guarded by a Sudeten German named Karl, they boarded a northbound service which crossed the Kozjak Mountains and the old border into Austria. Two stops after the border they alighted at Ehrenhausen, where a Herr Knaus was waiting. He was the *Ortsbauernführer* (village chief) of Ratsch an der Weinstrasse and wore stereotypical clothing – lederhosen and a Tyrolean hat with a feather – and a Nazi Party pin in his jacket. He also sported an impressive brush-like moustache and smoked a curved pipe. Owing to his resemblance to Joseph Stalin, the prisoners dubbed Knaus 'Joe'. An *Ortsbauernführer* was the head of the smallest rural unit of governance in the Reich. If the state needed anything from his village, or vice versa, Knaus was the man.[2] Ratsch needed farmhands, so prisoners were sent.

Knaus led the party away. On either side of the Kozjak Mountains, villages and towns were the same: centred around the local Catholic church, whitewashed cottages with red roofs shining brightly amid lush green grass. Morning mass was over, so the locals were at the cafes and taverns, regarding the prisoners with mild curiosity as the party made its way uphill.

Ratsch turned out to be a handful of smallholding farms. An Arbeitskommando was supposed to be a prison camp in miniature, but this one was a homely cottage bearing little resemblance to a prison. Within were a dozen wooden beds lined with fresh, bug-free hay, a table and chairs, a small stove, and a large copper pot. Since Ralph had entered captivity, such comfort had only been a dream. Knaus impressed them further, offering four brand-new blankets for each man. The cottage would be locked each night by Karl, who slept in an adjacent room, but at least they'd be warm and well fed.

Knaus let his new workers settle down for the night. Gerry set to lighting the stove, and Peter filled the pot with water for tea. Ralph and Wal cracked open a few tins of sausage and skewered the meat on sticks. Once roasted over the fire, the oily sausage was smeared on the bread and washed down with tea. Though he'd been discharged from the hospital, Ralph's stomach had not healed yet; he donated his sausages and nibbled only bread. He knew he couldn't keep the heavier fare down.

At 05.30 the following day, Karl woke the prisoners to meet their new employers. Each man tidied up as best as he could. Ralph had no comb, but tried to slick his hair back. At 06.00 at Knaus's house they were greeted by the man himself and a few other farmers. The eldest was a gentle-looking man with a shock of white hair and a wispy white moustache. Ortsbauernführer Knaus got the first and second pick. Peter Anderson was selected for his German, and Wal, for his size. Upon hearing Wal's surname, Steilberg, Knaus exclaimed, '*Ah, sie sind Deutsch!*'

Wal got off to a flying start. '*Ich nicht* fucking *Deutsch*,' he declared. '*Ich bin* Australian!'[3]

The other prisoners were then chosen one or two at a time until only Ralph remained. Smaller than his fellows and visibly malnourished, he was unwanted. He dreaded the prospect of being separated from his friends and returned to camp. Finally the old man, who had not yet chosen a worker, stepped forward. Through Peter he asked, 'Would you like to work for me?'

Ralph lit up. 'You bet I would!'[4] This old man seemed no Nazi.

The new employees hired, each farmer peeled off to his home with a worker in tow. Ralph went with his to a stone cottage with an attached shed and pigsty. In a courtyard next to the house was a stone square with waist-high walls, a pile of congealing animal excrement inside. Over time it would decompose, and when planting season came it'd be pumped into a barrel, loaded onto an ox cart and spread across a field. Ingenious, Ralph had to admit, but in the meantime it created an awful smell. Uphill was a more stately, whitewashed two-storey building.

Inside the old man's cottage was a homely scene. A large family were gathered for breakfast around a great oak table. The old man gestured for Ralph to sit. Ralph was asked to refer to his employer as *Vater* (Father) and his wife as *Mutter* (Mother). This was done in German, so Ralph believed the family were Germans. Mutter and Vater (their family name was Menhardt) had five children: three adults – Jakob, Maria, and Theresa – then sixteen-year-old Ferdinand and finally Friedrich. Ralph attempted an introduction but went astray. Somehow the family heard 'Konrad', so Konrad he was.

Despite the warm welcome, Ralph had issues. A pot of *žganci*, or *sterz*, was on the table. Usually based on buckwheat flour, not quite a dumpling, not quite porridge, with lard, crackling, or sour milk (if these were available), it was substantial and efficient fare. Father said a long prayer, and the children sank their spoons into the bowl. But Ralph was in a terrible bind: he knew he couldn't keep the thick žganci down, but he wanted to stay out of the camp. If he couldn't eat, however, he couldn't work and would be sent back for sure. As he attempted to explain with sign language, he could see Vater was concerned.

From the kitchen wafted the smell of Ralph's salvation. Fresh bread. That he could handle. A chunk of steaming black bread was handed over, and Ralph gnawed at it. It wouldn't be much, but it would help his stomach get used to eating again. As the family talked among themselves, Ralph's ear told him his hosts were not speaking German. They were speaking Slovenian. The language was alien to Ralph. Eventually, he would realize that they were bilingual, speaking German in public and to Ralph, and Slovenian in private.

When breakfast ended, Maria and Theresa set to helping Mutter with housework. Vater, Jakob, Ferdinand, Friedrich, and 'Konrad' prepared for the working day. Jakob handed Ralph a rake and they headed to a sunny field to pull scythed hay. Given Ralph's condition, it was hard work, but he felt liberated, almost a free man. After a few hours, Jakob called a break and handed out more chunks of bread and a water flask. Ralph went to take a hearty swig, and instead fainted.

When he came to, he would have been forgiven for thinking he'd gone to heaven. He awoke to a soft bed and a kindly, well-dressed aristocratic woman leaning over him. Her hand on his forehead, she said, in soft Austrian-accented English, 'Is there something perhaps I can do for you? The master tells me you have malaria. No? You are very sick, you must go to the hospital.'

The prospect of leaving his present company shook Ralph awake.

'I've been very sick, but I'm getting better now. Please don't let them send me back to Stalag – I will be much better here.' Ralph's English was not as accented as his fellow prisoners', and his carer smiled.

'I understand your English very easily. Where are you from?'

'Australia.'

'How sad for you, so young and so far from home. I will see what I can do.'

She went to leave. Ralph was confused. 'Who are you?' he asked.

'I am Frau Barta. My sister and I live with our mother in the white house across the road. Rest now – I go and get you something.'[5]

Frau Barta returned a short while later with some quinine. She was well connected; it was resourceful and kind of her to find malaria medication in rural Europe during wartime. It turned out that her mother owned the land that Vater farmed, so Ralph was working for the Barta family. She returned with another blanket and said she would check on Ralph again in the morning. Ralph thanked her and reflected on his stunning good fortune. He had found the kindest people he could have wished for, and they were well resourced and fluent in English!

Karl came to check on him, and Ralph feared the worst. But it was a courtesy call; Frau Barta had already interceded on his behalf. When Ralph scraped himself out of bed for dinner, the family too showed the utmost kindness. They gave Ralph valuable soft-boiled eggs and some bread, and a beautiful herbal tea to wash it down.

Ralph returned to his quarters later that evening, where Wal jokingly accused him of loafing, but they all knew Ralph was still not well. Wal was the subject of gossip himself. He'd immediately started trying to seduce Knaus's daughter. His fellows feared that he might succeed – and that the wrath of 'Joe' would descend and they'd all be back in Maribor, or worse.*[6]

Wal failed, or at least was not discovered, and over the following days and weeks Ralph regained his health. With Frau Barta, Vater, and Mutter's help, he received regular quinine and good food, which banished his malarial episodes. Father spared Ralph the most demanding work, giving him lighter tasks instead, to let the Australian build up his strength.

Settling into a routine, Ralph would begin his day at breakfast talking to Jakob, the eldest child and a bit of an odd one. Jakob was pro-Nazi, but also illiterate, which was unusual for a Slovenian at that time.[7] Ralph suspected Jakob might have learning difficulties. Jakob knew German as well as Slovenian, though, and helped Ralph to learn German. Ralph began reading the newspaper aloud to him while Jakob mimed the meaning of the words. Ralph took to the language like a natural. German verbs were intuitive for an English-speaker. To see: *sehen*; to feel: *fühlen*; to hear: *hören*. After a month, Karl announced that the prisoners would be going to visit the main camp to collect 'winter' clothing – until now they had only had the clothes on

---

* Amorous relations between Western POWs and Germans, if discovered, resulted in a prison sentence for both parties. See Raffael Scheck's *Love Between Enemies* for details.

their backs, without even a change of underwear. The POWs walked back to Ehrenhausen and boarded a train to Maribor. When they arrived, things at Stalag XVIIID didn't seem to have changed much: still poor conditions, still dull. The clothing distribution had not been sent by the Red Cross or their government, but was a motley collection of summer uniforms from conquered Allied armies. There were grey Yugoslav, Polish khaki, French, and a few British uniforms – cries of celebration went up when someone bagged a British kit. Each man also received a pair of underpants, a singlet, and some rags for foot bindings.[8] It wasn't much, but beat wallowing in your own filth. Ralph also got his hands on a green beret. He'd kept his precious Aussie slouch hat, but wanted to save that for special occasions. A camp tailor and a cobbler were operational by now, both well run, with men lining up to get their boots and clothes fixed or to have new shoes issued.

The Zollschuppenlager had ceased processing British Empire prisoners once the last batches captured in Crete had filtered through. The 'Slavic Section', though, was continuing to fill up with Slovenians, and now Soviet prisoners were arriving at the customs shed, though none had been processed to the camp yet. No one had seen any Soviet-crewed Arbeitskommandos.

Having returned to Ratsch, the farm crew laboured through the autumn. Ralph was getting twitchy. He resented both being captured and finding himself back doing farm work, though the scenery and the work practices were different.

His spirits were lifted by a new arrival, Frau Barta's niece Karla Todt. In her late teens, Karla was visiting for a fortnight, on a break from studying English at the University of Vienna. She asked Ralph if he would be happy to talk with her in English.

From the start they conversed with unexpected frankness. Practising her English with Ralph, Karla could air thoughts which in Vienna could get her imprisoned. She confirmed that, as Ralph had suspected, her relatives thought Hitler was a jumped-up nobody. Karla taught Ralph German grammar. During her brief stay, their conversations were Ralph's primary source of recreation. When she left, she gave him a pocket-sized English–German dictionary,[9] which he used to look up the words in the newspaper, before embarking on a regime of learning a dozen new German words a day.

Most farmers in the region owned stills to process fruit into schnapps or *slivovica*. Father's family instead tended a small vineyard for the Bartas, and Ralph joined in the grape picking. Mostly Riesling grapes were grown. Ralph had had only a brief acquaintance with wine during his time in Renmark and Wudinna, but he soon got up to speed in generous 'sampling' sessions. This nurtured a lifelong love affair.

Wages also began to be paid. Under the Geneva Convention, POWs were entitled to the minimum wage, which in Nazi Germany was fifty *pfennigs* a day.[*] The money was entered into an account run by the camp authorities: real currency could only be issued with the commandant's say-so; otherwise, the wages had to be converted into *Lagergeld* (camp money) coupons which could only be spent in-house on a handful of goods at inflated prices. Bottled beer could be purchased for a day's wage, while a hairbrush cost an entire week's earnings.[10] Ralph splurged on a hairbrush during a trip to Maribor to collect Red Cross parcels.

Autumn turned to winter, and brought hardship for all. Not

---

[*] 100 pfennigs constituted one *Reichsmark*.

long into autumn the first snows fell. Ralph was raking leaves for fertilizer when he heard young Friedrich cry out, '*Ach, schnee!*' Ralph smiled at the novelty. Though he'd seen snow up in the mountains in Greece, he'd never touched it before. The novelty wore off. Many of the Australians hadn't seen snow before the war, but now it reminded them of their bitter retreat from the Greek mountains. Though Ralph had retained his greatcoat, many had not, and they were all wearing summer uniforms. There were no scarves or gloves, so they improvised by cannibalizing the spare uniforms they'd been issued, and wrapping blankets around their torsos under their clothes before going outside. Wal and Gerry had more significant problems. Their shoes were falling apart, putting them at risk of frostbite. The two of them returned to Maribor to be issued new shoes by the camp cobbler; their replacements were uncomfortable, wooden-soled beasts, though at least now their toes wouldn't fall off.[11]

November rolled around, the snow piled up, the days grew shorter, and work ground to a halt. Soon they would have to leave their small cottage and move to a new Arbeitskommando. Ralph said heartfelt goodbyes to Vater, Mutter, Jakob, and Frau Barta. He could not have had better care. He was back to health, well fed and fit. Even Jakob's baffling Nazi thinking had helped Ralph grasp German. He hoped he'd be able to see Karla again and learn more of the language. There were promises from the family to ask for Ralph's services again come the spring, but he knew in his heart he would not return. Ralph cared about them and owed them much, even if the farm reminded him of what he'd tried so hard to leave behind. His mind returned to the same thought he'd had all those years ago roaming the paddocks picking wool from the wire: escape.

14

Resistance

Before Ralph even arrived in Maribor, the first successful escape had been made. Just an hour before their train pulled into Maribor, Abdul E. Krim and Mehmed Junis of the Palestinian Labour Corps broke out. They were picked up by and joined the Celje Partisan Company. With scarcely a dozen members, the company was one of many across Slovenia where existing Communist Party underground cells had taken to the field. Each gathered recruits, arms, and food, to fight the occupier. Men and women alike would fight for the liberation of Slovenia. For the prisoners of Stalag XVIIID, it could have been a way out, as the city of Celje was just sixty kilometres from Maribor. Sadly, the Celje Company, and many others, were quickly crushed. German looting had picked the country clean and few weapons could be found, other than the odd pistol. Recruiting was almost impossible as the Germans had an accurate census and had conscripted the entire male population into the *Wehrmannschaft* (military team). A part-time militia, its 85,000 members were in every town.[1] No one could slip away to the Partisans without the Nazis knowing and the Gestapo visiting one's family. Worse were the SS, who had regiments stationed across the country. Backing them were second-line rifle battalions from the Wehrmacht. The few battles

Mehmed, Abdul, and the Celje Company fought were more akin to gangland shootouts than military engagements. Over several firefights, both men were hunted down and killed by the SS.[2] The survivors scattered, joining other Partisan companies.

A little further west, one group of Partisans survived, even thrived. Several companies gathered together, forming a battalion. On 12 December 1941 those Partisans ambushed and killed forty-five members of the SS. The Nazis were stunned. This was one of the greatest acts of resistance yet. They gathered 2,000 men to pursue just 200 Partisans. The rebels fortified themselves in the mountain village of Dražgoše. The German attack began on 9 January 1942, and for three days the Partisans repelled the enemy; then in waist-deep snow they retreated into the mountains to lie low over the winter. Many civilians fled the village too. The other Partisans in the north disbanded; they had not the strength nor supplies to survive winter. Instead, they would keep a low profile and resume fighting in spring.[3] Eluded, the Germans turned to murder. Forty-one of Dražgoše's residents were killed, many children among them, and the entire settlement was burned.[4]

The Germans later returned and imprisoned every survivor. The foundations of the village were dynamited, and Dražgoše's fate announced: 'The German police are pursuing the bandits, anyone who went with them can expect death. The women and children who stayed behind have been sent to a camp . . . Whoever is with us has a secure future. Those who work against us, will fall into misery.'[5]

In the Italian-occupied Ljubljana Province, the Partisans were faring far better. They did not disband, but fought through winter. And alongside them were two more XVIIID runaways.

It was Christmas 1941 and Colin Cargill and John Denvir had been hiding in Ljubljana for weeks. The pair looked an odd couple; they might have passed for uncle and nephew. Colin was young, just twenty-two and tall, with boyish good looks. A plasterer from Queensland, he'd probably lied about his age to enlist for the AIF.* John was a few years older. A Glasgow Scot, he had migrated to New Zealand before the war. John had sharp features and a fearsome glare. John, unlike most of the Anzac volunteers, was already married with kids. The two had broken out from Stalag XVIIID and stowed away on cargo trains which brought them to Ljubljana, where for weeks, the pair were protected by some of the city's residents. Despite being under Italian occupation, the city enchanted Colin and John. It occupied one of the only stretches of flat ground in all of Slovenia, with old stone footbridges and cobbled streets lying in the shadow of a mighty fortress. Its charitable people had hidden the runaways, and furnished them with false Serbian identities. Under these identities, they had watched as support for the OF had swelled in Ljubljana, and a growing protest movement exerted itself.

Outside the city, Partisan bands were attacking the Italian 2nd Army, which occupied the province. Patrols were ambushed, garrisons stormed, and Italian soldiers taken prisoner. These prisoners were stripped of their weapons and boots (and sometimes clothes) and released.[6] They helped spread word of rebellion. Protests inside Ljubljana were likewise growing, despite violent crackdowns by Italian troops. The situation was more dangerous than Colin and John knew. The 2nd Army's generals

---

* His birth certificate lists a date of birth a year younger than that on his service record.

were terrified, and asked Mussolini for emergency powers to take hostages, attack the civilian population, and execute prisoners taken in battle.[7] These powers were not immediately granted. The generals' fear was well founded, though; the rebellion was expanding rapidly. Those unable or unsuited to fighting joined an OF underground, supporting and supplying the Partisans. Their numbers included a group of intrepid electrical engineering students who ran a secret radio station.[8]

Those who were suited to fighting slipped out of the city into dense, now snow-covered forests to the south, by Mount Krim. Colin and John were among them, joining a new Partisan battalion at the beginning of 1942. They were among over 2,000 rebels operating primarily in Ljubljana Province.[9] Despite the cold, all sorts had come: there were soldiers, tradesmen, lawyers, students, accountants, even a few orphans with nowhere else to go. Few gave their real names. The battalion Commissar instructed everyone to take a false name, to protect relatives from reprisals, and Colin and John decided to keep their false Serbian names. Colin was Ivan Glavić, and John was Franc Rabel.[10] The position of commissar was the exclusive realm of Communist Party members. As well as maintaining discipline, a Slovenian commissar had two primary duties. One, act as supply officer, and two, expand Party membership by recruiting Partisans.[11]

As professional soldiers, the Anzac Partisans were entrusted with a machine gun from the Commissar's stores. John served as gunner, and Colin as loader. Before going into action, they spent several weeks training, and learning enough Slovenian to comprehend battlefield commands. *Stoj!* – Halt. *Naprej!* – Advance, and so on. There were also several rules of Partisan warfare. One was always carry a spoon – you never knew when you'd get a chance to eat. Another was never take off your shoes, unless you were entirely certain the enemy would not arrive.

As Colin and John acclimatized, the 2nd Army's generals received the authorization they craved. New orders went out: carry out reprisals against civilians, interrogate and shoot suspects without trial, and do not take prisoners.[12]

The Partisans prepared to strike back. Colin and John's battalion assembled for their first major action on the night of 1 February 1942 under the light of the full moon. The eighty well-armed Partisans looked a motley sight, their clothes a mix of civilian garb, Yugoslav, and Italian uniforms. But all of them, Colin and John included, wore the sole uniform item of a Partisan, a cap bearing their symbol: the red star.[13] Their objective was a quarry and railway platform on the outskirts of the town of Vrhnika which were guarded by a few dozen Italian soldiers. The plan was to capture the garrison, seize weapons, destroy the machinery, and retreat before sunrise. Unfortunately an Italian patrol stumbled on the Partisans a little after 01.00 on 2 February, and fighting broke out. The Italians retreated into fortifications, and an hour of inconclusive shooting went by. Eventually the Partisans withdrew with little to show, though they managed to wreck some equipment, and take a prisoner (later released). The Partisans took a casualty also: one of their most senior officers had been killed.[14] The battalion retreated east to their camp, but imprisonment and winter had taken their toll on Colin and John. Colin was beginning to suffer frostbite, and John collapsed from exhaustion. The Partisans left John at a sympathetic villager's house to rest, and continued on their way. He would be spared the reckoning.

Three Italian columns had set out to hunt down the Partisan

battalion. The counter-attack began on 3 February. One column trapped a Partisan company in a barn, burning three alive and taking the rest prisoner. On the 4th, a second column, with artillery, moved on Colin and the main battalion. The Partisans were taken by surprise, scattering under fire. They fled straight into waiting Italian troops, who gunned down sixty-five Partisans. Despite frostbite and artillery fire, Colin was composed. He loaded the entire battalion's explosives cache on his shoulders and managed to slip through the Italian lines. His luck ran out later that day; the third column caught Colin near the village of Kožljek, and some locals identified him as a Partisan.[15] Despite local assistance, the Italians burned down part of the village. Colin was taken to an Italian garrison where he and the three other prisoners were asked to turn informant. All refused, so a firing squad was assembled, and Anzac gunner Colin Cargill and his Partisan comrades were murdered at Borovnica Bridge.

15

Thoughts of Escape

Towards the end of 1941 Ralph and the farm crew were transferred deeper into the Reich. Karl took the group to a northbound train, and they alighted twenty-six kilometres away at Werndorf, a small village at the end of the plain south of Graz. Marching across the river Mur, the prisoners sighted their new home, Arbeitskommando 410GW. It was a glorified pit: a small limestone quarry and cement factory fenced with barbed wire.[1] Karl led the column inside, saluted a young corporal, and bade farewell. The prisoners were sad to see the amiable Karl go. He had given them no trouble.

The new guard and camp looked unwelcoming. Hard limestone and wire fences surrounded every side. From a wall of rock, a small conveyor belt ran into a corrugated-iron shed. Across from that stood a timber hut, roofed and walled with tarred paper. The corporal shrieked at the prisoners to proceed to the hut, inside which were a dozen more Imperial prisoners and twenty-four bunk beds. There were no lights, no extra furniture, and no blankets. The only accessory was a small coal furnace, and the existing residents had already claimed the beds nearest to it.

The newcomers settled in as best they could. Though it

was still only November, it was already cold. Their work soon proved as tedious as it was miserable. A German sergeant commanded 410GW, but he was seldom seen. Responsibility was left to the corporal, another Sudeten German, dubbed 'Oozy' after his eyes, which were large, seeping, and looked on the verge of popping out of his skull.[2] If prisoners did not immediately comprehend his orders, Oozy would punch them in the head. As he had a shrill, high-pitched voice and a strong accent, this occurred often. Peter translated as best he could.

Oozy stomped about the quarry, jabbing prisoners with his rifle. To avoid beatings Ralph set himself to learning German orders, even though making out words in the dictionary was difficult in the shortening evening light. Only after several beatings did Ralph convince Oozy that he had a medical exemption from 'heavy work' assignments, which led to him being sent not to a different work camp but into the processing shed. Either way, work was miserable. When it stopped raining, it started snowing.

Gerry, Wal, and Peter all worked outdoors smacking at rocks. Ralph sorted stones inside the shed. The prisoners hardly spoke to one another, but Ralph managed to exchange pleasantries with a tall, thin, Australian man, though he seemed reluctant to talk much.[3] One of the few recreational activities available outside the hut was to 'buy' a conversation. When Oozy was not present, Ralph would offer a Red Cross cigarette to a guard, which bought fifteen minutes of chatting, a small break from labour, and the chance for Ralph to improve his German. Conversations went much like a high-school language class. 'Hello, my name is Ralph, what is yours? I am twenty-four years old; I worked in a bank. What was your job before the war?'

The guards were baffled by the Australians and New Zealanders. It confused them that men would come so far to fight. As Ralph's German improved, he learned more of the world outside. Some of the guards told him they were nervous about the Soviets, though most believed that Moscow must be about to fall, a Christmas armistice was imminent, and soon everyone would be able to go home – or at least the Germans could. The news gave the prisoners no cause to cheer.

When Peter was transferred out of 410, Ralph was thrown in at the deep end. The closest thing to a fluent German speaker, he was now the unofficial camp interpreter. It was improving, but Ralph's German was very one-way: he could speak the words he knew, but understanding anyone else was hard. This led the guards, who spoke in various strong regional accents, to think Ralph spoke better German than he did, and they would rattle off at full pelt, leaving poor Ralph scratching his head.

As winter deepened, the temperature plummeted, as did morale. It was always below freezing, the snow was metres deep, and sometimes it was as cold as -20°C.[4] Out in the shallow quarry the prisoners were completely exposed to the elements, and no winter clothing was issued. But before Christmas a new batch of letters came from home. Ralph received two. The first was from Ronte, containing good wishes and gossip. The second was from Ralph's mother and contained a devastating message. His sister Rita was dead. Her heart, weakened by rheumatic fever, had given out.

Gerry and Wal tried to cheer Ralph up with news of the war. Hitler had made a nationwide address: after the attack on Pearl Harbor, the Americans had declared war on Japan, and now Germany had declared war on America! The mood among the

Austrian guards changed; most had relatives there, and few had bad feelings towards the USA.

The good news couldn't stop Ralph's mental state deteriorating. It was always so cold, so dark. Stuck in the pit, he hardly ever saw the sun. Haul rocks, process rocks, warm your freezing hands, drink watery soup . . . on and on it went. Shortly after Christmas, Ralph walked off the job. He marched out of the front gate while the guards were at the other end of the compound and left, unchallenged. This was no serious escape attempt; it was a breakdown. Ralph had no food, no money, no documents, a British uniform, sloppy German, and no idea of where he was going. His only possessions were his photos, Karla's dictionary, and a small New Testament.

In what daylight remained, Ralph beat a path east through the snow and rested in an isolated barn. He slept, but awoke cold and hungry. Guided by his stomach, he walked into the nearest village and was arrested by a local policeman. A guard from Werndorf was picked out to escort him back to Maribor, where he was marched off to solitary confinement. A cup of water and a chunk of bread were pushed through his door. The cell was even colder than Werndorf.

16

The Extermination Camp

At dawn, Ralph's cell was opened. Along with half a dozen other prisoners from solitary cells, he was marched out to where a guard was pointing at a two-metre-square wooden box with an open top. Pick it up, he told them, and no talking. The prisoners knelt to lift the box and proceeded out of the camp under guard. Soon they reached their first stop: the Zollschuppenlager.

Ahead, in the middle of the yard next to the shed, was an enormous soup pot giving off a foul smell. It was no soup fit to eat, made of mouldy and rotting vegetable peel and ground straw.[1] Inside the wire, a group of German guards wielding batons stood by the customs shed. They opened the door and out poured hundreds of Soviet prisoners, skeletal, emaciated figures with bulging eyes. The Soviets surged forward, and the German guards on both flanks set on their captives with batons, making the prisoners run towards the soup while cracking skulls and shattering collarbones. There were no bowls or cups. Once the Soviets reached the pot, the guards backed off and left the prisoners to claw at each other over the food. In the doorway crawled the stragglers, now being trampled by their comrades. Men starving and collapsing, without even the strength to fight over food.

A gate in the wire was opened. A guard gestured to Ralph and his companions. While the Soviets were in the yard, Ralph was ordered into the shed to collect the dead. The German guards held handkerchiefs over their noses and gestured Ralph to get to work. Pick up the bodies, and put them in the box.

Inside the shed were dozens of corpses lying on a sheen of urine, excrement, and blood. Not yet thinking about what he was doing, Ralph grabbed a corpse by its hands. He didn't notice the frostbite on it. As he heaved, the skin from the deceased's fingers tore off. Ralph tripped backwards into the filth that saturated the floor. The guards kicked Ralph to get up, but did not shout: opening their mouths would let in the stench. Ralph lurched forwards but continued to dry heave even as he dragged bodies away. He and the other prisoners filled the box, then lifted it and marched out of the shed, gasping for fresh air as they emerged. The guards told them to put the box on a waiting horse cart. They followed it out of the camp, up the steep hill behind. At the top was a fresh pit. The box was laid down next to the trench and tipped on its side. The bodies came tumbling out with thuds and cracks as limbs snapped. The guards checked inside the mouths of the dead, then wrenched any teeth with gold fillings out with pliers.[2] Then they kicked the bodies into the pit. Ralph was handed a shovel to throw quicklime and dirt over the corpses. Then it was back to the shed to fill the box again.

Ralph saw a new group of Soviet prisoners arriving. They looked much as Ralph had done after Corinth and Thessaloniki: gaunt and almost broken. In the cold of winter, the Soviets stood clinging to their friends, some even holding hands in the pockets of greatcoats shared between two for warmth, a small reminder of their humanity.[3] There was a desperate glimmer of hope in their eyes. Here in Maribor, the suffering might end.

It would end in the Zollschuppenlager, but it would get much worse first. There was no sanitation, no water, and the food was more likely to kill than nourish. Soviet prisoners were not processed into working camps. They were not supposed to be: they were supposed to die. The Nazis murdered for the simple reason that they did not believe such lives should be preserved. Balt, Jew, Roma, Slav, gay, or Communist – in the Nazi plan, all had to die. To anyone with a sober mind and an inkling of what was happening, one truth was clear: this was a war of survival. If the Nazis won, they would enslave and kill every non-German from the Reich to the Ural Mountains. The customs shed was now an extermination camp: one of Europe's first.

Starvation and the journey had banished all strength to fight or resist. Only a base instinct to survive remained, and this would not last long. Colonel Ulbrich sent Soviet prisoners under guard on forced runs through the snow.[4] Hundreds died every week, and hundreds more would arrive by train to take their place.[*] This was the opening salvo of Generalplan Ost. In a little over six months, almost 5,000 people were murdered in Maribor.[5]

Survival was more likely in Stalag XVIIIA Wolfsberg, the next-nearest camp; the administration there was not as sadistic as Ulbrich. British Empire prisoners were better treated, which enabled them to organize. They pooled their Red Cross resources and began a smuggling operation into the Soviet Section. It kept alive scores who would have starved to death. In

---

[*] The death toll was, on average, twenty-six per day.

return, Soviet prisoners smuggled back valuables and trinkets as a small sign of solidarity.[6]

Despite these efforts, thousands died in Wolfsberg. Thousands more died in every POW camp across the Reich and German-occupied territory. A new chain of camps sprang up for Soviet prisoners. The Germans killed prisoners in forced marches, transit camps, trains, and camps, not because they could not care for them – the Reich needed the labour force – but simply because they believed those men should be murdered. As the majority died in POW camps, this genocide was carried out primarily by the Wehrmacht and not the SS.

Ralph and the others on punishment duty went back into the shed with the box. They returned time after time until the bodies were gone, and the shed was empty. Then they were sent to their cells for the night, and the following day were sent back in with the box. Dozens more had died, and the nightmare continued.

After days collecting Soviet corpses, Ralph was sent to a special punishment camp,[7] the standard sanction for escape attempts like his and other infractions. He was put to hard labour somewhere near Maribor. Though it is in his POW record, the trauma of the customs shed had so wracked Ralph's mind that he never remembered this. He had thrown away his only support network, and would never see Gerry or Wal again. A few weeks later he escaped once more – walked off the job, was immediately recaptured, and returned to solitary confinement.

As he was being led through Maribor, Ralph noticed something strange. The Soviet prisoners were being processed into Arbeitskommandos. After eight months of it, the slaughter was over. The war might not yet be lost: if Soviet prisoners were now needed for work, perhaps the outcome was hanging in the balance. In fact, desperate and determined resistance on the Eastern Front had indeed led Germany to reconsider its policy. It needed a workforce, and it needed to encourage the Red Army to surrender. Generalplan Ost and the murder of Soviet POWs would have to wait until the Soviet Union had been defeated. Even so, by the time the Nazis decided to delay the genocide, over two million had already been murdered.[8] Although Red Army and Partisan force of arms had halted Generalplan Ost for now, a greater force would be needed to end those designs forever.

The Jewish and Roma peoples of Europe were not so fortunate; their murder continued. Many of the camps built to murder Soviet POWs were converted into the first death camps of the Holocaust.[9] POWs were so neglected in Soviet history that many families have only in the last few years learned what happened to their loved ones. Valentina Oreh's father was a Soviet prisoner murdered in Maribor. She described concisely her family's experience in searching for him: 'Mother was left alone with six children. Father sent only two messages, then disappeared. We have been looking for him for seventy-two years.'[10]

Ralph spent seven days in solitary confinement in Maribor. Then he was taken under guard to a cold, furnished room. Before him sat an older, concerned-looking Austrian major and a clerk. Ralph looked and smelled a mess. He'd slept and eaten little in the past two months. The Major looked at a file, then at Ralph. When he spoke, Ralph had learned enough German to understand. 'Mr Churches. This was your second escape attempt in as many months. What did you hope to achieve?'

'I don't know, sir,' Ralph whispered.

'Normally, we'd send you to a camp in Poland. Nothing but

plains and no hope of escape. The duties required of you here have been difficult, I know. But, believe me, you do not want to go there.' The Major rose from his seat. 'You seem a reasonable young man. So I'm going to give you this final chance. I will assign you to a new work camp. But you will pull yourself together, keep your head down, and stop this nonsense.'

The Major ordered Ralph's release from solitary confinement, and his return to a normal Arbeitskommando.[11] Ralph was aware of his good fortune: thanks to the Major's kindness, he was out of Maribor.

17

Vengeance

Colin Cargill's death in February 1942 was a small part of a crushing of the Italian offensive that winter. By the time John Denvir recovered from the exhaustion that had taken him out of action, he was one of only 700 Partisans still fighting.[1] The Italian Army was determined to hunt him and the other survivors down, but they seemed unable to succeed. When the Italians pursued, the Partisans always managed to break or sneak out.* Sometimes Partisans vanished from inside an encirclement. After one such incident, Italian soldiers masked their failure by burning homes and reporting a 'conquest of the battlefield'.[2] Unable to deliver the killing blow, the Italians took their frustration out on the people of Ljubljana. On 23 February they fenced off Ljubljana with thirty-three kilometres of barbed wire. Italian commanders took hostages, systematically torturing and violating prisoners. One general complained about the latter – not because he objected on principle, but because he thought sexual violence damaged Italian prestige.[3] One in four Ljubljana residents were searched, and nearly 1,000 were arrested.[4]

---

* Sometimes hard to tell the difference between tactical retreat and running away.

They were the first to be sent to Italy's new concentration camps. One of the most notorious was Rab, an island in the Adriatic where thousands would starve to death in hellish conditions. But this did not stop the rebellion. Next, the 2nd Army enacted *Plan Primavera* (Spring Plan). Through January to April, they pulled all their forces back to just twelve garrisons. Effectively, they gave up and left the majority of Ljubljana Province to the Partisans. Slovenian soil was liberated. The Partisans tasted a strategic victory for the first time.

Success came at a terrible cost. As few Partisans had military training, they suffered staggering losses. One Catholic socialist described under-equipped 'Sunday trippers' wandering into the woods after mass.[5] Those Sunday trippers had seen their homes burned and their friends murdered. Many, Colin among them, had been killed because locals identified them to the Italians. There were scores to settle.

What transpired was a rampage that would stain the resistance forever. It took place in the same villages that had borne the brunt of winter fighting. Partisans went house to house, murdering those who had helped the Italians, and sometimes their families too. The Kiwi Partisan John Denvir saw one such execution: a villager who'd given testimony that led to the deaths of two teenage boys serving with the Partisans. He was shot, and his house ransacked, leaving his widow wailing over her husband's corpse that her spouse had only given up the boys because he had had an Italian gun to his head.[6]

The fight continued, and John found himself in a position of command. He led a company of mounted infantry for the Ljubo Šercer Battalion, which was named after a Partisan killed that winter. John became a legendary figure: 'Corporal Frank' (an

anglicization of his Partisan name), the POW who became a
Partisan. Still encamped at Mount Krim, and perilously close to
three enlarged Italian garrisons, he attacked wherever possible,
luring the Italians on hopeless pursuits.[7] He also learned that,
without heavy weapons and serious training, attacking garrisons
was foolhardy, so the battalion's attention switched instead to
convoys. On 5 May 1942 John and the Battalion ambushed an
Italian mechanized column, with the Italians taking over 100
casualties in bitter forest fighting.[8] Such attacks were the only
way for the Partisans to stay armed – their weapons stores had
been totally depleted.[9]

John was present for another stunning victory soon after, one
driven by moral necessity. On 24 June Italian troops had begun
sweeping Ljubljana again, arresting every male university student, ex-army officer, unemployed male, and anyone from the
lands annexed by Italy after the First World War. Many fled the
city, but a quarter of the population was detained, thirty-one
people killed, and 2,500 dispatched to concentration camps.[10]
For those arrested, a bleak future awaited, unless the Partisans
could save them. On 28 June 1942 a train carrying 600 people
departed Ljubljana, bound for a concentration camp. With the
help of friendly railwaymen and their signal lights, the train was
halted. Partisans opened fire on the guards' compartment, while
others rushed forward to break the padlocks on the passenger
carriages. The train arrived at its destination the next day, but it
did not carry a single Slovenian passenger.[11]

Sadly, these victories too were marred. Criminal actions by
Partisans were rarely punished if the perpetrator was a member
of the Communist Party. One such man was John's battalion
commissar, Mirko Fric Novak. Mirko had such a vile reputation

that Partisans from another unit threatened to kill him.[12] He picked out and killed a dozen perceived 'enemies of the people' from those liberated on the train.[13] Other Partisans committed crimes of ethnic hatred. A few dozen Roma from several families travelled through the village of Iška, which was held by John's battalion comrades in the 1st and 5th Companies. To the north, Roma were being sent to Nazi extermination camps; to the south, many took up arms to escape the same fate.* At Iška, none of this mattered: over fifty men, women, and children were butchered, and their bodies were dumped in the forest. A Partisan bulletin called the slaughter a victory over an 'organised gypsy spy and robber gang'.[14]

It was a thin line between rebellion and chaos. The independence and determination of individual units has given the Partisans early successes. Though their numbers had swelled to some 2,500 fighters, the Partisans were vulnerable; they had no clear strategic plan, and indulged infighting and atrocities. There were many incompetent or cruel officers. Units were small, poorly coordinated, and too close to Ljubljana and large Italian garrisons to ever plan and recuperate safely. This was the analysis of Commander Stane (real name: Franc Rozman), a veteran of the Spanish Civil War, and one of the Partisans' best commanders. He reorganized the forces under his command, with several battalions merging into a single brigade, although he was reprimanded for this unauthorized initiative.[15] The commander himself was embarking on an expedition, one that, if successful, could liberate Ralph and the other POWs. With 500 Partisans, Commander Stane was planning to cross the mighty

---

* Slobodan Berberski and Žarko Jovanović, for example.

Sava river into Nazi-controlled territory and make for Štajerska. The Germans reinforced the border and repelled multiple attacks by Stane's forces, so he was compelled to go on a long march via Gorenjska. And by the time they arrived in mid-1942, only 120 of his Partisans were alive.[16] The few other Partisans in the region were scattered and weak, as was the OF underground, relentlessly hunted by the Gestapo.

The Germans killed the Partisans they captured in publicly announced mass executions in Maribor and Celje. Ralph saw the death notices and didn't know what to make of them – the Germans spoke not of dead Partisans or rebels, but of 'Communist bandits' or 'bandit gangs'. The condemned were encouraged to write a final, uncensored letter to their loved ones as a perverse intimidation of friends and relatives. One young man wrote:

Dear Mother,

I love you, I love you, I love you, and Karla and Hansi . . . Dear Hans, don't forget me, I am thinking about you. Please greet Pop when you see him next. I am thinking of you, of my darlings, my dears. Mum I am so much yours, yours. Mum, Mum, I thank you for all that you have done for me. You are my everything, my everything, poor Mother. I would have so dearly liked to have given you some pleasant times in the autumn of your life. Unfortunately it will not be possible. I love you, I love you. I embrace you all and think about you all right to the end.

Your Erich.[17]

Although many paid a terrible price for resistance, the Partisans had one great triumph. Frightened of the possibility of full-scale

Partisan-led revolt, Himmler's mass deportations had ended.* However, under the rule of the Reich, young Slovenian men faced a more urgent problem: the Wehrmacht draft. Before, few would risk themselves and their families to fight and probably die as Partisans. But it became a more attractive option when the alternative was dying in Russia for Hitler. That summer, a few brave young boys left their homes and went to join Stane's Štajerska Partisans.[18] Striking opportunistically, Stane's forces kept their attacks small. They always stayed on the move, attacking lone trucks, cars, and high-ranking Nazis. Reinforcements arrived from all over the Reich and succeeded in mauling, but not destroying, the Partisans. Partisan battalions were split up, moved, and would begin again in a new area. Soon the war would come close to Ralph, to the mountain range south-west of Maribor: Pohorje.

---

* Though families of known Partisans were now deported, not to Serbia or Croatia, but into the Reich.

Churches family (including Ralph, *far left*), 1918 Kulkami.

Settlers in Murray Mallee.

Ralph about to begin
shoe repair sales, 1934.

Ralph starts at the
State Bank, 1935.

Wudinna, 1936.

Ralph (*far left*) and friends in Wudinna, late 1930s.

Ralph enlisted, 1940.

Men of 2/48th battalion AIF, 1940.

Ralph and Ronte on honeymoon, 1940.

Ralph (*middle left, second from front*) and A company, 2/48th Battalion, pre-embarkation, Adelaide, 1940.

AIF firing drill, Palestine, 1940.

Ralph (*right*) on leave in Athens, March 1941.

OPPOSITE PAGE
Top Lusterforce (2nd NZEF) troops retreating in Greece, April 1941.

Bottom Troops evacuated from Greece, April 1941.

Top Adolf Hitler visiting Maribor, 26 April 1941.
Bottom Red Cross inspectors at a Stalag XVIIIA Arbeitskommando quarry, 1941.

PART THREE

18

The Crow

At the end of February 1942 Ralph had arrived in his new home: Arbeitskommando 3GW, at Šentilj (St Egydi to the Germans), north of Maribor, next to the old Austrian border and a small tributary of the Drava river. It was too rural for Ralph's taste, but homely. Three or four barracks sat opposite a narrow green field, the railway line, and then the road. There was a cookhouse where meals were prepared, and the Drava tributary had several wooden footbridges running across it. Inside each barrack were metal-framed bunk beds, and feeble gas lights.[1] At least there was more sunlight, and the *Kommandoführer* (work camp leader) in charge was hostile but not violent – the Screaming Skull, the prisoners called him. At first he insisted all Red Cross tins be opened on arrival to prevent smuggled contraband, which had the effect of creating a weekly feast.[2] Once he'd accepted that the Red Cross was not smuggling, prisoners were allowed to store their tins.

Also good for Ralph's self-esteem was that he could now collect his special-issue Red Cross parcel that he'd missed out on in solitary confinement. Inside was a new British battle dress, a sewing kit, a shaving kit, and a toothbrush.[3] Ralph bathed, changed, and shaved. He also began the practice of writing a long letter to Ronte once a week. When his letters were delivered, Ronte replied weekly. The letters would usually arrive in bundles of six, but this correspondence helped ground Ralph's thinking about how to plan his future.

Through the end of winter and spring of 1942, as he became accustomed to his new camp, Ralph reflected on his failed escapes and took stock of what he knew. His escapes had been motivated by distress: they had been unplanned, unprovisioned, and in winter. Only a handful of flights had succeeded, all before the onset of winter, and all by men brave enough and crazy enough to fight and usually die as Partisans. As far as we know, Ralph had no idea if those escapes even succeeded. Prisoners generally didn't know when escapes failed either. Recaptured prisoners were usually transferred to a different Arbeitskommando, or another Stalag entirely. Their comrades remained in the dark about their fate. Then there was the problem of where to go. Getting out of a camp was easy; it was what came after that was the problem. Almost all of Europe was under Axis control. Transiting to a neutral country would require travelling through hostile territory for weeks. The nearest neutral nation, Switzerland, was 500 kilometres of patrolled mountains away. That left Sweden, Turkey, and Spain, all about 1,500 kilometres away. Passage would require excellent language skills, forged documents, ample food, money, and contacts.

One decent attempt that Ralph may have been aware of was Harvey Harold Pepper's attempt to escape from Maribor. He'd saved food, procured a water bottle, obtained civilian clothing, and broken out and travelled south-west into the rugged hills of Pohorje. From there his plan was vague and ill-conceived. He hoped to cross the border into Italian-occupied Ljubljana Province. From there, he'd move from east to west across Italy, cross into France, and then presumably Spain. Harvey was caught moments after leaving Pohorje, challenged and arrested by a policeman in the city of Celje.[4]

The only escapes since Colin and John that had been successful were joyrides. 'Jock', a prisoner in Maribor, had bartered his Red Cross parcels for a pair of overalls, a ladder and some German money. Posing as a civilian labourer, Jock had walked out of the main gate carrying the ladder. He was not challenged, so he'd stashed the ladder in a bush and gone for a night on the town, spending the whole night drinking and eating and pretending to be an Italian merchant sailor on holiday. No one had challenged him, and in the morning Jock had returned to the camp, carrying the ladder. Again he'd not been challenged, and had resumed life as a prisoner.[5]

Officers had it easier: their camps were secure, and they were not put to work. They could spend all their time planning escapes and could also pool a dazzling array of technical and linguistic skills, as well as having the intelligence services on their side. MI9 had been created in London to help escaped prisoners and downed aircrews, and after 1940 all officers and aircrew had received instructions on what to do if captured. They had to form a secret escape committee and get to work.[6] MI9 created fictitious aid organizations to smuggle equipment into prison camps: blankets made of fabric like that used in German uniforms; silk maps hidden in Monopoly boards, ink wells in chess pieces. This never involved Red Cross parcels, the supply of which could not be jeopardized.[7]

The men of XVIIID, on the other hand, were enlisted men, regarded as of little importance to the war effort, and no help was offered. None of those captured had received an MI9 briefing, so there was no escape committee. Ralph did not know about MI9, but he knew an unplanned escape was a fool's errand. Success needed planning, fair weather, outside help, and skills he did not yet have.

Arbeitskommando 3GW also had a *Vertrauensmann* (man of confidence) and an *Übersetzer* (translator). The Vertrauensmann was elected by the prisoners to represent their interests to the camp authorities and to any company for whom they worked. Ralph was furious when he learned this was standard practice: a Vertrauensmann would have gone a long way in Werndorf's quarry. 3GW's Vertrauensmann was a New Zealander, Sergeant William Fagan.[8] Bill was a kind and gentle man, who everybody liked. He never tried to assert himself with the Germans, seeming to lack that instinct that bolshiness can work, but he often succeeded with the gentle touch.

The Übersetzer was another Kiwi, Lance Corporal Roy Courlander. Very tall and slightly odd-looking, Roy was popular, keeping his comrades entertained with his incessant leg-pulling and far-fetched tales. Highlights included his mother being the beloved cross-dressing singer Ella Shields, that he was the child of Baltic nobility or White Russian émigrés, and that for a short while he'd lived in Germany and had been a member of the Hitler Youth.[9] His stories kept the men amused, though a few gullible prisoners believed every word. The Hitler Youth anecdote particularly upset those prisoners, and confused others.

At 3GW Ralph turned his attention to learning more German. Soon after his arrival, there was an escape attempt. A member of the Šentilj crew, New Zealander Jeff Stuckey, made a break for Switzerland. He did well, getting nearly halfway in a week, surviving on a few stashed tins, berries, and an unfortunate hedgehog. But Jeff was recaptured near Villach. He was briefly put in solitary confinement in Stalag XVIIID, but spent a few days out in the general camp population before being transferred. In that time, he met a member of the working crew who had returned to XVIIID to see the doctors, and news of Jeff's exploits were passed along.[10]

Ralph found 3GW to be similar to Wudinna: small, isolated, and strange. Wal and Gerry were gone, probably still in Werndorf, and there was little hope of a reunion. However, there was one man he did recognize: the tall, skinny Australian he'd sorted limestone with. The fellow seemed shy and nervous, so Ralph determined to do them both a favour and make a friend. He introduced himself: Ralph from Adelaide. The lanky man looked at Ralph and paused for a moment before responding. Kit Carson, he introduced himself: Tamworth, New South Wales. It was clear why he spoke so little: poor Kit had a stutter like a machine gun. With a shy grin and a lot of concentration, he managed to call Ralph a c-c-c-crow eater.

'Crow eater' was Australian slang for a South Australian, the myth being that the first European settlers there had taken to eating crows and cockatoos. 'Crow Eater' had a much flashier ring to it than 'Ralph', and soon, even to the British, he was 'The Crow Eater', and then 'The Crow'. Ralph's unkempt state when he arrived had helped the label stick.

Shaving became a dividing line in 3GW, between those meticulous about their toilet and those who weren't. Guys like Courlander shaved once a week and didn't bathe enough for their comrades' liking.[11] Soon Ralph fancied himself the flashest man in the camp. Griffin Rendell, a tall New Zealander, begged to differ, and the pair of them ended up in a grooming competition.

Ralph grew a moustache and styled himself on Hollywood's Ronald Colman – he'd already modelled his 'Adelaide posh' on Colman, so this was a natural progression. Kit, also a farming man from a farming family who had been sent to the 'family school' in the city, was in the neat squad too. He'd boarded at the prestigious King's School in Parramatta, west of Sydney, a school of strict discipline and with a military uniform that included a slouch hat. The pair stuck close to each other on the worksite.

The nature of the work also lent itself to camaraderie. The prisoners were not confined to the same pit all day or split among individual farmers, but were digging out an enormous bend on the road that ran south from Austria to Maribor, to make it straight. Removing a minor obstacle to traffic seemed a waste of 100 men, but they didn't mind working on a white elephant – after all, who were they to question the wisdom of the Reich? Work was supervised by a few guards and civilian workers from a local construction firm. Red Cross parcels supplemented German rations, so they ate well, and morale was high.

Bill Fagan was a keen rugby player, so he marked out a small field near the barracks and procured a ball. Whether this was homemade or sent through the Red Cross is not known. Locals would sometimes look on in bafflement at this strange foreign game. Ralph studied German, though the only German books available were propaganda pieces. With a bit of flattery directed at the camp guards, however, he was able to get hold of a German grammar book.[12] Ralph read it obsessively in the hope of bringing his grammar up to the same level as his vocabulary. Karla Todt's lessons had given Ralph a refined *Hochdeutsch* accent, a German 'Adelaide posh'. Ralph hoped it would be the tool to get him out, and get him home.

19

El-Alamein, Stalingrad, and Slovenia

To the south, John Denvir and his fellow Partisans had been successful. It was July 1942. In North Africa, the Italians and Germans prepared for the climactic battles with the British. In the Soviet Union, the Italians sent hundreds of thousands to prop up the faltering German offensive and hold the German flanks at Stalingrad. Yet something strange was happening. Instead of supplying further reinforcements against the British or Soviets, Italy diverted 80,000 troops, aircraft, and its newest tanks to Slovenia.[1] They were determined to destroy the Slovenian Partisans.

By 15 July they were ready. By Italian order, no one was to move between villages. Possession of arms or false documents would carry the death penalty. Any homes containing contraband would burn, and sympathizers would be sent to concentration camps. The Italian 2nd Army set fire to Slovenia. Entire communities were annihilated. In a little over a month, the Italians reported they had killed in battle or captured 3,600 Partisans.[2] If this were accurate, the rebellion was over and the Partisans were all dead – but it was not true. Murdered civilians were usually counted as dead rebels, as was the case in the town of Sodražica. A fire there sprawled out of control, consuming the village. Italian officers fled, but their men moved into the flames and committed grave atrocities. To cover their crimes, the commander reported, 'Rebels killed in combat: six. Thirty-five executed by firing squad.'[3] Sometimes, the dead were indeed rebels. An Italian military chaplain described the execution of a Partisan:

> He died as well as all true rebels. He didn't fret and didn't beg. He was very calm, although they had beaten him until he was swollen. While walking he said to the soldiers, 'Today you will shoot me, tomorrow someone else will shoot you.' He received absolution, and kissed the crucifix with great devotion, and he too died reciting Hail Mary.[4]

Outnumbered thirty-two to one, John and the Partisans never stood a chance, so they did the only thing they could: they ran. Often they broke out at night, swallowed by noise and darkness, and with Italian positions visible from their gunfire.[5] With the Partisans unable to defend liberated territory, civilians were left behind to suffer to consequences; 26,000 people were sent to Italian concentration camps.[6] Swathes of land were left barely populated. Many who remained had been broken by the trauma. One old, ethnic German man appeared in a number of villages where there had been fighting. He busied himself as a grave-digger, telling passers-by the number of people he'd buried. He was aiming for a hundred. Then, he could sing *Nunc dimittis*: 'Now, Lord, you let your servant go in peace. You have fulfilled your promise.'[7] Still the Partisans fought on, though their worst deficiencies had been laid bare. If they were to triumph, they had to change.

As summer turned to autumn, another force made itself felt. The Slovenian Communist Party had downplayed the fact that it was not actually an independence movement but was subordinate to a larger Yugoslav Communist Party, led by the enigmatic Josip Broz Tito.[8] He commanded his own Yugoslav Partisan Army. In 1941 they had fought in Serbia and Montenegro, now they were strongest in Bosnia and Croatia. To assert his own authority and fix the Slovenians' problems, Tito dispatched his Chief of Staff and a dozen experienced officers to reorganize the Slovenians.[9] The surviving battalions merged into larger units: brigades. Criminal or incompetent officers were demoted and sent to remote postings with high fatality rates. This fate befell John's battalion commissar Mirko – given a remote posting in Gorenjska and later killed in action.[*][10]

Competent officers were retained, or promoted. John was just such a man. He survived the Italian offensive but his poor horses had been worked to death, and John himself had sustained many minor wounds. The cavalry was disbanded, and John took a new commission as company officer, 2nd Battalion, 2nd Strike Brigade Ljubo Šercer.[11] Finally, the Partisans made themselves felt as an effective force. They moved further away from Ljubljana and linked up with their Yugoslav comrades in Croatia. As the battles of El-Alamein and Stalingrad began in autumn 1942, the Slovenians continued to do their part for the Allies. Several large ambushes each caused more Italian casualties than the whole southern summer offensive had.[12]

Things were also looking up in the north. Commander Stane

---

* Though it's not clear what the Gorenjska Partisans had done to deserve him.

had set his sights on a new goal: Pohorje. A vast massif of dense forest, sparsely populated mountains and few roads, Pohorje was the key to the north. It had rural smallholdings and food in plenty. If the Partisans could hold it, there were many avenues of entry or escape. Anyone fleeing the Germans in Maribor could be deep in Pohorje's embrace within a day. It could be a source of new recruits. And for Ralph and the other prisoners, it could be their way out. In late 1942, Stane assigned ninety Partisans to the newly formed Pohorje Battalion, and ordered them to storm the hills. The battalion ran amok for four months, fighting the same brutal and ghostly battles they always had. They were not the only ones to recognize Pohorje's importance. Their activities drew the personal attention of Hitler himself.[13]

The Partisans held the area through until New Year 1943, but they made a calamitous error: rather than keep moving, or break up over winter, the Pohorje Battalion built a fortified camp deep in the woods where they holed up. Trenches were dug, tents erected, and stores gathered. It would be the battalion's grave. German reinforcements brought in over the summer still remained in the region. Tracking the battalion through winter snow was straightforward enough. On 6 January 1943 German operational orders were issued and 2,000 troops from the Wehrmacht, the Wehrmannschaft, and SS moved on Pohorje. By 8 January the Partisans' camp was surrounded. It was a slaughter. Though a few dozen Germans died with them, the entire battalion was butchered, save for a single survivor, later executed.[14] News of the victory was conveyed to Hitler, while hopes of a Partisan escape line from Maribor lay dead in the snow.

20

In the Papers

Through 1942 Ralph's camp, 3GW, found a measure of peace. They were well fed, away from danger, away from death. Most were getting several postcards or letters each month.[1] In June Ralph surprised Ronte on their second wedding anniversary, organizing through the Red Cross for an enormous vase of red carnations to be waiting for her when she returned from her factory shift.

3GW was also buoyed by the news that Colonel Ulbrich's reign had ended. The Wehrmacht took conditions for Western Allied prisoners seriously, even if they had no qualms about murdering prisoners they considered less than human, and Ulbrich and Stalag XVIIID had become an embarrassment. In October 1942, Stalag XVIIID closed down, with responsibility for all Arbeitskommandos in Slovenia handed initially to Stalag XVIIIA/Z Spittal. As this camp was too far away, authority was transferred again to XVIIIA Wolfsberg.[2]

Ralph also had a growing friendship with one of the few other men on site with any language skills. Leslie Laws was a jazz pianist by trade. He was a bit older than Ralph, in his early thirties, with a wife called Rose, and four young children back in England. When war broke out, he joined the Royal Engineers and became a driver. His closest friend was a Scotsman and fellow Royal Engineer, Andy Hamilton. The pair had trained together, shipped out to Greece together, and, like so disproportionate a number of their ranks, were left behind together. As with Ralph, those who did not belong to intact combat units had often been left to fend for themselves. Les was restless, and had probably the best luck in camp. He'd attempted escape four times, yet somehow had not been sent away to Poland. Andy was even on the crew with him. Les had good looks, a strong jaw, soft blond hair, and a trimmed moustache; like Ralph, he styled himself on Ronald Colman.

Among men who had mostly finished school at thirteen, he and Ralph were both 'Renaissance men'. Leslie could speak French fluently and ran a well-attended class for his campmates, Ralph being one of them.[3] He'd also started to pick up a bit of German. Later, thanks to the Red Cross, Leslie was able to renew his passion for music. He cobbled together a small band with donated instruments, playing the piano accordion himself.[4] It wasn't much, and nothing like a real piano, but it kept Leslie occupied, and the camp entertained.

Life at 3GW improved further when permission was granted to trade at local markets, supplementing an already generous diet. Toiling on the roadworks, Ralph and his fellows qualified for the 'heavy worker' ration, which brought with it larger portions, and meat. Red Cross rations made this practically a feast. With access to the local market, they could trade for fresh fruit and vegetables, herbs, and, of course, alcohol. Because Courlander was needed at the work site, Ralph became responsible for the market transactions, both collecting the official ration and trading with local farmers. He began to converse with locals, and to understand the difference between the ethnic Slovenians and ethnic Germans (though, with the Slovenian language suppressed, everyone spoke German in public). Only through careful sounding out could one work out who belonged to which group. Eventually, Ralph befriended a Slovenian, Jan. He was an engineer, a civilian from Maribor who worked onsite with the prisoners.

Otherwise, Ralph simply toiled away on the roadworks, and improved his German. He knew Šentilj was not an ideal place for an escape; there were an unusually large number of German troops nearby, not just the Wehrmannschaft but also, unusually, border guards. Although German-occupied Slovenia had for all other administrative purposes been absorbed into the Reich, the official annexation never took place.[5] Partisan resistance had deterred this. As a result, there was still a border, and still troops patrolling it.

With so many troops around, the POWs were even more eager to hear news of the war, most of all from North Africa, where almost all the prisoners had served. Most news was from the local paper, the *Marburger Zeitung*. Though it was propaganda, useful war information could still be gleaned from its coverage of North Africa and the Eastern Front. Ralph knew the Germans were on the defensive back in Africa. The paper wrote on 2 November 1942, 'The major enemy attack in Egypt, defended by the German and Italian defensive front of El-Alamein, had already caused extraordinarily high losses of tanks and airplane losses.'[6] For days Ralph, Leslie, and all the other POWs waited with bated breath to see who would win the battle of El-Alamein. Then, on 7 November the following was printed: 'The Italian Army has announced: that Italian and German divisions were in fierce fighting with enemy tank formations in the Fuka–Marsa Matruh area.'[7] Marsa Matruh! That brought back memories. Ralph had been based at HQ there while he was mapping Libya; he knew it was some 200 kilometres west of El-Alamein. That meant the Allies had broken through! In the coming days the papers did not admit defeat, but spoke of rearguard actions and German forces moving west. Knowing the tide had turned in the theatre where the prisoners had fought, the camp was jubilant. Normally depression swept POW camps during winter. Not this time.

Preparations for Christmas and New Year now began in earnest. The POWs had little trouble from their guards. Most of the young Nazis had long since been shipped to the front. In their place were Austrian men in their forties and fifties, too old to fight, too young to retire. The prisoners were warmer now too, since the Red Cross also sent fresh winter uniforms. Ralph outdid himself gathering food and alcohol for the festivities; no one had partied so hard in years.[8]

At the new year 1943, while Ralph still nursed his hangover, he noticed something was different. All the border guards and local Wehrmannschaft had gone. The puzzle gnawed at him for days, until a week into January 1943. Ralph was doing some trading in the village when one of the border guards – a local resident – returned. He was drenched in blood: not his own. Hushed whispers darted across the street. An older woman stormed onto the road and screamed at the guard. She was furious, crying and shouting in Slovenian, which meant Ralph could not understand a word. Finally, she spat in the guard's face and stormed off.[9] Ralph later asked some locals what had happened. The guard had been sent to Pohorje, where Reich forces had killed a great many 'bandits'. It was not clear whether the woman had a son among the dead, or was just a wholehearted supporter. Ralph thought about this, and the German notices regarding 'Communist bandits'. That a country under occupation might have problems with banditry, he didn't doubt. But, seeing that woman so passionate in defence of the so-called bandits, Ralph began to suspect there might be more afoot. For its part, the newspaper did not celebrate the slaughter of the Pohorje Battalion. It carried only a quiet piece on the funeral of a few German soldiers killed fighting the 'gangs'.[10] Ralph determined to gain Jan the engineer's trust, and try to learn what was really going on.

The end of winter brought more good news, with the German defeat at Stalingrad. Then spring 1943 brought change. Roy Courlander left the camp to visit the dentist in Maribor, and did not return. This was not unusual: men were transferred in and out (usually out) every few weeks, and the once 100-strong working crew was closer to half that now. Ralph now became the Übersetzer, meaning he was exempt from manual labour and could practise his German full-time. Hopes of getting any information from Jan, however, were dashed. Jan did have a connection to the Partisans. For that, the engineer had been arrested and either executed, or sent to die in a concentration camp.[11]

Jan's arrest led to a sea change in Ralph's thinking. First the woman in town, now this? Disappearing a Slovenian engineer didn't fit the German narrative that the Partisans were simply bandits. Ralph began to suspect that the Partisans were most likely Slovenian patriots. More importantly, they could be allies.

133

21

The First Spies

In early 1943, British intelligence was thinking the same thing as Ralph. Total victory was near in North Africa, and attention moving across the Mediterranean. The British knew that Italian forces were tied up in Slovenia. Yet aside from that, they knew little about Slovenia except what they received through a secret line from the old politicians of the SLS in Ljubljana, via the Vatican.

The SLS were in a bind, playing both sides, but as the Italian summer offensive faltered, their fear of the Partisans triumphed. The SLS paramilitary underground, the Slovenska legija, remained dormant during the occupation. Meanwhile a few local militias had formed following Partisan reprisals. The SLS leveraged their underground to expand the militias and create a pro-Italian, collaborationist army, dubbed *Vaške straže* (the Village Guards).[1] Slovenia was now in a civil war. The SLS tried to convince London that this was nothing to worry about, and that the Partisans were the enemy. In a single baffling message, the SLS told the British three competing conspiracy theories: that the Partisans were Nazi agents, that they wanted to resurrect Austria-Hungary, and that they wanted to form Communist super-Germany.*[2] The SLS also claimed that the Partisans were gone, not worth British attention. 'The Partisans are slowly disappearing . . . [they are] now solitary bands fighting for their own lives.'[3] The British determined to find out for themselves. The Special Operations Executive (SOE), the intelligence agency responsible for espionage and resistance, would go into Slovenia.

The Slovenian Communist Party, meanwhile, seeing Slovenia's international importance rising, wanted total control of the OF. More or less at gunpoint, the leading non-Communist rebels were forced to sign the 'Dolomite Declaration' at the beginning of March 1943:

> other founding groups of the OF will not organize independent political parties or political organizations. Corresponding to their national, political, and social aspirations, which are identical in all respects to the aspirations of the Communist Party, they do not feel or see any need for their own specific parties or political organizations.

It also emphasized the Slovenian Communists' links to Tito's Yugoslav Communists, while trying to hold the mantle of Slovenian patriotism. 'As an integral part of the Communist Party of Yugoslavia, the Communist Party of Slovenia is the only party . . . which correctly understood and represented Slovenian nationalism.'[4]

The first British agents led by Major William Jones arrived a few months after this coup within the OF. Jones was from

---

* Technically, it was a 'Central European Republic under Austrian leadership' they referenced, not Austria-Hungary.

Newfoundland, and a veteran of the First World War. Somehow, at nearly fifty and missing an eye, he convinced SOE to parachute him into the Balkans. He immediately saw that the SLS were lying, and the Partisans were doing all the fighting against the Axis. The rebels were by now very strong, and the Italian 2nd Army was all but defeated, Italian troops rarely leaving their garrisons any more from fear of the Partisans. One Italian colonel said, 'I haven't moved, ever. I'm waiting to go home and if I manage to get there, I'm going to light a candle to the Madonna.'[5] Jones also met John Denvir, now commander of Ljubo Šercer's 2nd Battalion.

Major Jones's primary job was to supply John and the other Partisans. At first this was all by parachute drops, but there were ambitions to build an airstrip. One of the last things on the Major's mind was POWs. That was MI9's area, not SOE's – but that would soon change.

On 8 September 1943 Italy capitulated. The Allies had invaded Sicily, and Mussolini was spent. His armies in the Soviet Union and Africa had been destroyed. His army in Slovenia would fight no more. Three Italian divisions in Slovenia surrendered their weapons and were granted safe passage home by the Partisans.[6] In Ljubljana, the SLS held an emergency meeting. They decided to take control of the *Vaške straže* and defect to the Allies. But the orders never went out. German forces seized Ljubljana and took over from Italy before the *Vaške straže* could be organized.[7] The Partisans also made sure against any defection: *Vaške straže* garrisons were attacked, and the OF's Communist leadership ordered the execution of any prisoners taken.*[8]

---

* Senior prisoners were first put on trial, but proceedings were by no measure fair.

The Partisans liberated the Italian concentration camps, took on 10,000 new recruits, and formed nineteen new brigades. These were grouped three or four into a single Partisan division.[9] John and the Ljubo Šercer Brigade joined the 14th Division.* They seemed victorious but they were grossly outmatched against what was coming: Hitler pulled the formidable II SS-Panzer Corps off the Eastern Front to take what Italy had lost. The predictable happened. With tanks, planes, and overwhelming numbers against them, the Partisans took devastating casualties and were unable to protect the civilians against reprisals. Towns that had only just been liberated were lost again.[10]

Major Jones had his hands full trying to maintain supply during an enemy offensive. Worse, the region was so devastated it was on the brink of famine.[11] Then, in November 1943 came more work. A few dozen POWs who had escaped from camps across northern Italy found their way to him. Jones could offer little besides weak soup. He had no plan for evacuating escapees. Instead, he asked the group, exhausted by two months on the run, to join the Partisans. This nearly triggered a mutiny, and the senior POWs vowed to report the Major.[12] Eventually, Jones arranged to send the POWs south by way of a Partisan courier line. There, they evacuated from the Croatian coast to southern Italy, now held by the Allies.[13] Once returned, the POWs were debriefed by MI9, who began to think SOE and the Partisans would make useful partners.

Though, following the SS offensive, the situation again looked bleak for the Partisans, Commander Stane's resourcefulness led

---

* The division numbering included all the Yugoslav Partisans; there weren't fourteen Partisan divisions just in Slovenia.

him to be recalled south to take overall command of all Slovenian Partisans. Before he left, he had reorganized the northern forces. A small group of Partisans returned to Pohorje after the battalion there was destroyed. They did not fight – rather they established an escape line from Maribor for Partisan supporters and sympathizers. Over 1943 several hundred Slovenians fled into the hills and formed into three groups. The largest group was smuggled south along the secret courier lines, where it formed a fresh brigade, armed, and trained. A second group formed the Koroška Odred, a Partisan force that would go high into the mountains bordering Austria. The third formed what later became known as the Lackov Odred, the new permanent presence in Pohorje.[14] If brigades and divisions were wolves that would cooperate with each other to strike hard, then odreds were bears. Lone scavengers, they would operate stealthily across a large territory.

With the south near famine, not all the Partisans could remain. So Commander Stane assembled the 14th Division. They were to march north, cross into the Reich, link up with the odreds, and liberate Štajerska.

22

The Combine

By mid-1943, Ralph's work as Übersetzer was getting in the way of escape planning. His primary duty was to help prisoners slack off. If a prisoner didn't want to work, he milled about with a confused look. When a German foreman directed him to get back to work, the reply would be '*Nicht verstehen*' – don't understand. A great deal of time would be wasted while The Crow was brought to translate, and then eventually work would resume.

Ralph didn't last long as Übersetzer. Vertrauensmann Bill Fagan received a 'Dear John' letter. Separated from him for years, and with no end of the war in sight, Bill's fiancée had broken off their engagement. Break-up letters were so common that there was a noticeboard in the main XVIIIA camp that was full of them, posted as a form of group therapy.[1] The appearance of 'Dear Johns' always caused ripples: even where relationships had been rock solid, years of captivity brought doubts.

Bill Fagan folded in on himself, wouldn't leave his bunk or talk to anyone. This was a problem. The camp guards and foremen had to be stood up to with threats of the Red Cross: 'Keep this up, and I'll have the entire Swiss legation of the Red Cross jumping down your throat. You'll lose your cushy posting and wind up freezing on the Eastern Front.' A camp meeting was called, but Bill was so distraught he couldn't bring himself to attend. No one else fancied the job, and Ralph was the only person with the nerve and the German to shout down Nazis, so The Crow was elected as Vertrauensmann unopposed.[2] To the Germans, he would now be Herr Vertrauensmann. The prisoners did not know that they had given Ralph a licence to release a reconstructed version of Rory. Ralph's public persona was now The Crow. Leslie Laws, who had passable if not fluent German, took Ralph's place as the Übersetzer.

The Crow's first act was to form 'The Combine', a collective pantry of Red Cross parcels.[3] On a volunteer basis, prisoners would submit their parcels to The Crow; cooks appointed by the prisoners would use the German ration and supplement it with tinned meat, sugar or margarine from the parcel, and a cauldron of strong tea on the side. Breakfast, lunch, and dinner were all provided on this basis. Half of the hygiene and confectionery items were kept by the men. All other items with black-market value also went to The Combine. Non-smokers donated all their cigarettes, smokers only half. The real high-value commodity was coffee: few in the British Empire were coffee-drinkers yet, but Europeans couldn't get enough of it, and for most Germans coffee had been unobtainable even before the war. The Crow had a larder filled with soap, toothpaste, chocolate, cigarettes, and coffee, and he was able to buy anything he could get from local farmers, usually by bartering with these goods. He ran a double-entry ledger; all goods had to be signed in and out by a prisoner and countersigned by Herr Vertrauensmann. There were two padlocks on the store room door and only Herr Vertrauensmann had both keys. The produce acquired was consumed as fast as possible, thus destroying the evidence of black market trading.[4]

In all, he and his comrades' diet was hearty and nutritious; they were probably the best-fed men in town. The Crow was quickly also known as The Con Man; cultivating an image to all and sundry of being content with his lot, keen to turn a quid.

The Crow's second venture was, as he had done back in Australia at Wudinna, to build a swimming pool. In the last hot days of 1943 part of the nearby river was dammed to give the crew a place to cool off. Then came the wonderful news of Italy's surrender. But celebrations, and maybe hopes of a rapid Allied advance and liberation, were short-lived. The Allied attack through southern Italy bogged down, and Germany had asserted control over Italy faster than anticipated. The Germans were now transferring the occupants of Italian POW camps to the Reich.

On 10 October fifty of these prisoners arrived in 3GW.[5] Most had been taken prisoner in North Africa; a handful were from the Allied invasion of Sicily only a few months earlier. The Crow made the newcomers welcome and gave a speech explaining the nature of the camp and The Combine. He didn't push the latter too hard: most new prisoners were protective of their parcels. On the other hand, membership of The Combine meant a cooked breakfast; the alternative was a generic German ration topped with uncooked Red Cross tinned meat. Most came round after a few weeks.[6]

Earlier in September, 3GW had been dissolved altogether. The crew would now work for a firm called Fritz Schlie that sub-contracted for the German state and be put to work reballasting the railway line that ran from Maribor west to Klagenfurt.[7] They were now Arbeitskommando 1046GW. Still living in the Šentilj barracks, the crew had a four-and-a-half-hour return journey – changing trains in Maribor – every day, to whichever part of the line needed work.[8]

Becoming 1046GW brought a new camp *Kommandoführer*. This responsibility usually rested with a mid-ranking NCO of the 891st Landesschützen Battalion. It was always an Austrian man in his forties or fifties, who was not at risk of being sent to the front, but the position changed hands roughly every six weeks. Kommandoführers in Štajerska tried to get transferred back to Austria as soon as possible. The prisoners identified two types. There were the 'screaming skulls', and those who believed in *gemütlichkeit* (cosiness). The 'skulls' resented having to spend time among enemies of the Reich and Slavs; the '*gemütlichs*' resented being away from Graz, where the 891st was headquartered.

Johann Gross of Vienna, however, was neither of these. Some of the men jested that 'this one's come all the way from Whitechapel' – referencing the Jewish community of London's East End – and 'Whitechapel' was the name that stuck. Gross looked the antithesis of Nazi depictions of 'Aryans'. Even under an *Unteroffizier*'s[*] cap, Johann's baldness was evident. So was a smattering of curly dark hair on the sides. He wore small round glasses and had a heavy five-o'clock shadow.[9] Gross surveyed the camp, then established himself in an office near the barracks. A short time later, a guard shouted for Herr Vertrauensmann. The new Kommandoführer would like to see him, The Crow was told.

Ralph freshened himself up and dropped by The Combine to put some coffee grounds in his pocket – from trading in town,

---

* Roughly equivalent to sergeant.

he knew the aroma was helpful in difficult negotiations. The Combine offered the prisoners more money than they could spend, without even counting the wages paid by the Reich, and much depended on having the Kommandoführer onside. Black marketeering may have been rife – and since Stalingrad the value of Red Cross goods had been reaching absurd levels – but it sometimes attracted the death penalty.[10]

Having been invited in and offered a seat, Herr Vertrauens-mann sat, noting the cup of *ersatzkaffee* on the desk and a thin cigarette in the ashtray. They probed each other's background; Kommandoführer Gross seemed particularly pleased with Herr Vertrauensmann's clerical experience. Herr Vertrauensmann mentioned that prisoners were permitted Sunday recreation walks, during which small, discreet trades may have occurred with the local farmers. If such Sunday activities resumed, the guards could, of course, take a portion of these trades. Herr Ver-trauensmann was, naturally, just considering everyone's health. It turned out that Herr Kommandoführer had already had discus-sions with his guards on this matter. A price was agreed: a tin of coffee per excursion for Herr Kommandoführer – equal to several weeks' wages for an Unteroffizier. Herr Vertrauensmann assured Herr Kommandoführer that the paper trail would stand scrutiny: all Red Cross goods would have a legitimate POW consumer signing them out of the store. Gross was satisfied and The Combine had a handy new partner.

With Gross's help, The Combine would expand. Then, come spring, Ralph could think about escape. The western railway line they'd be working on lay south of the Drava River, against Pohorje, a perfect first step into the wilds.

23

The Greatest Show in Maribor

Unfortunately for Ralph, some of his crew didn't wait for spring. Six Australians, most of them transfers from Italy, were bitter at having been recaptured in the chaos after Italy's surrender. They were determined to try again. While working the railway line, James Hilliard, Noel Hammon, Eric Davis, Jack Davis, 'Bluey' Murray, and Robert Tellrock slipped off the tracks and into Pohorje, where they hoped to make for Allied lines in southern Italy.

Jack Davis was the only one who hadn't come from Italy. He'd been in the Reich since 1941 and had a personal mission: he wanted the world to know what happened in Wolfsberg and Maribor. They must be told that Soviet prisoners had been murdered by the thousand. Jack had a photo of Soviet prisoners arriving in camp before their deaths, a picture of real people, with hope and fear in their eyes. It was only a tiny piece of evidence, but it was worth more than the recollections of a few traumatized enlisted men. As far as Jack knew, it might be the only physical evidence that any of those men had even been there.

The escape did not succeed. The group had no contacts to help them travel south even though there were, unknown to them, actually a small number of Partisans nearby. Those Partisans were lying low, running their own escape line and courier network. Only blind luck would have enabled the escapees to reach them. Instead, German patrols recaptured all six. They were returned to Šentilj and locked in one of the barracks while the authorities worked out what to do with them. The escapees were fortunate to arrive back at night, with the rest of the crew there to see them, enabling Jack to palm the photo to another Australian, Alexander Connor, a meticulous man who had lied about his age to join the Australian Imperial Force.[1] *Abwehr* (German Military Intelligence) officers arrived in the morning and turned the camp upside down in search of contraband. Gross followed with a notepad to ensure all confiscations had receipts issued and would be returned.[2] The Abwehr did not find the photo, and Alex kept it safe until the end of the war and donated it to the Australian War Memorial.[3]

The Crow was furious at the escape attempt. It was an amateurish effort that was not the result of mental distress, nor well planned enough to justify the risk. He also feared that such a large escape attempt would lead the camp to be shut down and transferred. After the search Herr Vertrauensmann had a quiet word with Gross, who agreed to try to soothe his superiors. But, for a while, escape dominated camp conversation, along with speculation about the 'bandits'.[4] The Crow gathered the men for Sunday parade and tried to suppress the chatter. 'Right, you lot! I don't want anyone else making stupid bolts for the exit. There's no way you'd make it home: winter is setting in, and we've got the Germans breathing down our necks. Next thing you know, we'll all be packed off to Poland. At least here we're safe.'

The crew shifted with unease. Some agreed with him; others

murmured dissent. Leslie Laws eyed Ralph up and down, unsure if he'd let luxury and a safe billet get the better of him, but The Crow was only doing what was necessary to protect the crew. Unknown to Ralph, however, the six's example had revived Leslie's hopes of flight. Somehow, at some point, he resolved, he would escape.[5] Five of the bolters were transferred to other camps; Eric stayed and joined Leslie's band as a violinist.

1046GW was not shut down, but it did move quarters. On Thursday 28 October the prisoners gathered their possessions and boarded a southbound service to Maribor.[6] Their new home comprised two large wooden barracks in a railway yard fenced with barbed wire. Outside was another barrack where the guards would sleep. There was a storage area for Red Cross parcels, not only for this camp but also for distribution to all the Arbeitskommandos in the region. Herr Vertrauensmann and Herr Kommandoführer would be responsible for their delivery.

Inside the wire was a large concrete-walled shed. The colour drained from Ralph's face when he saw it. He was back at the Zollschuppenlager. The shed still crawled with bugs and the foul odour of the thousands murdered. The two wooden barracks, all that was left of the old XVIIID camp, had fallen into dilapidation. Ralph snapped. He gave the guards, railway employees and the Fritz Schlie company foremen the tantrum of their lives. Gross agreed to disinfect the shed just to stop him from yelling. Ralph was able to pull out a man from the crew to carry out renovations: Len Austin, a cheerful Londoner dubbed 'Eggy' who was a handy carpenter. Len would stay with Ralph in Maribor to make the barracks comfortable while the crew worked.[7] The venue was lousy, but the change to Maribor was agreeable, cutting two hours off the daily commute.

However, the move meant The Crow had to rebuild the camp's black-market network – with even bigger plans. As winter set in, the men needed entertainment, so he organized amateur dramatics in the camp. As in Wudinna, he would put on a spectacle to remember: The Crow would be MC and producer of a Christmas variety show. He set about recruiting acts. George Shaw was a stout, balding Australian recently arrived from Italy who led a group of half a dozen preparing *Fair Em – the Miller's Daughter of Manchester*, a Shakespearean-era romantic comedy.[8] George transcribed the entire script from memory (as best he could). Others prepared slapstick routines, monologues, and drag romantic duets. More music was needed, though, and while Leslie could still remember a few songs off by heart, they needed some hits. For some time Ronte had been trying to send her husband sheet music in the post, but the Germans always destroyed it for fear of sheet music's potential for coded messages. Herr Vertrauensmann had a conversation with Herr Kommandoführer: would it be possible to allow it to pass through? Gross considered his options. Yes, if Herr Vertrauensmann immediately transcribed a copy and destroyed the original. That would avoid trouble with the Abwehr.

In this way Ralph was able to get copies of 'Elmer's Tune' and 'Maria Elena', both current jazz band hits in Britain and Australia.[9] Leslie was delighted when Ralph passed him a copy; any ill-feeling or doubts over Ralph's attitude to the escape attempt was forgotten, and Ralph was invited to sing in the band, which by now had ballooned to seven men. Leslie squeezed the piano accordion, Phillip Tapping blew a trumpet, the Hoffman brothers were a guitar rhythm section, Eric Davis played silky violin, and now they had The Crow on vocals.[10] Leslie was the

musical director to Ralph's artistic director. Both believed themselves in charge, but responsibilities were divided to avoid any
conflict.

For those not interested in the show, The Crow leveraged
resources to keep the men engaged. The Combine allowed an
Australian, Eric Edwards, to borrow a camera from one of the
Fritz Schlie foremen and to buy some film to photograph events.
For exercise, an indoor badminton court was constructed. The
net was improvised from Red Cross parcel packaging, and
crude wood cut-outs were used for racquets.[11] Seeing their
production preparations, Gross approached The Crow with a
surprising offer: they could rent sets and costumes from the
Maribor Opera House. The old Slovenian producers had long
since been replaced by members of Graz's Austrian Provincial
Theatre.[12] Gross had ingratiated himself with the new management and was able to offer Ralph the goods in return for
a few discreet payments. Ralph jumped at the chance. On one
December Sunday, the production team hauled props from the
Opera House to 1046GW. There were tuxedos, tweed jackets,
jackboots, mock officers' uniforms and epaulettes; for the drag
acts there were beautiful black dresses and convincing blond
wigs. They also had a few painted backdrops, including one
mimicking an Alpine manor house.[13]

The only thing left was to create food for a Christmas party.
Ralph worked hard, hitting up the local farms and businesses
in town; Gross exchanged some of their Lagergeld into *Reichsmarks*, and Ralph had an ongoing parole into Maribor. It was
rarely a pleasant experience: having been under an iron grip for
years now, the townsfolk were cold and unwelcoming.[14] Most of
Ralph's interactions were with Germans secure in their lives. 'Ah,

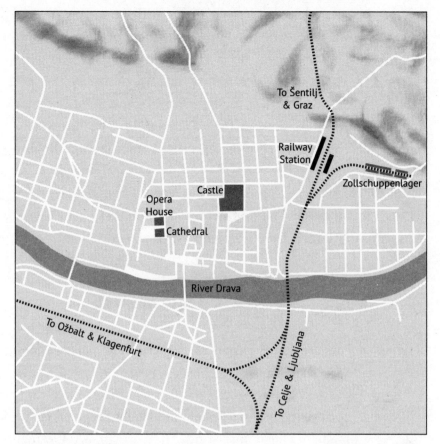

Map 8. Maribor City

you have such beautiful Hochdeutsch!' remarked the proprietor one day at a bakery where Ralph was arranging a special commission. 'It is a pleasure to listen to you. Your German is so pure no one would ever believe you were actually German!'

Ralph laughed, but he was shocked by the revelation. He'd worked so hard at proper German that he'd over-reached! With thoughts of escape uppermost in his mind, he made a note to learn the local rural dialects. There was one Slovenian he managed some pleasant conversations with, a young woman called Kristina Tinka who lived in an apartment behind the camp.

Christmas Eve arrived on a cold Friday night. The prisoners and their guards crammed into a room in the old Austro-Hungarian barracks at the centre of the defunct Stalag XVIIID camp. The curtain parted, revealing The Crow in a white jacket and black trousers at a mock microphone. Behind him, the band stood in two rows. Give a warm welcome, he asked the audience – to the Marburg Vaudevillians! The crowd erupted in applause. The first item was Ralph and Leslie's band performing 'Elmer's Tune'. A bouncy jazz tune struck up.

Why are the stars always winkin' and blinkin' above?
What makes a fellow start thinkin' of fallin' in love . . .

The show had the same format as the Wudinna review. Each song was followed by a sketch. First, a prisoner called Willie Walshaw performed a solo sketch as a British officer. Then came a Chaplin routine, and so on. Musical interludes included Ralph singing Comedian Harmonist songs in German. (A German close harmony and comedy ensemble, Ralph had seen the Comedian Harmonists perform in Adelaide before the war.) Len Hewlett, stunning in a black dress and blond wig, sang a romantic duet, 'Green Eyes', with Jock Inglis. Sketches and songs gave way to the *Fair Em* production, a campy tale of comic love that followed several lovers, including William the Conqueror, in various contrived situations. Isolated for so long, the men craved this sort of absurd escapism, where everyone in *Fair Em* bonded with a partner: the happy ending sent the audience into raptures.

With everyone in high spirits, The Crow picked his moment;

he hadn't actually asked the men before the show if they were willing to pay for the props, and now he appealed to the crowd to cover the costs. When he stepped down, Leslie got a good laugh in by commanding the band to strike up the tune 'No, No! A Thousand Times, No!'[15] The show later closed with the band playing 'Maria Elena'. After several rounds of applause, the audience and performers adjourned to the Christmas feast.

The Crow had outdone himself: all the best Red Cross food had been saved, the camp cooks had baked some marvellous cakes, and The Crow had procured monstrous quantities of wine, cider, and spirits. Even a barrel of beer was produced! The Maribor baker had come through as well and delivered a fresh batch of white bread.[16] White bread was hard to come by, but it was a taste of home that swelled the prisoners' hearts. Leslie and Ralph were overwhelmed by the show they'd pulled off. Ralph loved the applause, and Leslie was ecstatic to have a proper gig again. They all ate well and drank, toasting that 1944 might bring great things.

24

The March of the 14th Division

At New Year 1944, the 14th Partisan Division regrouped in a collection of villages north-west of Novo Mesto after the II SS Panzer Corps' offensive. The Ljubo Šercer Brigade was joined by two other brigades – the 1st and 13th Brigades, known as the Tomšič and Bračič Brigades respectively, altogether numbering 1,112 fighters. With them was a collection of couriers, medics, clerks, typists, and even a chaplain, barber, and dentist.[1] Their objective was to move north to fight the Germans in Štajerska. It would be a brutal winter march from Dolenjska, but Štajerska had manpower, food, tall mountains, dense forests, and a population desperate for liberation. Getting there would not be simple. It could be reached in a week or two, but the direct path led over the Sava river. Going west via Gorenjska was also unappealing, as Stane's experience in 1942 had showed. Instead, the 14th would march east into Croatia, turn north, and cross back into Slovenia from the east. Were he fit for action, John Denvir might have returned to Maribor. Sadly, he had been badly wounded during the SS offensive. He was smuggled to the Adriatic coast, evacuated to southern Italy, and then to an Allied hospital. John Denvir survived and went home to New Zealand.[2] The last of the XVIIID Partisans was out of the fight.

On 6 January 1944 the division set off in a five-kilometre column. Croatian terrain was forgiving, but bad weather meant it took a whole month to loop around to Štajerska. The *Ustaše* (the fascists governing Croatia) were weak by now and only fought minor skirmishes against the division, and German attention was far away. Still, injuries and illness led to nearly 100 casualties by the time the division crossed into Štajerska.[3] Luck was against them; they entered Kozje, where thousands of ethnic Germans from Ljubljana Province had been resettled, and these locals raised the alarm as the weather took a harsh turn. Moving west in deep snow, the Partisans were easy to track. Their pack mules were dying from cold, and fighters were succumbing to frostbite. Then came the enemy under Colonel Egon Treeck, the perfect man for the job. An experienced mountaineer, Treeck received the Knight's Cross for a bold attack against Anzac and British forces in Crete and had also seen harsher weather than even the Alps could offer, fighting the Soviets inside the Arctic Circle.[4] Treeck pursued with a force of 3,000.

The Partisans were now mired in snow, wedged between the Sava and Savinja rivers and deprived of the element of surprise. Over two weeks the 14th Division fought running battles, crossing the Savinja river and passing Celje. To hold off Treeck, they set up a defensive position on high ground in the ruins of the medieval Lindek Castle.[5] A single valley now separated the 14th Division from Pohorje, where they could regroup and link up with the Lackov Odred, but they might not make it that far. Night temperatures were -20°C, supplies were nearly exhausted, the pack mules were dead or had been given to local farmers, and the gun lubricant was freezing weapons shut. To survive, the Partisans had to make a bold play.

On 18 February they got their chance: a heavy snowstorm. The march would be hell, but the storm would mask their tracks. The division tried to break out into Pohorje but were spotted on a major road crossing, and Treeck's forces attacked. Only 162 Partisans succeeded in getting through; 360 were killed, captured, or went missing during the fighting. Many more wounded would die soon after.[6] The survivors retreated west, climbing Mount Basališče in deep snow. They hoped to rest and recover, if only for a day. Treeck would not allow it; he deployed his last reserves to the Partisans' west and sent ski troops up the mountain. They caught the 14th Division unaware. Retreating further

Map 9. Štajerska region

west, the Partisans used their last ammunition to smash through German encirclement, make for the Kamnik-Savinja Alps, and link up with the Koroška Odred.

The 14th Division was divided across two mountain ranges and had suffered heavy casualties. But Treeck's forces were exhausted too. Believing the Partisans all but destroyed, the German offensive ended on 25 February.[7]

Blocking any path for the Partisans back south was a new enemy. Following the German takeover in Ljubljana, new collaborators had appeared. In spite of the fact that they had attempted to join the Allies in 1943, once German forces arrived, the SLS had bent with the prevailing wind and reorganized their forces into an SS auxiliary: *Slovensko domobranstvo* (the Slovenian Home Guard). However, the SLS could see that the Nazis were losing the war, and they did not want to be bound to a sinking ship.[8] The Germans were also hesitant to hand any power to an established political party. So they appointed Leon Rupnik, a sixty-four-year-old Slovenian former general in the Yugoslav Army, as figurehead president of Ljubljana Province in late 1943.

Positions of power around Rupnik primarily went to the Slovenian members of a small, pro-Nazi group, Zbor.[*] Their members were mostly ambitious students, believing in their own superiority. Due to this group's youth and behaviour, the SLS called them 'the kindergarten'.[9] Their leading propagandist was a slender and charismatic twenty-year-old called Lyenko Urbančič. His rabid speeches earned him the nickname 'Little Goebbels'.[10]

---

[*] Zbor was a Yugoslav fascist organization whose Serbian members had closely collaborated with the Nazis in Belgrade.

Urbančič's recruitment drives swelled Domobranstvo* ranks, which, despite the moderating influence of the SLS, proved an effective Nazi puppet. The Domobranstvo participated in German offensives, held garrisons and key infrastructure, and assisted in the Holocaust, hunting down the survivors of Ljubljana's small Jewish community.[11] At the end of June 1944 in a radio broadcast that launched the 'Great Anti-Communist National Assembly' in Ljubljana, Urbančič outlined the new collaborators' ideology:

> It is not important if I speak over the radio in these times as the youngest Slovenian journalist. What is more important is the truth, which is centuries old. This is the truth about all the mean designs of the chosen people – the 15 million of the tribe of Israel . . . [we wish the English] would taste German weapons so fundamentally that they shall see that their place is only in togetherness of European nations with Germany against Asian and Jewish Bolshevism . . . Does the American and English soldier know what he is fighting for? Negroes, Chinese, and Indians are [fighting against Europe] for a free block of land in America.[12]

Urbančič also devoted part of this speech to condemning the SLS. He let everyone know that when Italy had surrendered, the SLS had decided to fight the Axis. In the following days the Gestapo began arresting SLS members, along with 500

---

* Conjugated as *Domobranci* when referring to the actual soldiers, for simplicity we have used Domobranstvo when referring to both soldiers and organization.

'politically unreliable' Domobranstvo members.[13] Others who opposed the Nazis were kidnapped in the dead of night and taken to Sveti Urh, a converted church east of Ljubljana. Here the victims were tortured and murdered.[14]

For the Partisans in the south facing the Domobranstvo and the SS, the situation was tenuous. They badly needed food and new recruits if they were to triumph. Their hopes, and the hopes of thousands in Štajerska, lay on the battered shoulders of the 14th Division. The division had only 440 battle-worthy fighters left, but recovered as best it could through March.[15] Supplies were gathered, and recruits taken on. A novel tactic was developed for the latter: the Partisans halted rail services in an isolated spot and took on new members from the passengers.[16] Soon the 14th Division was back up to 800-strong, although many lacked weapons. In Pohorje, the Lackov Odred yielded a whole new brigade, the Zidanšek or 11th Brigade, via the escape line from Maribor. Many Wehrmacht conscripts defected while on leave, either alone or in small groups of fellow Slovenians. Zidanšek comprised 300 such defectors. They brought their own weapons, uniforms, and training.[17] There were, as always, black sheep, in this case the Bračič Brigade. The most inexperienced of the 14th Division's brigades, a high fatality rate induced a psychotic atmosphere. While other Partisans prized Wehrmacht deserters, here seven such men were executed on suspicion of spying. The evidence was deranged, including accusations of 'placing scrunched-up twigs in a suspicious manner', supposedly some sort of code.[18]

In late March 1944, the division was ordered by 4th Zone HQ – responsible for all Partisan forces in Štajerska – to defeat several German garrisons, creating a 'liberated area', a permanent

Partisan base in either the Savinja Valley or the twin towns of Velenje and Šoštanj. The Maribor OF underground had been infiltrating the towns, and the division was nearby, so Velenje and Šoštanj became the aim.[19] Preparations went on all April, but the Partisans had little ammunition and no heavy weapons, and the attack on 1 May went poorly, particularly at Šoštanj. There, some Partisan officers got drunk before the attack; one tried to burn a Nazi office by mixing gasoline and hay, with the resulting explosion killing the officer and two others. Exasperated, 4th Zone ordered most of the division to retreat to Pohorje.[20] It seemed to be a hopeless pantomime. But help was on the way, in the form of a daring American spy . . .

25

Bombs and Recreation

The first big snowfall of 1944 triggered wild scenes on the worksite. The prisoners leapt from the railway to pelt snowballs at their fellows. Kit Carson, who'd cultivated a reputation as a quiet, serious man, took no part. He muttered, 'If the other chaps want to have some fun, they may do so . . . I have neither the inclination nor the energy.'[1] But he could not escape the crossfire. A snowball hit Kit square between the legs. He was enraged, reaching for snow to retaliate. Sometimes guards, foremen, or passing civilians would be hit, and then join in themselves. The crew's merry attitude led them to be affectionately dubbed '*Churchill Kinder*' by their guards.[2]

It was not all so happy, though. Since November Allied bombers had been seen overhead, flying north. Initially they brought cheer to the prisoners, then, on 17 January Maribor was targeted for the first time. The men were resting in the barracks when air-raid sirens sounded. The guards rushed to open the wire gates and take the prisoners and themselves to an air-raid shelter.[3] It was an eerie moment for the prisoners; the sounds of bombs and bombers were their first 'contact' with comrades in arms in years – yet if those same comrades struck their targets true, the prisoners would be killed. Their shelter was not hit, but by the time the raid was over, fifty-three of Maribor's residents were dead.[4]

The mood soured everywhere. German soldiers were beginning to accept that the war was going badly for them. Maribor's residents found their own homes and lives were in the firing line. For the first time since arriving in Maribor, the prisoners were in mortal danger. Nothing could be done about the bombs, but something could be done about winter malaise. Though conditions were good at 1046GW, suicides were common in other Arbeitskommandos. Captivity and boredom bred depression. A solution had to be found.

First, a library was established. Supplemented with local purchases and packages from families, the bulk came from a special Red Cross programme headquartered at the Bodleian Library, Oxford.[5] Then, Gross came again to their aid with an incredible offer to Ralph: money from camp wages with black-market sweeteners could fund various excursions. Each prisoner generated a modest income, but everyone knew it was unlikely that the German Reich would ever pay out the money – even less likely that Reichsmarks would be worth anything by the war's end if Germany lost. Gross's suggestion therefore would 'liberate' these funds before it was too late. The first of his schemes was a trip to a photo studio. A couple of gifted Slovenian women ran *Jana Foto* in Maribor, and The Crow and Gross arranged a booking for the whole camp. The men assembled one Saturday in groups of six, had a photo taken, and copies were printed to be mailed to the prisoners' families. If someone desired an individual photo that could be purchased separately.[6] The men grouped themselves by nationality, hoping their families could share copies. Eric Edwards enquired as to the cost of a Leica camera: 5,000 Reichsmarks was the answer. As the POWs were paid in pfennigs, this was an eye-watering sum that even black-market trade would struggle to overcome.

Gross followed this up with an offer even more expensive than a Leica. 'Herr Vertrauensmann, I understand your Herr Laws is quite the pianist. Would you like to buy a grand piano?'[7] The Crow was rarely short of words, but this took even him aback. How much does it cost? he asked. 10,000 Reichsmarks, was the reply. Ralph gulped and ran his arithmetic: that was a third of their total earnings, a fair chunk of which had already been spent on vegetables, photos, and alcohol.*[8] Herr Vertrauens-mann didn't even bother to consult the other prisoners on this potential purchase, only Leslie Laws. Leslie was delighted with the prospect and went with Ralph and Gross to an apartment in central Maribor, where they found a Bechstein concert grand piano. It had been three years since Leslie's fingers had touched ivory. He tried some scales and played jazz tunes.

Ralph, meanwhile, surveyed the apartment and chatted to the seller; the German owner had done well from the occupation, though Ralph wasn't given the details. By the look of things, all his belongings were now being packed up in quite a hurry. Ralph learned that the owner was moving to Salzburg. Any suggestion that he was in haste created noticeable tension. While he played, Leslie kept an ear on the conversation. Both he and Ralph were convinced there was an obvious explanation for the flight. The

---

* Day rate was 4.02 Reichsmarks per day. Fifty-six of the men had been working for two and a half years, another thirty for four months. This puts total earnings at just under 30,000 Reichsmarks. A considerable sum would have already been expended on excursions, food, and in early years of captivity on inflated prices for goods.

Slovenians were getting bolder by the day; if Germany were defeated, those who had profited from the occupation could expect no mercy.

To Leslie's delight the piano was a fine instrument and was purchased. Soon the band were starting to sound like a serious jazz outfit! However, the other prisoners were taken aback to learn of the purchase, and that everyone would be contributing. It became the subject of gags to Ralph's face and behind his back. 'If you buy a car for each of us, will we have to pay for it?' Or on the worksite: 'A bit of work now, chaps, think of the piano!'[9]

Gross also offered grand days out every Sunday, which proved universally popular. They would begin at the local cinema, known before the occupation as *Grajski Kino*. The film would be followed by trips to the tavern and an afternoon's drinking. Alcohol was in short supply all over Europe, but not in Štajerska – here copious amounts of almost every kind of alcohol were produced. The Laško brewery lay not far from Maribor, and as Allied bombing intensified, the beer had a hard time moving out of the region.[10] Someone had to drink it all. There were many teetotallers in camp, and after the film, the prisoners would split into drinkers and non-drinkers, with one group heading to a tavern and the other to a cafe.[11] Many of the other Arbeitskomanndos were also let out on Sunday. Some would take trips to see old friends in other camps, often farms, and drink and gossip the day away.[12]

At the cinema, few could follow the German dialogue, but it was a pleasant distraction and warmer than in barracks. Audiences in the German Reich had long since lost their taste for war films. Like the prisoners cheering *Fair Em*, they craved cheerful escapism. Musical comedies such as *Gasparone* and *Der*

Weisse Traum were shown, and eagerly consumed. Less cheery were the twenty minutes of newsreel, *Die Deutsche Wochenschau*, before every film. Most, local and POW alike, waited outside, smoking, while the 'advertisements' played, but for those who hoped to glean some information on the war, the *Wochenschau* was useful. Leslie and Ralph paid attention, as the last ten minutes were always devoted to the fighting. The newsreel of the second week of February 1944 was particularly enlightening. It showed Anglo-American troops attacking German lines south of Rome. German forces in the east were retreating: a map of Ukraine showed the front line had been pushed 1,000 kilometres back from Moscow. German sappers were filmed blowing bridges and railways while foot soldiers were digging trenches in the frozen ground.[13] Ralph and Leslie had seen this kind of desperate defence before, by Anzac troops in Greece. They knew what it meant: the Germans were crumbling in the face of the Soviet advance. The newsreel added fuel to their desire to escape, though neither knew the other's plans. That would change at post-cinema tavern drinks a few weeks later.

That day the pub bustled with prisoners; the local patrons had adjusted to the new reality and the barmaids did their best to avoid the lecherous advances of some prisoners. The general mood was festive, but Ralph wasn't. The show was over, the snows thawing, the tides of war turning, and yet he was still a prisoner. Leslie sighted his creative partner in the corner and brought fresh drinks. Ralph reached a hand into a coat pocket and produced the day's *Marburger Zeitung*. 'They Wanted to "Liberate" Štajerska', ran the headline – 'The End of a Bandit Division'.

The article referred to the three weeks of fighting it had taken

German forces to 'defeat' the 14th Division, claiming the Partisan division had been wiped out.[14] But to the two POWs this German interest in the Partisans meant the threat the resistance now posed was very credible. For the first time, they debated escape plans. Leslie was surprised Ralph had any. He appreciated the conditions Ralph had created in the camp, but after Eric Davis and his mates made a break for it, he'd assumed Ralph was content with the quiet life.[15] In truth, memories of Corinth, Thessaloniki, and above all the customs shed meant Ralph would never be content with sitting idle. The pair revealed to each other their previous escape attempts and agreed to find a way to contact the Partisans.

26

Thieves and Traitors

It was still early spring, and at 05.00, the sun wouldn't rise for another hour. Thanks to 'Eggy' Len Austin, the carpenter, the barracks was well heated and divided into sections of eight, which gave some semblance of privacy. This section had the old-timers, who had been together from Šentilj all the way back to the Maribor work camps. It had two Australians, Ralph and Kit, then three Kiwis, Bob McKenzie, Griffin Rendell, and trumpet player Phil Tapping. The northern hemisphere was represented by the three Britons: Leslie, Len, and Leslie's best mate Andy Hamilton.[1]

Some of the other sections slept in while the cooks prepared breakfast. In the old-timer section, everyone rolled out their kits for a shave. Ready for the day, they had a hearty breakfast washed down with hot tea and assembled outside the barracks at 06.30.[2] The guards made a count, checking no one had gone missing, fallen ill, or overslept. Ralph, Len, and two cooks stayed behind in Maribor.

The other prisoners, with another cook, 'Shorty' Humm, then moved out and, along with twelve guards and six Fritz Schlie foremen, boarded a little two-carriage train to take them to their day's work as a tracklaying party on the railway. The carriages were ancient, with dusty wooden bench seats. It was first light when the steam engine came to life. It puttered across the Drava to south Maribor, then turned west to follow the river upstream. Some men snatched a little sleep; others watched the valley go past. White frost dusted the pine trees. The Drava surged through its narrowing valley, fuelled by the spring thaw.

The locomotive halted at the town of Ruše, where 'Shorty' Humm stayed behind to prepare a lunch for the workers.[3] The train continued on another few stations before its passengers disembarked. Most stations here were seldom used or staffed; they consisted of a standing area and a small office for railway technicians. South of the track lay a sheer ascent up Pohorje. North lay the river and, beyond that, Austria. The foremen ordered the prisoners to start work, and tools were retrieved from locked sheds. The guards got a fire going and settled in to play cards and pass the time.[4]

Arbeitskommando 1046GW was a model of non-work. The crew could disassemble, strip, and relay ninety metres of railway track a day at a modest pace. An official agreement was made with Fritz Schlie to this effect. The prisoners worked backwards from there. Ninety metres would be the most daily progress. Generous delays were taken for any snowfall, rainfall, or air raids. The guards had no desire to work in these conditions – and, like the prisoners, they were subcontracted to the company, which made the prisoners and their guards working-class comrades.[5] If the firm did not look after the guards, the prisoners would drop tools until the matter was solved. This bought an enormous amount of goodwill, and gave the prisoners leverage to get their way with work grievances.

The prisoners lost tools at an astonishing rate: the Pohorje side of the track was lined with dense shrubbery, and men tossed railway jacks and pickaxes into the bracken, then wandered about, remarking how clumsy they'd been to mislay an expensive tool. Others were more active in sabotaging the track. They hammered nails into holes where screws should have gone. Workers from the railway would inspect the track, whacking the new rails with a hammer, and would have fits of apoplexy when the whole line wobbled. The prisoners understandably had little faith in their own work: when a freight train passed, the whole crew would scatter up the hill, fearing derailment.[6]

Leslie did not partake in the manual labour. He'd persuaded the guards that his precious pianist's fingers could not lay track. As the Übersetzer, a somewhat infrequent responsibility, he would try to convince the railwaymen and foremen that the wobbly track was an honest mistake, though sometimes his German wasn't up to the task, and The Crow would have to catch a train and come out to resolve the situation.

Aside from that, his duties on the working party were to fetch water and make tea.[7] Once the crew were getting down to work, Leslie would take two wooden pails and head off to get some water, often ignoring colleagues' wolf whistles. His journey used to be made under guard, but by March or April he went alone. The nearest water well was in the yard of a railwayman's cottage up the slope, opposite the village of Ožbalt.

He became a familiar figure to the cottage's residents and, hearing Leslie approach, two small children would often come running out. When they came up to him he embraced them as though they were his own. The little boy, who was called Stanko, was six; his sister, Mitsi, three. They reminded Leslie of his four

167

children so far away. Les would bring Red Cross sweets for the children, who would chase him around the yard as soon as he brought them out of his pocket.[8]

Their mother's name was Elisabeta 'Lisa' Zavodnik. Her husband Avgust was usually away working on the railway. Once Les had got to know her and her family during these days out with the working party, he would enjoy a coffee and a chat in passable German with Lisa while the crew's tea was brewing.[9] Sometimes he brought Lisa some Red Cross soap, and she would teach him some Slovenian. He agonized over how to gather information from her about the Partisans and resolved to continue to earn her trust.

While the men were working on the railway, back in Maribor The Crow had his hands full. He was responsible for Red Cross parcel delivery, not only for 1046GW but also to all other Arbeitskommandos in the area.[10] Farms, factories, lumber mills, and others were scattered across the region, each with anything between ten and a hundred prison labourers. The entire economy of the region depended on Allied prisoners of war. The Crow would pay visits, deliver parcels, and pick up gossip, though it was never very useful. Everyone whispered about the Partisans, but no one had any solid facts.

Ralph also had to deal with more attention from a tougher German intelligence service: the Abwehr had been superseded by the SS intelligence service, the *Sicherheitsdienst des Reichsführers-SS* (Security Service of the Reichsführer-SS), or SD.[11] The Crow's paperwork showed the prisoners consumed all their Red Cross coffee – the evidence of black-market purchases had been eaten or drunk. But now the prisoners' quarters were searched with regularity by the SD. Kit Carson found these searches particularly uncomfortable because SD uniforms reminded him of those of his boarding school, the King's School. It was like vengeful prefects bullying him all over again. Gross, however, endeared himself further to his charges by insisting that all quarters be left as found: if an SD agent took a bed apart looking for contraband, he had to put it back together again.[12]

Australian Sergeant Ernest Stevenson, chief Vertrauensmann for Stalag XVIIIA and head of the camp's new secret escape committee, was a man held in high regard across all Arbeitskommandos in the region. His deputy, both officially and on the escape committee, was Padre John Ledgerwood. Ledgerwood had travelled to Maribor in April to conduct an Easter Service, and it was probably he who brought Stevenson's unwelcome news:[13] Roy Courlander, Ralph's predecessor as Übersetzer, had defected to the Germans. Roy was free and traversing POW camps, recruiting members for a British unit to fight the Soviets on the Eastern Front. Stevenson was notifying all Vertrauensmänner that Courlander was considered a traitor.[14]

What have you got yourself into, Roy? thought Ralph. Ralph had always taken Courlander for a misfit too fond of leg-pulling for his own good, but a traitor? Ralph didn't know how to process this. He feared Roy would turn up in Maribor and attempt to recruit. That could start a riot. Ralph hoped that, with Gross's help, the German authorities might be convinced to bar Roy.

A few weeks later he had a chance to ask. He was attending a peculiar event: a business conference in Graz that brought all Vertrauensmänner and their Kommandoführers together in one forum where working and living conditions, pay, safety, and other issues could be discussed. The conference was led by

Stevenson and Major Benedikt from 891st Landesschützen Battalion. The latter was responsible for the main XVIIIA camp and, therefore, all Arbeitskommandos under it. Ralph and Gross arrived on a pleasant passenger service from Maribor. There are no detailed accounts of the occasion, but two incidents were recalled by Ralph. Courlander did indeed try to show his face, wearing an SS uniform with a British flag on the sleeve, and was chased out by the first man who recognized him.[15] Gross also arranged for Ralph to meet Benedikt.

The Major had a complex relationship with the prisoners. Unlike in 1046GW, conditions for most POWs in the area could still be hellish if the Germans in charge willed it. Benedikt did not lift a finger when, on 15 April, an unstable German NCO murdered two prisoners.[16] Benedikt was also suspected of pilfering Red Cross aid, handing parcels instead to Graz locals, though this may have been an act of mercy to provide help after an air raid.[17] Whatever his attitude towards the prisoners, however, Benedikt had no love for turncoats. He told Ralph that no orders about Courlander's activities had been received. However, if Roy showed his face in Maribor, POWs must do no more than give him the cold shoulder.[18] Roy did not make a visit to Maribor. Instead, orders came for Gross to distribute a pamphlet to the prisoners, which read:

> As a result of repeated application from British subjects from all parts of the world wishing to take part in the common European struggle against Bolshevism, authorisation has recently been given for the creation of a British volunteer unit.
>
> The British Free Corps publishes herewith the following short statement of its aims and principles of the unit.

1. The British Free Corps is a thoroughly British volunteer unit, conceived and created by British subjects from all parts of the British Empire who have taken up arms and pledged their lives in the common European struggle against Soviet Russia.
2. The British Free Corps condemns the war with Germany and the sacrifice of British blood in the interests of Jewry and international finance, and regards this conflict as a fundamental betrayal of the British people and the British Imperial interests.
3. The British Free Corps desires the establishment of peace in Europe, the development of close friendly relations between England and Germany, and the encouragement of mutual understanding and collaborations between the two great Germanic peoples.
4. The British Free Corps will neither make war against Britain or the British crown, nor support any action or policy detrimental to the interests of the British people.[19]

The pamphlet met with nothing but abuse. The 'repeated applications of British subjects' were an invention. The British Free Corps' strength never reached more than a few dozen. It was a collection of fascists, oddballs, and naive depressives – and, in some cases, individuals who simply wanted not to be tortured any more.[20]

27

Looking for the Connection

Ralph was scratching his head for ways to make contacts among the Partisans. Conversations with Kristina Tinka, the young Slovenian woman living near the camp, had gone nowhere, though in the meantime Ralph had managed to assemble a few escape aids. He'd stolen a compass from Gross's office, an act Ralph expected they could work out between them if caught. A riskier steal, in public no less, was a map of the region which Ralph tore out of a school textbook left open on a cafe table.[1] What he needed was to get out into the countryside, where Slovenians could speak in private, away from Nazi ears.

Such an opportunity arose in regrettable circumstances. The prisoners were now barred from pub and cinema trips, after several drunk lecherous men had sexually harassed a waitress.[2] The non-drinking group were particularly annoyed to lose their privileges. The Crow therefore needed to keep dozens of thirsty prisoners in high spirits, and so he expanded Sunday shopping operations. He'd head out with three or four others – usually Leslie, Len, Kit, and Andy – and travel with a guard to farmhouses, where the prisoners would barter for meat, fresh vegetables, cider, spirits, and wine. Payment was in Red Cross cigarettes, coffee, chocolate, soap, and tinned goods. Len's services were provided too: he'd bring his carpenter's tools and fix doors, windows, furniture, or roof leaks in exchange for goods.[3]

For contacting Partisans, however, this too proved a dead end. The farmers hated the Germans, and Ralph's language skills actually put him at a disadvantage: by now he had learned the nearby southern Austrian dialect well, but this turned out to make him sound so much like the Nazi officials from over the border that it spooked the locals. Having a guard nearby didn't help either.

For the guards at least, these trips proved fruitful. Ralph's favourite was Gustl Breithof, a middle-aged man from South Tyrol, a German-speaking region that had been annexed from Austria in 1919 by Italy. In 1939 it had been an awkward point in relations between Hitler and Mussolini. The resolution was an ultimatum: Tyrolians could either stay in the region and give up their name, culture, language, and 'become' Italian (like Slovenians in Primorska), or they could emigrate to the Reich. Gustl had chosen to emigrate.[4] For Gustl and the other guards, the prisoners were the only source of alcohol: guard wages were pitiful, and prices too high to afford much in taverns or shops – by now, in any case, most Slovenian farmers refused to sell to Germans. Many times, Gustl and the other guards sampled the purchases with such enthusiasm that the prisoners would carry their guards' rifles while they all staggered back to camp.[5] The rest of the prisoners were also delighted by the alcohol.

There was more cause for celebration. On 6 June 1944 came D-Day. The Western Allies had invaded France. The Germans were now fighting on four fronts: France, Italy, the Soviet Union, and in the Balkans against the Partisans. The *Marburger*

Zeitung carried the news of D-Day with unexpected honesty: 'The long-awaited British and North American attack against the northern French coast began last night . . . the enemy, with simultaneous heavy bombing attacks, dropped strong airborne units . . . protected by heavy and light warships, a number of enemy landing craft also advanced.'[6] For Leslie and many of his fellow Brits, though, the jubilation was muted by concern for the safety of their families at home. For the past two years, German cities had been pulverized: under the premise of focusing 'on the morale of the enemy civil population'; like the Luftwaffe, Allied air forces were authorized to kill civilians in their homes.[7] Hundreds of thousands of people were killed this way by the war's end. And in recent months, German radio and newspapers had started talking of 'wonder weapons' and 'retaliation'.

Leslie took German propaganda about the V1 flying bombs launched against southern England after D-Day to heart. A typical example of such propaganda declared:

> a fiery circle has been drawn around London, which has been fighting for days for its life against a terrible weapon of attack. In the centre of the town at the bend of the Thames fierce fires must be raging. A thin veil of clouds over London is coloured dark red . . . in London the fires will never be extinguished.[8]

Hearing about the threat to his home, Leslie went ballistic. Cursing the Nazis, he seemed ready to tear down the wire barehanded, so much did he fear losing his family.[9] The war was coming to a head, both abroad and in Maribor.

The railway worksite was now having visits from a cheerful and good-looking Slovenian man with brown hair: 'Flash Harry' or 'Harry the Bum', depending on which prisoner you asked. He wandered in and out, sometimes speaking with the guards, who told the crew he was a forest warden making a timber inventory.[10] It was clear that what attracted him to the site was the chance to pinch a meal or a cigarette. He'd pester the whole crew trying to bum a cigarette. Sometimes Harry would look for conversations in German. Leslie indulged Harry in conversation but rarely in cigarettes.

Through their daily work on the railway the prisoners were aware that services in Štajerska were in disarray. Partisans had been blowing up bridges, derailing trains and halting services, and Maribor Station was clogged with trains caught in bottlenecks.[11] Leslie and Ralph were now convinced that the 14th Division was still in business. Exactly where, however, was the question to which no one had an answer.

Summer, meanwhile, was moving along, and with it their window of escape. On a pleasant July day, Leslie finally popped the question to Lisa over tea. 'Lisa, do you know where I could find some Partisans?'

Lisa froze. Her eventual reply was cryptic: 'I do not. They are over the hills somewhere.'[12] Leslie took the hint and felt unable to press her any further. He was reluctant to let Lisa risk her and her family's lives on his behalf.

Ralph and Leslie felt a sense of urgency, but camp life needed to go on. They both continued the music and drama, developing new acts. Everything had to appear normal. Keeping the show going was complicated by regular transfers, though. Connor – still bearing the photo of the Soviet POWs – had been transferred along with many others central to camp life. Replacing them was a group of twenty from Stalag XVIIIA in

175

Wolfsberg, which brought their number to around eighty. Previous newcomers had been from Italy, captured in North Africa. But many of the arrivals here now were older hands caught in Crete. A short show was put on to keep up the happy impression and distract the newcomers. Henare Turangi, a Maori soldier also in the Ronald Colman moustache club, had developed a musical axe-juggling routine. It made a great impression on the new arrivals.[13]

Some of the newcomers to Maribor did not believe in fanciful tales of the Partisans, but others had come determined to escape. Colin Ratcliffe was one such man.[14] A young New Zealander, he'd spent two years on the run. He had lived in a cave in Crete, subsisting on wild plants, snails, and local help. Finally caught in 1943, Colin and his fellow runaways had not been sent to a Stalag, but to the notorious Mauthausen concentration camp, where they endured labour designed to work them to death.[15] The authorities then realized that these prisoners were supposed to be in an army camp and transferred them to Stalag XVIIIA. Now Colin had been moved on to Maribor and, like Leslie and Ralph, hoped to escape to the Partisans.

Those hopes seemed dim. Little indicated that there was a chance of establishing contact. For all their scheming, Leslie and Ralph had not made much progress – nothing to show besides a compass, a map, and a vague sense that the Partisans were nearby. It was late July already. If the Germans kept retreating, the prisoners would be moved deeper into the Reich. Their plan seemed dead in the water.

28

The Escape Network

In late spring 1944, an American agent boarded a Halifax bomber, bound for southern Slovenia. His mission was on behalf of three intelligence agencies. MI9 had realized how useful the Slovenian Partisans and SOE were to rescuing POWs and downed airmen, known in the business as 'escapers and evaders' (E&Es). Undercover as 'A Force', MI9 cut deals with Tito and the SOE to allow their agents to be attached to SOE missions in Slovenia.[1]

The Americans had become interested in Slovenia too, and the Office of Strategic Services (OSS, the American equivalent of SOE) cut a deal to join SOE missions. This culminated in OSS Major Franklin Lindsay being appointed to head an SOE-led joint mission with OSS and MI9 to Štajerska. Its codename was Cuckold.

Lindsay was an outsider to SOE, whose recruitment process had often consisted of hiring chaps met at a bar, with the old-school tie playing its part. Not infrequently candidates were capable individuals used to brutal privations, but also barking mad. Major William Jones had been recalled for just such eccentricities. As well as trying to convince escapees to fight, in a fit of revolutionary enthusiasm, he had donated all of his operational funds to the organization of Anti-Fascist Women of Slovenia, on behalf of the invented-on-the-spot 'Anti-Fascist Women of Canada'.[2] Lindsay, a tall, thin man with a radiant smile younger than his years, wasn't without elite (or inside) connections himself: a twenty-eight-year-old Princeton engineering graduate, he was originally a supply officer with a desk job. He went then with US Army Engineers to Iran, working Anglo-American–Soviet supply lines. Lindsay craved adventure and talked his way first into OSS, and then onto the mission by exaggerating his skill in German and Russian.[3] His second officer was OSS Lieutenant Gordon Bush, skinny and very short, with a fine moustache. They'd become a great double act. There was also an MI9 man aboard: Captain Jack Saggers, a polite and professional Brit. He was not going with Cuckold. Instead, he was to build an airfield and holding centre for E&Es in southern Slovenia.[4] If successful, planes could land rather than parachute supplies, and take Partisan wounded and E&Es on the return journey.

As the Halifax reached the rendezvous late at night, an air of anxiety prevailed. This was their third attempt to parachute in. One attempt failed due to bad weather, the other due to Partisan failure to light the correct fire signals on the ground. Tonight, all was well. Sighting the correct light signal, the Halifax flung its cargo and passengers into the night. Parachuting down, Lindsay hit the ground with bruises but no broken bones. A Partisan officer emerged from the dark and embraced Lindsay like a brother. The agents were plied with spirits while Partisans gathered the supplies.

The agents had brought a few guns and munitions, but the most precious cargo was three large portable radios. One had shattered during the drop, along with Cuckold's only bottle of Scotch. Their superiors at SOE's 'Force 399' in Bari in Italy were going to drop an extra man with two more radios once the mission was in Štajerska.[5]

Cuckold had landed near Semič, a small town in southern Slovenia held by the Partisans. Nearby was Partisan HQ, while the OF's political HQ was a day's march away in Kočevje forest. Cuckold's mission was simple. Contact the 14th Division, blow things up, and make life difficult for the Germans. In more detail: establish supply sites and get weapons and explosives to the Partisans. Lindsay also had responsibility for MI9 matters, to look after E&Es and gather intelligence from them.[6]

He could not begin his mission yet. A small German offensive was blocking the way north. While they waited, Commander Stane paid Lindsay a visit to offer advice on the realities of war in Štajerska. His advice was to travel light and always stay on the move. Lindsay promptly gave away much of his luggage, including all his spare clothes save a pair of socks. Soon the 14th Division had defeated the small offensive, and the way was clear. Cuckold would follow secret Partisan courier lines north, travelling only by night. The Kamnik-Zasavje Odred, the 'Sava Navy', was responsible for getting Cuckold across the Sava river in crude canoes made from rough planks, but one of their Partisans deserted, and likely reported their position to the enemy. Several days of pursuit ended in a safe house high on a hill south of the town of Gornji Grad. No one had been killed or injured, but one of the radios had been left behind. If the last one broke, all contact with SOE would be severed, along with any hope of supply.

Lindsay saw Štajerska by daylight for the first time while they were resting at the safe house. The whole region sprawled out beneath him, a kaleidoscope of colour. Fields and forests were a vibrant green, fed by spring rain. Red roofs were soaking up the sun under a rich blue sky. With the white peaks of the mountains and the purple bloom of crocus flowers, it looked like a peaceful paradise. He could see why the Partisans were fighting so hard for it.

He also got his first taste of MI9 duties, receiving a group of American airmen being rescued by the Partisans. They had little intelligence to pass on, except that their intended bombing target had been the Maribor railway yard.[7] The Partisans sent them on south, where they hoped Saggers could assist them. Lindsay was then taken to Pohorje, where the 4th Zone HQ had encamped following the failed attempt to create a liberated area. The camp was rudimentary, but had all the typists, officers, and couriers needed to run an army. An honour guard ceremony greeted Lindsay. Slovenian and Yugoslav tricolours bearing red stars were unfurled, and HQ troops stood to attention. As each Partisan possessed different uniforms and weapons from each other, it was a peculiar sight. Then it was straight into conference with Partisan commanders.

4th Zone HQ had realized their poor planning and lack of heavy weapons needed urgent correction. They had two ambitious operations to execute. They still had to create a permanent 'safe' area, but first, they were ordered to destroy the enemy's railway lines. Summer fighting was about to intensify on the Eastern Front, and Pohorje was the perfect staging ground for a sabotage operation: along every edge of the massif lay a railway line. East was the main route south from Vienna via Maribor and Celje. West was a secondary line south from Wolfsberg to Celje. North was the Maribor to Klagenfurt backline. South of Celje was the junction at Zidani Most. Two bridges there carried all the lines from Belgrade, Vienna, Zagreb, and Trieste.

Four targets were chosen: three bridges and a tunnel on the eastern, southern, and western lines. Lindsay's task would be supply and explosives. Later, in order to take German garrisons and create a 'safe area', the Partisans would need more guns, ammunition, and portable artillery. For the railway sabotage they would need high explosives, and lots of them. If they could do this, they'd cripple German supply for the entire southern section of the Eastern Front. It would stop the Germans there from reinforcing against the Red Army. It could be a monumental contribution to the war at a critical moment.

Lindsay arranged a successful airdrop of high explosives, and the operation was a partial success. On 8 June 1944 the brigades fanned out to their four targets, though one operation had to be cancelled when the Partisans spotted a reinforced German garrison with flak defending the target. Lindsay was with the Zidanšek Brigade, tasked with blowing up a vast viaduct on the western line. He soon suspected that Partisan sappers, usually former mineworkers, might not be well qualified. They insisted on taking the bombs from Lindsay and almost caused a disaster by placing the charges in sequence around the campfire when they stopped for dinner – 'They work better when heated up,' one of the sappers assured Lindsay.[8] By luck, they didn't explode and kill the whole brigade. Reaching the bridge, they dug holes at the bases of three of the seven columns and laid their charges. As the charges were blown, a battalion of Partisans opened fire on a nearby enemy garrison, keeping the defenders penned in. Unfortunately, the explosions did no more than damage the pillars, leaving the bridge standing. Lindsay had a few hundred kilos of explosives left and little time. Knowing a German relief force could be heading up the railway, the sappers went back to digging. It took an hour to set the new explosives, the Partisans working as their comrades kept up their fire on the garrison. Drenched in sweat, Lindsay and the sappers laid and triggered the last of their explosives. This time the columns crumbled, and the railway with it. The Wolfsberg to Celje line had been completely destroyed. On the eastern line, a tunnel had been blown, knocking it out for a month, although the same sappers who successfully blew up the tunnel botched the charges on one of the target bridges and no damage was done.[9] Still, it was a demonstration of strength that encouraged first hundreds, and later thousands, to join the Partisans.

Now, for Lindsay and the Partisans in Pohorje, weapons were the priority. They camped on Rogla, an isolated high-altitude grazing area, and received an airdrop there the night of 25 June. The cargo contained British guns – Lee Enfield rifles, Bren machine guns and Sten submachine guns – but, to Franklin's dismay, no extra radios. An attempt the week before to supply another radio had failed because it had been dropped late, into German hands.[10] This time SOE, or the Royal Air Force (RAF), refused to drop the radio, insisting that the first drop test the site's safety, and a second drop a day or two later deliver the radios. This was against Lindsay's specific instructions for single, large drops with no follow-up.[11] Any drop would risk exposing their position to the Germans. The prudent response was to gather the supplies and immediately move elsewhere.

Lindsay was also learning how difficult it was to persuade SOE, the RAF, and the Partisans to coordinate. Paranoid over security, SOE would change fire signals with less than twenty-four hours' notice, which led to the cancellation of all drops, because it took up to three days to pass the new signal codes to the drop sites by courier. Even if time, place, and cargo could be coordinated, the drop ultimately depended on the skill and nerve of the RAF pilots who were becoming more and more skittish about low flying in the mountainous terrain. Frequently blanketed in fog, they feared flying into a mountain. Stuff-ups were getting worse, and Lindsay's rage would be clear from his messages to SOE: 'Planes strewed chutes over a fifteen-mile area in mountains' was a typical complaint, or: 'You loaded Cuckold Mission supplies on plane to [incorrect drop site], most lost and some dropped to Huns. This is gross negligence.' SOE also did not deliver Lindsay a new radio. Cuckold was always on the brink of falling out of contact, and no contact would mean no drops, no weapons, no ammunition.

While awaiting the follow-up on Rogla, Lindsay was joined by several escaped prisoners from Maribor, though not from 1046GW. Among them were Alfred Ashely and Owen Peterson.[12] Maribor district was littered with Arbeitskommandos – and they'd escaped from one in western Maribor, probably bringing the information that Stalag XVIIID had been disbanded and its working camps subordinated to Stalag XVIIIA.

They probably also passed on the information that one camp commuted far out along the railway line but was based in the Maribor railway yard. Ralph and the crew, Lindsay realized, were living under an Allied bombing target. The prisoners were in mortal danger. He had no direct contact with the RAF, and SOE didn't seem to be listening. To save the prisoners, Franklin had to act. He consulted 4th Zone and radioed MI9. With Partisan help, he planned to spring Arbeitskommando 1046GW.'[13]

---

* That the arrival of Ashely and Peterson led Lindsay to signal MI9 his intention to stage a rescue is not confirmed, but is the most likely explanation.

It wasn't even Lindsay's primary job but, if successful, it'd be the biggest escape of the war.

More than that, Maribor was littered with Arbeitskommandos, and tens of thousands more POWs were over the mountains in Austria. Lindsay had his hands full with sabotage and supply, but if a dedicated agent could be brought in, MI9 and the Partisans could establish the most outrageous escape lines.

MI9 mounted a search for such an agent and found one of the finest His Majesty's Secret Service had to offer: Major Andrew Anthony Vincent Losco. Hailing from a Maltese family in Egypt, Losco had been working for MI9 since early in the war. First, he had infiltrated enemy-occupied Corsica, with orders to create an escape line for POWs escaping camps in northern Italy. This proved unsuccessful, but he was evacuated and sent into Italy in December 1943 to retrieve POWs still at large after Italy's surrender. Even as II SS-Panzer Corps secured the region, Losco located fifty escapees and made his coastal evacuation rendezvous. The transport never arrived and Losco was captured bearing arms but managed to convince his captors he was also a runaway. For taking up arms during escape, Losco was sentenced to fifteen years in prison in Macerata. Despite being in prison rather than a lightly guarded camp, Losco quickly masterminded a successful escape. Tracking the German and Italian guards' routines, he rallied the other prisoners and overpowered the guards at an opportune moment. They liberated Italian political prisoners in the process, and Losco returned to Allied lines by boat in May 1944.[14] Rested and briefed, now Losco would drop into Štajerska, under the cover name 'Major Matthews'.[15]

29

A Partisan Agent

Leslie dawdled his way up the hill, water pails hoisted across his shoulders. Reaching the cottage, he was taken aback to see Lisa chatting with Harry the Bum. Noticing Les, Lisa smiled. True to his nickname, Harry was finishing a cigarette and gestured to Les for another. Les was reluctant to pass a cigarette to this shady character, but Lisa's smile eased his concerns. 'Hello, Leslie, this is my cousin, Anton,' she said.[1] Les wasn't surprised they had got his name so wrong and passed him a cigarette.

Anton lit it up and inhaled deeply. 'I hear you want to meet some Partisans?' he said.

Les was almost breathless.

'I'm meeting three tomorrow, a short distance from here. Please come if you wish.'

As Anton continued chatting to Lisa, Leslie was left with tea and his thoughts. He'd have to tell Ralph that evening.

Back at the camp, Leslie pulled Ralph aside for a walk inside the wire and told him the story. Ralph had to work very hard to keep his cool and not attract attention.

Leslie made the rendezvous the next day without issue and met Anton and three Partisan fighters in the woods near the cottage. Each Partisan was almost a human armoury, wrapped in bullet loops and grenades. One held a small, odd-looking gun Les had never seen before: a Sten submachine gun, courtesy of a British airdrop. Les thought the Partisans resembled operetta bandits from *The Maid of the Mountains*.[2] The trio explained that in a few weeks the Partisans would move into the area in strength. When that happened, a Partisan force would come to the railway and rescue the whole crew.[3] Anton had most likely been sent at Lindsay and 4th Zone HQ's behest to put this plan into motion.

'We'll be ready,' Leslie declared. In an instant, the plan had gone from Leslie and Ralph escaping to the entire railway crew.

There would be major logistical problems. Corn and fruit were ripening all over the country, so they might have enough food to survive on, but living off the land for survival and fuelling potentially strenuous marches or a long winter in hiding were very different matters. The best hope was that the Partisans would be able to provide some food. Leslie and Ralph weren't relying on this. If it were to be a rescue, then everyone would be breaking out, no matter what, and they needed supplies and co-conspirators. They both wanted to bring their best friends, Andy and Kit, in on the scheme, but they knew that once they had done so it would be impossible to keep the secret from the rest of their section. They decided to bring in Griff, Bob, Phil, and Len too.

To start with the response from the other six was lukewarm, but the frequent air raids and mounting German losses helped them warm to the plan.[4] However, Leslie and Ralph kept their companions in the dark about the Partisan raid: as far as the other six knew, it'd be them alone escaping.[5] Most likely this was for security. If word got out that eight of them were trying to escape, their fellows might not take issue. But a full rescue – that would cause problems. A cosy life had been built here, and many would be unhappy to go on the run with dangerous 'bandits'. So, under a shroud of secrecy, the eight set to work. To ensure supplies, each man would have to smuggle food on site. The Crow could withdraw food from The Combine for special projects, which took some creative accounting. For Ralph and Len, the plan entailed resigning their posts to get places on the railway crew. This in turn meant Ralph would no longer control The Combine. Soon getting supplies would require creative signouts from the storeroom.

First, though, Ralph had someone he needed to protect. He took an almighty gamble. He marched out of the camp and off to Gross's office. He could feel his heartbeat and the rhythmic thumping of his boots on the ground. Standing at the door of the Kommandoführer's office, he gave two sharp knocks.

'Come in, please, Herr Vertrauensmann. Have a seat.'

Ralph sat down, doing his best to appear calm. In truth, sweat was pouring off him. He inhaled and looked hard at Gross. 'Herr Kommandoführer, I intend to resign as Vertrauensmann, and I believe you should leave too. You have been with us four times longer than any of your predecessors. You should seek a transfer. It's only fair you should find new pastures.'

Gross's jaw dropped, disbelief transparent. 'Why? Why resign? Why should I leave? For what possible reason?' He lowered his voice. 'We've got a wonderful thing here; here we can sit out the war.'

Ralph took a moment to compose himself. Gross's case was compelling. Whatever came out of Ralph's mouth now had better be good. 'Herr Kommandoführer, if we try to hold on to our good thing for too long, it will go bad. Circumstances will change, and things will sour. This cannot last forever. I wish not to jeopardize the respect we have developed.'

Gross was silent, processing what Ralph had just said. They watched each other across the table; Ralph used all his willpower to seem at ease. Unteroffizier Johann Gross looked at him from behind his glasses, the gears turning. He knows, Ralph thought; he knows – please take the hint.

'Thank you, Herr Vertrauensmann. I will do as you suggest.'[6]

Ralph left the office without another word. It wasn't until he was back in the barracks that he felt he was breathing again. Les returned to hear that Gross was out of the picture, but seemed less than thrilled at the risk Ralph had taken without consultation. Ralph wasn't fazed. Matters of camp and Kommandoführer were his domain – why shouldn't he take decisive action? He felt he had had no other choice. That week a group of Wehrmacht officers attempted to assassinate and overthrow Hitler. They failed, but paranoia was rife, and the SS were wreaking bloody vengeance. If the entire camp vanished, Ralph expected Herr Kommandoführer would face execution.

The gamble worked. Three days later, Gross had organized his transfer and departed. He met Herr Vertrauensmann for the last time by the camp gate. Gross had been the best friend the prisoners could ever have. Kind and cunning, he had made sure his charges' internment was as comfortable as that of any prisoners in the Reich. He had actually worked against his regime, aiding and abetting a highly successful black-market racket right under his superiors' noses. Herr Kommandoführer had also found the courage to stand up for the prisoners against both the Abwehr and SD. In turn the prisoners had made him relatively rich – to amass more wealth than any Unteroffizier could hope to see. Ralph and Gross had always addressed each other by the formal German *Sie* – Johann Gross had always been Herr Kommandoführer, and Ralph Churches, Herr Vertrauensmann – but now Johann used the intimate *Du*.[7] 'Good luck, Ralph. Please take care.'

Ralph took Johann's outstretched hand with both of his own. 'I will, Johann, likewise to you.'

Then Johann Gross, a great friend and ally, departed.

Now Ralph had to resign as Vertrauensmann without arousing suspicion. Everyone knew The Crow liked being in charge, was fond of rash action, and asking others if they were game after the fact.

The new Kommandoführer was an officious hard-arse, closer to the 'screaming skulls' of old, and described by one prisoner as 'gun happy'.[8] For Sunday parade, Ralph prepared a speech he hoped would make Shakespeare blush. He would hit his usual talking points – lack of discipline, poor presentation – but then he'd add the stress of working with the new Kommandoführer, working himself up until he seemed on the edge of exploding. He knew that would sell it. The crew assembled. Many were out of uniform, unshaven, and wearing homemade shorts and casual shirts.

'Right, fellas, there are a few things I want to talk about today . . .' Ralph began. 'The army sends you a brand-new uniform every year, a beautiful pure wool uniform, and you go slobbing off to work. Not like British soldiers, but like ragtag bums with homemade shorts. For heaven's sake, walk out there with pride! You can wear that stuff under your uniform and strip down on the worksite![9] I'm grateful that you put your trust in me, and I thank you for that, but I'm through. We've lost our camp commandant, and I have to deal with this new bastard. I've had a gutful. I want to get out into the fresh air. You'll have to elect a new Man of Confidence.'

His bewildered comrades duly elected a new representative, Robert Shuttleworth, an Englishman with decent German and no enthusiasm for the job who agreed out of a sense of duty.[10] 'Eggy' Len resigned as the camp carpenter, to be replaced by another Len, Leonard Hewlett, the star of the Christmas revue's 'Green Eyes' duet.[11]

The next Monday, Ralph and 'Eggy' joined the railway crew on the commute for the first time. Many marched off in shirts and shorts, expecting a hot day of work. By contrast, the escape eight dressed in full British battledress. Each brought a rucksack with tinned food and biscuits, and when they went off to pee found somewhere in the undergrowth to stash it. More tins were added each day until they could escape. Only Ralph and Leslie knew this would have to be shared by the whole crew. The pair prepared an indignant rant should they be challenged by the guards, a variation on the theme of insufficient rations for such hard work, but it was their fellow prisoners who were more likely to notice the unusual behaviour. The Crow had made a fuss about the last escape, berating his fellows for risking reprisals and a loss of privilege with their escape. He hoped it hadn't set a precedent; before that, the attitude had usually been, 'Your business, not mine.' The guards didn't challenge the food but were hardest to convince on the resignation. 'You bloody Englishmen,' Gustl had remarked to Ralph as they headed out. 'We'll never understand you.'[12]

On the railway, the heat of the day rose. Ralph stripped down to the shorts underneath his battledress. He had his escape supplies in a small army haversack. It was waterproofed to the best of his ability and stowed within a larger homemade rucksack.[13]

On every tea run, meanwhile, Les grew more nervous about Lisa. She had given them a chance, and he hoped her life would not be endangered because of it. Succeed or fail, Leslie knew his visits would be over. Most likely, he'd never see her again. He would miss Lisa, Stanko, and Mitsi.

The days were not without their drama. While bathing in the Drava, Eric Edwards was caught in a current. A poor swimmer, he only survived thanks to rescue by Andy Hamilton.[14] As for Anton, there was no sign of him or the Partisans. Days of waiting turned to weeks. Ralph began entertaining ideas of escaping anyway. The Balkans were on fire from Slovenia to the Black Sea as the Germans retreated on all fronts – if an air raid didn't strike the prisoners in Maribor, they'd be evacuated deeper into the Reich. If that trip resembled the transfer from Corinth, many would die.

Ralph's fears were to come to pass for others in the coming weeks; the rations for all prisoners would be halved. A further month on, all camps would be put under the authority of the SS, and then, in winter, the prisoners would be sent on brutal forced marches into Germany, conducted in much the same way as in Greece, with little to no provision of food or water. Temperatures were freezing, and many died.[15]

Late in August, the conspirators' anxieties eased and then rose again. The whole railway crew were given a day off because a bomb had gone off on the line.[16] That meant the Partisans were nearby – but what if today was the day for escape, and the would-be rescuers arrived to the site empty? Should Ralph, Leslie, and the others break for it and hope to catch up with them? They decided that would be too risky and waited it out. Nevertheless, Ralph ended a letter to Ronte in July with 'look to see me with the birds of spring'.

A few days later, their prayers were answered. As Les made his way up the hill to the well, Anton emerged from the trees. He said two words before departing: 'Stand by.'[17]

30

The Battle of Savinja Valley

The second drop with the radio never arrived. While waiting in Pohorje, Lindsay heard the sound of gunfire. Thinking the Partisans were having fun, he stormed out to lecture them on the prudent use of the weapons and ammunition that had only just been dropped! Crossing a hill, he found two Partisan brigades dug in, holding off 1,200 SS.[1] He withdrew to a hasty 4th Zone HQ meeting, where it was decided to hold until night, then retreat west. The Partisans would gather their full strength, Lindsay would arrange new drop sites on the way, and together they would liberate the Savinja Valley. For any of their future plans to work, they needed a liberated area, somewhere they could defend in strength, take airdrops, rally and train recruits, and shelter E&Es on their way south.

The Partisan forces were in place to attack Savinja Valley on 30 July, but Lindsay's part had not gone well. Some ammunition, but no arms, explosives, or light artillery had been dropped. It would all be on the Partisans. The targets were German garrisons in two small towns in the Savinja Valley: Luče and Ljubno. The valley was deep, with narrow winding roads, a few back paths out of the valley, and a single main road east to Celje.

Each garrison was held primarily by Wehrmannschaft troops, supplemented with Wehrmacht and SS personnel.

Taking the garrisons' central fortifications was the key. The task fell to locally recruited troops: the Šlander Brigade, composed of Partisans smuggled out of Pohorje in 1943, and the Zidanšek Brigade. The 14th Division, meanwhile, would blockade the eastern road, and a feint would be launched against a town just outside the valley: Gornji Grad.[2]

Lindsay, his second man Bush, and 4th Zone HQ established themselves on the mountain range between the three towns and watched the attack begin. This time the Partisans were meticulous in their assault. At Ljubno, grenades were thrown into pillboxes, and explosives set against fortifications under covering fire. The enemy retreated into their central garrison as dawn broke on a glorious summer day. Lindsay and Bush watched from the hills, indignantly taking cover when an enemy soldier spotted them from a window and opened fire. No longer shrouded by darkness, it looked as if the Partisans would again fail. Lindsay hadn't been able to drop weapons capable of breaking the last fortifications. Then six Partisans pulled a 75mm Italian gun up the main street. It had been disassembled and carried by hand all the way from the south, thanks to the Sava Navy.[3] The first round blew a hole in the garrison wall. A second exploded inside, and a Partisan assault team stormed the breach. The German garrison surrendered.[4] The next day the other garrisons surrendered too, including the one at Gornji Grad where the feint became total victory.

The Wehrmannschaft survivors accepted an offer to join the Partisans, while the forty-five surviving German defenders had their lives spared. For propaganda value, they were stripped and sent walking naked to Celje.[5] The Partisans had their liberated territory and had captured enough German guns to arm 500. Recruits rallied by the thousand, and they now hoped that all the other arms they needed would be dropped by air.

The Partisans did not linger; orders came from Tito for Operation Ratweek. Slovenian Partisans would operate in synch with their Yugoslav colleagues, destroying German lines of transport and communications all over the Balkans. That meant going back to Pohorje, and making a second attack on the railways. Lindsay stayed in Savinja to coordinate, while Bush accompanied the 14th Division. They would seize Pohorje, take a large airdrop of explosives at Rogla, and destroy the railways. Major Losco would be dropping too, ready to take up his MI9 duties and begin rescuing POWs.[6]

PART FOUR

31

Getting Away

On Wednesday 30 August 1944 Ralph, Les, and the men in their section made their preparations, away from the prying eyes of fellow prisoners. Ralph stashed a razor blade and a toothbrush in his hip pocket. Expecting cold nights, he wore layers of wool beneath his uniform, thick socks, and heavy boots. The others dressed the same. It could be a tricky bluff – eight men in heavy gear among a lightly clad crew on a hot day – but being out at night in the forest almost naked had no appeal.

The team assembled at 06.30 for a headcount and set off. Marching to the station, the guards were their usual docile selves. The carriages pulled in, and everyone boarded. The train puffed out of the station, clattered across the Drava river bridge. Ralph looked across the town that had been his home of sorts for the past three years. 'Ta-ta, Marburg. See you later.'

It was a crisp morning in the shade of the river valley; the sun had not yet cleared the southern edge of the hills. Stopping at the siding at Ruše, the train dropped off 'Shorty' Humm, and clattered off to the worksite. At Ožbalt, the carriage doors opened, and prisoners, guards, and foremen began their routine. Ralph and his fellows were soon sweating buckets. An observant man would have wondered why they had not changed into shorts, but they were not challenged. Leslie made his morning tea round. No sign of any Partisans. Then a second tea run; nothing. Ralph was getting twitchy when, with Shorty well on the way with lunch, Leslie went to brew a third lot of tea.

To his profound relief, Anton was there to meet him. The spy looked as if he meant business. 'Leslie, we have seized Lovrenc, over the hills from here. We'll hold it a short time and withdraw before the Germans can counter-attack. Meet me at the chestnut tree west of the cottage, 16.00.'[1] Leslie nodded and returned to the railway.

Did Anton mean he'd be the only one there? Had the promised Partisan raid been cancelled? Les had not the time nor privacy to convey his concerns to Ralph; he passed Anton's message along. As the afternoon wore on, each conspirator fretted about how to slip away. Go without a word? Take a toilet or cigarette break? All eight couldn't go to piss at once – it would attract attention.

As 16.00 approached, Ralph saw Len had come up with his solution. Dry heaving, staggering, and making a great show of being ill, Len lay down in the shade near a thicket. Kit and Andy were grasping sheets of paper and moving off for a toilet break. Les gathered his pots and went up the hill to prepare the afternoon tea. Ralph couldn't make out Bob, Griff, or Phil. Deciding on stealth, he moved to retrieve his haversack and walk away without a word. But as Ralph pulled his bag from the thicket, he glanced to the left and saw a guard moving down the line. Ralph froze, but his wits returned in time to realize it was Gustl bearing down on him. Ralph threw his haversack over his shoulder, adjusted his hat and faked his best smile.

'Gustl, old boy, at the house up there, there are plenty of eggs,'

200

Ralph said, gesturing up the hill. 'I'm on my way to do a little business to get some eggs for tea. Stick around, and I'll cut you in for a couple, okay? Have a smoke while you're waiting. I'll be back before you've finished them.' Ralph grabbed Gustl's hand and palmed an open packet of British Capstan cigarettes, two left in the pack.

Gustl's suspicion turned to satisfaction. Two cigarettes and some eggs for sitting around for fifteen minutes? It was an outstanding deal. He lit up. '*Danke schön!*'[2]

Ralph felt relief but also guilt at taking advantage of this gentle soul. He suppressed the thought and turned into the forest. He dared not look back. If Gustl saw any of the others, he would guess, and it would all be over.

Ralph arrived by the chestnut tree at 16.00. Les, Bob, Griff, Kit, Andy, and Len had already got there. Anton was with them. There was no Partisan force. Ralph shot an exasperated look at Leslie. Then he realized they were a man short. 'Hang on . . . Where's Phil?' The group shuffled with nerves.

'He was stuck on the other end of the track. A guard was chatting his ear off,' said Len.[3] Phil would be hard-pressed to prise himself away from the conversation.

Anton guessed what was being said and forbade any delay. 'We have to go. Now.'

The group set off, making a straight ascent south, up a steep forest path. Leslie and Ralph were nervous. This whole plot didn't seem so bright now. If the Partisans were unable to pull off the rescue of the whole crew, had they been weakened? Was there any way the Partisans could get even the seven of them home? Would they be expected to take up arms and fight as Partisans? Neither Ralph, Leslie, nor most of the others had been combat troops in Greece. All of them had been without military discipline for three years. Ralph especially had been traumatized by the transit camps, as well as by the genocide of the Soviet prisoners. His nerves were unlikely to withstand combat.

All these thoughts rattled around in Ralph's head as the small column made its way south. Their destination was known to the Germans as Sankt Lorenzen am Bachern, a market town atop a plateau in Pohorje. It had no railway connection and only a single road leading up from the Drava. Anton was not following the road but discreet forest trails. Dense cover created ample shade, but in their thick garments they were still overheating. They begged Anton to halt to allow a change. Their guide relented, and the seven changed into summer clothes.[4] Without the weight of several layers, some of the anxiety left; they were free men. Ralph felt the mountain air in his lungs and breathed deep. At last, he was working against the Reich, not for it.

Anton's physique was lean and his pace tireless. The escapees, on the other hand, well-practised at heavy lifting though they were, were not fit for this sort of exercise. Anton urged them on, hoping to make their destination before darkness fell. Passwords and sentries would be easier if all parties could see each other: a nervous sentry's trigger finger was dangerous in the dark. As the sun began to sink, they pressed on. On their flanks, they spied small meadows dotted with farmhouses. Anton took care to avoid the grass and stick to the woods. Ralph glanced at his pilfered map, feeling sure they were nearing the goal. Stepping over a small stream, the escapees froze as a young man in German uniform stepped into their path.

32

Meeting the Partisans

'*Stoj!*'[1]

Thank Christ, Ralph thought, he's Slovenian.

Breathing again, the seven examined this strange figure as Anton exchanged passwords. The sentry wore a German uniform but was holding the same odd kind of gun that Leslie had seen the Partisans carrying. He also wore a khaki side cap with a red star sewn into the front, the only uniform marking him as a Partisan. Leslie had seen the same headwear on the three men he had met in the forest. For good or ill, the escapees had reached the Partisans.

Every 500 metres, they were challenged, again, again, and again. Partisan security impressed them. Woods and sentries gave way to level paths and small streams, and then the escapees were making their way down to the town. It had reclaimed its Slovenian name, Lovrenc na Pohorju. The evening sun warmed steepled churches and light-coloured buildings.

Within minutes they were in the centre of town. Partisans milled about the streets, along with small groups of curious townsfolk. Some seemed apprehensive, some ecstatic, some curious. Others, if they had favoured the Germans, were terrified.

Les's baffling *Maid of the Mountains* reference began to make sense to Ralph. A few of the Partisans were in civilian clothes but most wore an array of uniforms, either looted or ancient. Some wore Wehrmacht green-grey, some the old Nazi-style brown shirts of the Wehrmannschaft. Others sported blue-grey Italian uniforms that the escapees recognized from North Africa. There were even a few Royal Yugoslav Army greys. All were adorned in bandoliers, bullet loops, pouches, and belts; many were also covered in grenades. They sauntered about, explosives jiggling, with a nonchalance that made the escapees nervous. These were people used to combat. They expected no new supplies in battle, using what they carried with them.

Among the Partisans' ranks were many women, also well-armed. They seemed to be comrades in arms, which shocked the escapees' sensibilities.

The Partisans were preparing a party. Food and liquor were being carried to the town hall, and everyone except Leslie and Ralph were invited to join the festivities. Anton led the two ringleaders to the local tavern. Inside were four men: Ljubo Šercer Brigade deputy commander Jože 'Silni' Boldan, 3rd Battalion commander Ivan Kovačič,[*2] and two Allied officers.[3] Who these two officers were, and what they said, is not known; their presence was later covered up. It is almost certain they were members of Lindsay's Cuckold staff, and one may have been Lieutenant Bush, but Major Losco was not the other. Like the new radios, fuel, and now even explosives for Ratweek, SOE had failed to deliver – either due to their own incompetence, RAF nervousness, or Partisan mistakes with the signals. Things

---

* Not to be confused with Ivan 'Efenka' Kovačič, another Partisan officer of the same name.

were particularly grim at SOE's Force 399 HQ in Bari, Italy. Dr Rogers, a New Zealand surgeon running a secret Partisan hospital, described the HQ as a bureaucratic merry-go-round where stores were plenty, but apathy high. So high that Rogers wrote that SOE did not seem to care if its operatives lived or died.[4] It is likely that the mission to rescue the whole crew was cancelled due to Losco's absence. The Cuckold staff had their hands full with Ratweek and supply, and needed a dedicated MI9 agent before embarking on an ambitious rescue.

Boldan and Kovačič beckoned Ralph and Leslie to sit down. Neither spoke German very well, so Anton translated where necessary.

'Nice to meet you,' said Boldan. 'Want a drink?'[5] He was only a year or two older than Ralph, but younger than Leslie, and here he was, deputy commander of a whole brigade. Boldan seemed much more youthful than the other officer. Kovačič was a tall, stern man with a skinny frame harried by guerrilla warfare. Ralph nodded and took a glass of Riesling.

Leslie turned his attention to the matter at hand. 'There are seven of us. Can you get us to safety?'

'Oh, yes, we can send you south back to your people. We're doing it all the time. It's not a problem at all.' Boldan raised his glass. '*Na zdravje!*' They toasted and drank.

'Seven of us, no problem?' Ralph asked. He wanted to be sure he wasn't dreaming.

'No problem. Cheers again!' The Commander refilled their glasses. 'We're doing it all the time. Your airmen get shot down over Austria or Slovenia. We pick them up and get them out. Here – try this.' Small glasses appeared, along with a bottle of plum brandy. *Slivovica* or schnapps, depending on which part of Slovenia you asked in. The hard spirits were poured. Food emerged, washed down with yet more wine and spirits. Boldan and Kovačič regaled Ralph and Leslie with the story of how they'd seized the town several days ago with a few hundred men. The local authorities and police had been detained, the armoury was now emptied, and all local records burned. The Partisans were on a recruitment drive. Kovačič commanded the new 3rd Battalion; the 1st and 2nd Battalions were going village to village, taking on recruits.[6] The Partisan officers suggested Leslie and Ralph go into town. Well-fed and lubricated now, they should enjoy themselves. Everything would be all right.

33

Dutch Courage

Ralph set off on his own for the town square. There, a commissar was spruiking the cause to the locals. Ralph didn't know what he was saying, but it sounded optimistic, and full of hope. He assumed the Commissar was painting a glowing picture of Slovenia once they had defeated Germany. Ralph figured the taking of the town was as much a political operation as a military one. He'd read the propaganda decrying the Partisans as bloodthirsty bandits and thieves, and even when you knew the Nazis lied through their teeth, it didn't mean there wasn't some truth in the stories: right now the Commissar was giving a human face to a movement the locals had only heard about from rumour and propaganda. It was a peculiar reality, he reflected, that it was now the Communists who held the mantle of patriots.

The Commissar done with his speech, the rally gave way to festivities. Up the street in the village hall, folk joined a happy crowd. Drink flowed, music played, and voices rose in the cold air. A *schuhplattler* dance in the Austrian style was getting going, the men slapping their hands on their legs and stamping the floor, the women spinning around. A tall young woman in uniform grabbed hold of Ralph and hurled him into the dance, and Ralph found himself stomping and slapping with a vigour he hadn't felt since before the war. His improvised dance may have been comical, but it didn't matter – he was free, spinning round in circles with a woman for the first time in over four years.

Running out of steam and not wanting to embarrass himself too much, he bowed out to his dancing partner, got himself another drink, and sat by the wall to watch the proceedings while the sweat ran off him. To his left, he spotted Len drinking like a fish. On his right, he saw the Commissar having a stern word with one of the Partisans. The latter wore a small hammer-and-sickle badge over the red star on his hat, and the Commissar was jabbing at it. 'Slovenian, not Russian!' Ralph managed to make out the Commissar's words. The badge was removed.[1] It seemed essential to the Partisans that they were their own thing.

He sat pondering his own situation. Would he make it home? He was feeling more confident: the Partisans seemed hardened, committed, disciplined, and well supported. But there was an itch in Ralph's head, a dangerous one. The dancing had plied him with an explosive mix of adrenalin and alcohol. Here he was, having a ball, while the rest of the Arbeitskommando were still locked up. The original plan had not come off, and his mates had no way home. The strength of the Partisans and the nonchalance of their officers were inspiring – to them, seven prisoners were nothing – but could Boldan and Kovačič be convinced to go back for the others?

Ralph pulled away from the wall and went in search of Anton. The spy had disappeared. His interpreter gone, Ralph began approaching strangers, asking if they spoke German. By now he was not looking his best: quite drunk, he may even have come across as frothing mad. An elderly farmer rebuffed Ralph without a word. A middle-aged woman also fled, wanting nothing to do with him. On his third attempt, Ralph interrupted the evening of a young Partisan who said yes. Ralph grabbed him by the arm and led him to the tavern where, much to the young man's alarm, Ralph stopped him right in front of his commanding officers. Fortunately for Ralph's plan, the Allied officers had gone. 'Excuse me, you're sure about getting seven of us out?' The nervous Partisan translated the message. The officers were still drinking and smoking and looked up at the interruption. They maintained a polite air.

'Yes, yes, it's no problem. We are happy to help.' Boldan tried to wave Ralph away.

'Could you handle more?' Ralph asked.

The officers looked quizzical. 'How many more?' asked Kovačič.

'Seventy.'

The Partisan commanders stopped their conversation and looked at Ralph with interest. Ralph could feel they needed a little extra push, like Gustl had. They did not invite him to have another drink; instead, they indicated that he should explain himself. Ralph pulled his map from his pocket, laid it on the table, and described the worksite and crew. 'We came from the railway at Ožbalt – here. Tomorrow morning at 08.00 the whole party will arrive at the worksite by train. It'll have minimal protection: a dozen elderly guards, and a few civilian directors.' The officers eyed the map for a moment and moved to talk in private. Ralph and the interpreter stood by, waiting for a decision.

Ralph knew there were grave risks in returning. The Partisans had the provisions, the knowledge, and the men to take a larger group, but it would delay the brigade's plans and move them closer to Maribor. It would put them on a railway line less than ten kilometres from the Reich itself. Ralph had stated that the work party would be lightly guarded. But with seven escaping, and Partisans in the area, how did he know the SS wouldn't be combing the area? They could be walking into a trap. Even if they weren't, the Partisans might stumble into the enemy by chance. Including those already escaped, shepherding nearly eighty POWs to safety could hardly be the most productive use of their time; on the other hand, it could get the Partisans kudos with the British, who had supplied all the new weapons they were sporting. That could lead to more arms.

Ten minutes later, the officers returned. They needed more details.[2] Ralph explained the schedule, the guards, terrain, cover, nearest local inhabitants, aware his accent sounded far too Austrian to put them at their ease. He offered as much detail as he could to allay their suspicions.

His charm and attention to detail won out. Boldan and Kovačič were brimming with enthusiasm at the prospect of the rescue.[3] They had a fresh, well-armed battalion and operational considerations: if the prisoners were still there, the Partisans could gain serious prestige from getting them out, and it could also be an excellent way of diverting German attention from Ratweek. The 14th Division had still not received explosives, and the Germans knew by now that the Partisans had returned to Pohorje. Recovering an airdrop of explosives, then destroying bridges and tunnels, was risky anyway, and far more dangerous now with the enemy on alert. A whole Arbeitskommando of runaway prisoners was a perfect diversion. If the prisoners were not there, and a troop of SS came instead? Then the 3rd Battalion would lie in wait and gun them down as soon as they left their train.

'We will move out tomorrow morning, but you will have to come with us, along with your other leader. You will help rally your men,' Boldan declared. Ralph was ecstatic. His early efforts had come to little – results so far were all down to Leslie – but now *he* would be doing something.

'I didn't think that you would go without us,' he said. 'The men would probably jump into the Drava in fright. I'll go talk to the others.'

Ralph strolled out of the tavern and into Lovrenc. A passing Partisan directed him to a barn where Ralph's comrades were settling down. It was past 23.00 now and his fellows were in various states of inebriation. Len had drunk himself silly, and the others were pretty sloshed too.[4] Leslie looked in better condition. Ralph told them the plan.

Leslie was furious.[5] They had already got seven men out. That was far more than any other escape from Maribor had even attempted. To go back was reckless, and another example of Ralph taking rash action without consulting any of the people concerned!

Those who were still conscious backed Leslie, especially his best mate Andy.[6] The Scotsman thought Ralph was out of his mind: they didn't know if they'd make it home even with seven. There was a long road yet to freedom. Len, now unconscious, had got drunk on his misgivings about even their small group escaping.[7]

Ralph talked them through the situation. 'Look, fellas, these guys are the real deal. They've survived and fought all this time, they're in contact with our boys, and they say they can do it. They'd know better than us, and I trust them. Besides, it's not our decision. The Partisan commanders have told me they're doing this. The troops are already being prepared.' Ralph set about easing Leslie's fears in particular – he needed his support. 'And, Les, look. One of us is going to get a serious gong for this. And it was your contact who got us out, so it's going to be you. So how about it?'[8]

Leslie relented. Not at the offer of an award, but because Ralph had outmanoeuvred him. There were probably many thoughts burning in his mind. Ralph's efforts had yielded some fine black-market fare but nothing of value to the escape. It was Lisa who had got them out, and Lisa who had risked her life. Now nearly eighty men were going to be disappearing near her doorstep. The Gestapo would come. Leslie had seen the lists of murdered Slovenian hostages in Maribor and Šentilj: he knew the Germans wouldn't hesitate to kill the entire Zavodnik family. Now Ralph was risking all their lives by confusing his ego with his conscience.

Leslie found himself dragged back to the tavern as Ralph, Boldan, and Kovačič pored over maps. 'You will go with Ivan and his battalion before sunrise,' Boldan told them. 'We'll set up in the forest and ambush them once your train has left.' Ralph twitched at the mention of combat, feeling pangs of guilt. He didn't want Gustl's corpse on his conscience.

'What will you do with the guards?' he enquired.

Boldan gave Ralph a hard look. 'What do you suggest? The Germans don't take Partisans prisoner, except to torture them.'[9]

Ralph understood the implication. He knew he was bartering for the lives of Gustl and a dozen others, the guards who had been so kind, their comrades in labour disputes. 'Gentlemen, the guards are not young Nazis. They are old Austrians stuck doing guard duty because they are not fit to fight. They will offer no resistance. None of us wants to be involved in killing men who have treated us well.'

Boldan considered this. 'Okay. If they offer no resistance, we'll cut them loose after a few days.'[10]

Ralph remembered one last thing from when he was distributing Red Cross parcels. A farm where a dozen British prisoners were held, guarded by a single man, lay not far from Ožbalt. Could the Partisans spring them too?

Boldan and Kovačič would be not drawn on this. They gave their order. 'Be ready at 04.00.'[11]

Ralph and Leslie retired to snatch what sleep they could.

34

The Raid at Ožbalt

Thursday 31 August 1944 was the last day of summer, but the night before was a cold reminder that the first snows were not far off. Ralph and Leslie had only slept an hour or two; both were still a bit drunk. Lovrenc was abuzz. Partisan cooks prepared breakfast, while others pulled themselves together to face the day. Those with hangovers took turns splashing cold water on their faces. Ralph decided they were on to a good thing and did likewise. It was before sunrise when the 3rd Battalion prepared for departure. Kit, Andy, Bob, Griff, and Len would stay behind with a Partisan skeleton crew. Kovačič gathered his troop and mounted a dark horse to lead.[1] Boldan trumped Kovačič by getting on a stunning white gelding, a Slovenian *Lipica* horse, a breed made famous by the Spanish Riding School of Vienna. He might as well have driven a sports car into battle.

Led by the Lipica pride of Slovenia, Ralph, Leslie, and the 3rd Battalion departed for Ožbalt. The sun rose as the column reached the treeline. It was a crisp and clear morning. To avoid detection near any open ground, the Partisans broke into groups of ten. They moved in turn from one thicket to another, each group giving the all-clear for the next to follow.

The wisdom of these tactics was soon proven. A German

Fieseler Storch reconnaissance plane buzzed overhead. The Partisans had done this many times before; they knew how to move without being seen. Yet a sense of anxiety scratched at them. Was the plane scouting the way for a German attack? Were they walking headlong into an enemy offensive? Past the scattered meadows and into forest cover, the Partisans reassembled the column, and a little after sunrise they were all in position at the top of the ridge over Ožbalt.

Well before the train was due, Boldan and Kovačič dismounted, tied their horses at the top of the hill and ordered the battalion to advance with caution. Partisans crept from tree to tree, taking positions behind the dense shrubs that led to the edge of the railway.[2] It was 07.30 now – would the train come? Ralph and Leslie weren't sure. Ten per cent of the crew had vanished. The SD might be interrogating the crew and searching the barracks by now.

Come 08.00, they felt a distant rumble: the chugging of an engine and the squeal of metal on metal broke the morning quiet. The carriages stopped in front of the battalion; the doors opened. Peering through the undergrowth, Ralph breathed a sigh of relief. The crew were here: yesterday's escape appeared to have caused no bother. The men and guards got out as usual, the foremen waved the driver all-clear, and the locomotive reversed to Maribor. Ralph nodded to Kovačič that everything was in order. Once the engine was out of earshot, Ivan put a whistle between his lips, took a deep breath, and blew.

As one, the battalion emerged. Dozens of Partisans, weapons in hand, shouting '*Hände Hoch!*' The guards were so surprised that none of them even unslung their rifles. They knew they were in no position to disagree and were soon disarmed.

At first the prisoners were confused and scared of these armed men who had emerged from the bushes. Then Ralph stood up, identifiable by his slouch hat. 'C'mon, you jokers, get up here!'[3] Leslie's presence helped, but Ralph had swung back fast into The Crow as Vertrauensmann. Some of the prisoners were ecstatic; others remained dour or confused. The guards were terrified, though Gustl was philosophical enough to call Ralph a 'great rogue'.[4]

But while The Crow was enjoying the attention, Les gazed towards Lisa's cottage. Should they bring the family with them? Lisa would never leave without her husband, and if they did go without him, Avgust would be killed by the Nazis for sure. Leslie felt a great weight in his stomach: the whole family were in terrible danger now. But they would all have to take their chances. Les hoped he would see them again.

Time was short and the column was soon moving uphill. It pushed its way through dense, green shrubland and into the forest. There, the canopy was so thick that any undergrowth was deprived of light and gave way to countless tree trunks, and a red floor of fallen leaves. This would be the view for much of the journey to come. Suddenly, one of the captured guards turned and fled back down towards the Drava.[5] The Partisans held back from firing, scared that gunshots would alert any German forces that were nearby, and having learned by now that hitting a fleeing target through dense forest was difficult.[6] Even if it took the runaway a while to reach his lines, however, urgency was prudent: the SS would be apoplectic at the escape. The Partisans preferred to move by night, a tactic that had always served them well, but that wasn't an option now. They would have to make like the wind for the most remote and dense terrain available.

Once they were all on their way, the new escapees' lack of pre-paredness bothered Ralph. At least half wore nothing but shorts and a shirt and carried no other supplies. There would be noth-ing for warmth on rainy days or cold forest nights, and Slovenia had both in abundance. The supplies the original conspirators had with them would not feed everyone.

By mid-morning, they had bypassed Lovrenc. They turned south-south-west, all the way marching uphill, and stopped at a farmhouse for an early lunch. Here, food had been prepared by a few Partisans who had not joined the raid. Andy, Bob, Kit, Griff, and Len were there too. Several Partisans threw buck-wheat flour from a large sack into a cauldron, and added water and dollops of pig fat.[7] It was žganci, Ralph's old friend from the farm, and the fuel that would drive the rest of the escape. The žganci presented a problem, though: the Partisans wanted to eat and move on, but the new escapees had no cutlery. Borrowing a few spoons from the Partisans, The Crow organized a rotation. They would all line up, take a few mouthfuls, pass the spoon to the next man, and move to the back of the line. He hoped no one had a cold.

The spooning delay at least allowed Ralph to take stock. There were many prisoners here he did not recognize. The Partisans had raided the farm![8] But they had raided the wrong farm first, finding twenty French prisoners. A mix of forced labourers and POWs taken in 1940, these Frenchmen were now closer to civil-ian workers than prisoners. They had been living leisured, almost free lives – many had relationships with local women – and they were furious to be 'rescued' against their will. No wonder – they were going from a summer in green fields with their girlfriends to become fugitives alongside armed rebels. Leslie, as the best French-speaker, had to bring them into line.[9]

Leslie and Ralph were relieved to see Phil among the railway crew and got the other side of the story. Their luck had defied belief. The guards hadn't noticed anyone was missing until roll call yesterday evening. Time was bought during roll call when one POW handed in the POW identity plate of a man who'd been transferred out twelve months earlier.[10] The flustered guards counted again and again. By the time it was confirmed that seven were missing, the Kommandoführer had left for a night out with his girlfriend, and he hadn't returned in time to stop the prisoners departing the next morning. Unauthorized to act without him, the guards had kept to the schedule.[11] When the Kommandoführer finally returned, he rang his superior to inform him seven prisoners had escaped.

'Only seven?' the Kommandoführer's superior replied. 'That's nothing! You've lost another seventy-seven this morning.'[12]

It was not quite a clean sweep, though. Bob Shuttleworth and Len Hewlett, as well as Shorty Humm and the two other cooks, had been left behind. So too was Eric Edwards. Tired of working onsite, he had accepted an offer from Bob to be an administrative assistant. Keeping track of The Combine after The Crow (and his creative accounting) was proving a difficult task. Those left behind would be transferred to other camps in Austria a few days later.[13]

With almost all of 1046GW and the two farm crews, the escape party now numbered 105. They surveyed the Partisans with the same awe Leslie and Ralph had: the eclectic uniforms, the knives, the bullet loops, and grenades had menace. Most of the 3rd Battalion being unshaven and hungover from the night before helped the rugged image. 'I'm bloody glad these blokes are on our side,' mused one of the Australians.[14]

The female Partisans were a baffling prospect to a number of the escapees, some of whom were deeply sexist (and likely the same men who had harassed the pub waitress). One of the Partisans was Josefine Lobnik, a dark-haired Maribor native and former Partisan courier and spy. Discovered by the enemy and forced to flee the city, she now worked in the field. Josefine scouted the way ahead. Her assistant was Dušan, a Partisan with a reputation for brutality.[15]

While Josefine scouted, the 3rd Battalion took stock. A Partisan doctor inspected the German guards captured and decided one was too old, slow, and sickly to accompany them any further. The guard was set loose, and returned to Maribor bearing the doctor's note reading, 'This man is unfit for military duty.'[16]

A little after midday, 200 Partisans, escapees, and prisoners headed south-west, deeper into Pohorje. Josefine reconnoitred the column's ascent 1,000 metres up, east of the mountain Črni Vrh.[17] She and Dušan descended the other side to an isolated farmstead, whose owner was known to be a staunch ally, often providing shelter and food to Partisans. The pair knocked at the front door: no reply, so they knocked again. There was movement inside. This wasn't right. Dušan took his rifle and slammed the butt against the door. A distressed older woman opened up. Josefine explained the situation: they had 100 British prisoners on the run and needed her help. The woman seemed unmoved. Her husband was away, she explained. Was the farmer's wife not as sympathetic to the cause?

There was no time for this, Dušan decided, forcing his way in.

Josefine followed, her eyes focusing on the religious icons in the hallway. Catholic images were common in Slovenia, especially in the homes of rural folk, but tucked away in the corner of the shrine was a picture of Adolf Hitler. Dušan grabbed the woman by her hair and held a knife to her face. The occupants had been Partisan supporters, she blurted out, but they'd disappeared – murdered or sent to a concentration camp, no one knew. She and her husband were Germans relocated from Ljubljana Province, and the house had been gifted to them by the Reich. Dušan detained the new homeowner and prepared for the column to arrive.[18]

This was not only a pit stop for the escapees and 3rd Battalion; it was also here that the whole Ljubo Šercer Brigade reformed. Hundreds of Partisans came from all directions. There was little room in the house, so Partisan and escapee alike camped in the open. With the 1st and 2nd Battalions came seventy-one recruits.[19] Some were apparently eager rebels, others terrified refugees. One of the latter, a man in his forties who'd been issued with one of the camp guards' rifles, Ralph recognized as a businessman from Maribor. He got talking and it turned out the man had been under suspicion from the Gestapo. Tipped off that his arrest was imminent, he'd fled to Pohorje and been taken in by the Partisans. Now he was in despair: in the rush to get away he'd abandoned his wife and children in the city, to the constant anxiety that they'd be arrested in his place and deported to a concentration camp, or worse. Ralph offered what comfort he could, but his words felt hollow. This man could now only live out the rest of the war as a Partisan and hope against hope that his family survived.

Exhausted by the twenty-kilometre upward march, everyone

settled where they could. Cold and out in the open, few of the escapees slept well. Ralph and the rest of the original seven, warm in many layers, managed to drift off.

The peace was broken by the blast of a lone gunshot. Unable to bear his guilt, the man from Maribor had put the barrel of his rifle in his mouth and pulled the trigger.[20]

35

Into the Mountains

Friday 1 September 1944[*]

In the morning mist, Les and Ralph stood near the suicide's corpse. Nothing had been done about him during the night, so the pair helped bury the man from Maribor now. Those who'd had experiences like Leslie and Ralph's knew the sort of war that was being fought. Others, caught up in it like this man, weren't ready to see the reality up close. The Partisans' hit-and-run tactics meant entrenching tools were low on the inventory, but two Wehrmacht deserters provided Les and Ralph with small standard-issue shovels. They tried not to look at the body while they dug. The hole left by the rifle bullet was huge: the man's face had collapsed in on itself. The rest of the crew threw nervous glances as Les and Ralph slid the body into a shallow grave.[1]

Ralph tried to get his mind off it by organizing the spoon rotation again. Between mouthfuls, the men quenched their thirst at a small mountain stream. They may have lacked flasks

---

[*] Dates from this point onwards are taken from the diary of British escapee Kenneth Dutt, written during the escape.

but they wouldn't want for water. Today was a rest day of sorts with Brigade HQ. Hidden in thick forest, the rest of the 14th Division gathered down the hill at Rogla, awaiting an airdrop. The escapees tried to snatch some daytime sleep, but heavy rainfall put paid to that.[2] Their Partisan counterparts gathered branches and leaves, improvised shelters, and started campfires; the escapees followed their example.[3]

That day also saw the release of the guards. The most ragged of the Partisans exchanged clothes and boots with their captives and a small group of Partisans then led the guards off back northwards.[4] To their dying day Leslie and Ralph believed that Boldan was true to his word, but others suspected that the guards were taken to a quiet spot in the woods and murdered.[5] That was what Alexander Connor, who was now working at a different Arbeitskommando in Maribor, heard.[6] Eric Edwards, on the other hand, confirmed that at least one was released. Given the nature of the war and previous atrocities, it could be either. The truth of what happened to Gustl and the other guards remains a mystery.

It was time for the escapees to part ways with the 3rd Battalion. Kovačič, its commander, mounted his horse, bade farewell, and ordered the battalion to move out. Seeing their rescuers departing, The Crow turned to his resting escapees. 'Come on, fellas – three cheers for the 3rd Battalion!'

The 3rd Battalion formed up with the rest of Ljubo Šercer Brigade, heading east. Boldan, with his Lipica, was staying with the escapees, who remained with Brigade HQ while they waited for nightfall and an airdrop. More žganci was eaten. When planes were heard, the Partisans rushed frantically to put out their fires to prevent the pilots picking up the wrong signals. The cargo was dropped – but again it turned out to contain only weapons and uniforms.

SOE had once more failed to drop explosives or radios. It was hoped that secondary drops would be used to supply these essential items, but no other planes arrived that night.[7] Franklin Lindsay was furious that SOE or the aircrews had either failed to follow his instructions or were just not up to the job. Without explosives, the whole of Operation Ratweek in Štajerska was in jeopardy.

SOE did succeed in finally dropping Major Losco.[8] He parachuted with the supplies to 14th Division HQ late that night. He was too late to aid in the escape, but they hoped there would be many more rescue missions for him to organize.

Meanwhile, the good soldier Švejk had received his orders: he was to take ten men of the Lackov Odred and escort a band of escaped British soldiers to the Savinja Valley. His real name was Franc Gruden, but he resembled another long-dead Partisan who had had the moniker 'Švejk' and the name had stuck.[9] Švejk was also the name of the famous anti-hero of the satirical Czech novel *Good Soldier Švejk* about a subversively simple soldier during the First World War. The latest Švejk scratched his face, reflecting on the irony.

It had been a long war already for him. He'd joined the Partisans in the south over two years ago and seen unrelenting service against the Italians and their collaborators, then the Germans and theirs. He'd seen the majority of his comrades killed, most recently on the march to get here, to Štajerska. The death toll of Partisans in the field was high, and few who joined in 1941 or even 1942 would survive the war. Švejk had been transferred

224

from the 14th Division to the Lackov Odred, helping oversee recruitment in Pohorje. New fighters were flocking there, most of them green recruits, teenagers who had come of age under the fascist occupation.

Where Švejk was sitting on the peak of the mountain had once been a tavern, Ribniška Koča, the highest in the whole Pohorje mountain range, but over the past years it had been the scene of bitter fighting. The tavern had long ago been burned (it is rebuilt and operating again today). Camped with him by the ruin were 100 fighters of the Lackov Odred. As a commissar with the Partisans, Švejk had a range of responsibilities, but was often called upon to perform duties more suited to an officer. Unfamiliar with this odred, Švejk formed them up and called for volunteers to help him bring the British POWs to safety.[10]

First to step forward was Alojz Volern. A teenager, he'd had a lucky escape already. Drafted from Štajerska into the Wehrmacht, he'd been posted to Normandy on the English Channel, but had fortunately been given home leave a fortnight before D-Day. While in Vienna, he fled and defected. He'd already received a promotion of sorts with the Partisans, being made a machine-gunner wielding a British Bren gun. Alojz's motivation for volunteering was personal: he was from the Savinja Valley, and he hoped to see his family again.[11] The young corporal brought both good military training and local knowledge. To have him on board meant Švejk's unit had got off to a good start.

Next was Franj Vesenjak, 'Franjo', another teenager. Fresh-faced and handsome, Franjo had done a year of underground work in Maribor before taking up arms this summer. He'd seen the murder of the Soviet prisoners and watched the men being forced to bury them. The rest of the squad filled up with local youths eager for action.

Švejk was relieved when Karl Čolnik, 'Čolo', also stepped forward. Čolo had been watching the other volunteers sign up and knew some more experience was needed if Švejk's unit were to survive. Čolo had joined the Partisans alongside his brother two summers before. He was one of the few to regroup in Pohorje, after the Pohorje Battalion's destruction in 1943.[12] Švejk didn't know him, but could tell he was an experienced soldier; from what Švejk knew of the war in Štajerska, Čolo had had to endure even more of an ordeal than he had. Švejk thought he could do a lot worse.

Saturday 2 September 1944

Come daybreak the escapees moved with Boldan and a few other HQ staff a short way west up to Ribniška Koča, crossing the meadows to the camp of the Lackov Odred. Though the rain had passed, threatening clouds still lurked. On a clear day, one could see near half of Slovenia from here. In the woods was the smoke from several campfires, each topped with a big cooking pot and shielded by a small bivouac. Salutes were exchanged between Švejk and Boldan.

The former prisoners were invited to more žganci. After the luxuries of Maribor most escapees found it foreign and unpalatable, but it was the fuel that had kept generations of mountain farmers going and it did the job. Ralph hoped the Partisans wouldn't notice how low the prisoners' morale was after years of captivity; their legs were not fit enough for marches. Yesterday had involved no walking but had been cold and wet. The first day's thirty-kilometre forced march with an ascent of 1,300 metres had also caused a lot of soreness. The decline in the quality of the food didn't help – The Combine and the Arbeitskommando had treated the crew very well, despite the air raids. Indeed, with the exception of Nazi Party officials, the men of 1046GW might have been the best-fed men in the Third Reich. 'What do you think you're doing spoiling our nice billet?' hissed someone at Leslie after a spoonful of žganci.[13] There were a few grumbles of support, though with so many well-armed Partisans around the complaints weren't going to get too loud.

'You're welcome to try finding your way back,' retorted Les. One of the odred saw the state of the crew and passed round a bottle of schnapps.[14] Grog to wash down the buckwheat helped reduce dissent a little, though the French escapees were particularly morose.

Ralph and Leslie went to meet Švejk. Franjo was standing next to the new commander. 'Hello,' he said in German. He had an air of mischief that told Ralph that they were going to get on well. 'I am Franjo. I will be your interpreter.'

With Franjo, Ralph had an instant connection. Franjo was full of a vigorous youthfulness. He had a handsome face, a thick head of soft brown hair, and a shining pair of German infantry boots. Franjo's hair was so precious to him that he never covered it with the typical, red-starred Partisan cap. 'This is my commander, Švejk,' Franjo said. It would be another twenty-five years before Ralph knew Franc Gruden as anything other than 'Švejk'.

Ralph looked their new commander up and down. Švejk was gaunt and thin. He wore a pilfered Wehrmacht tunic that might have fitted him once, but no longer. He wore glasses under his Partisan cap, giving the impression of an exhausted scholar.

227

'Švejk, as in *The Good Soldier Švejk*? I'm Ralph Churches, and this is Leslie Laws.' Ralph didn't know how much German the Commissar understood. He must have got the gist, but remained dour at the question. Ralph took him to be a serious and humourless commissar. He had read *The Good Soldier Švejk* and wondered if the Partisans were pulling his leg. Literary Švejk was good-humoured but often deliberately incompetent. This one didn't seem to have any of the character's enthusiasm.

'We usually use nicknames in the Partisans,' explained Franjo, 'to protect our families.' Švejk had good reason to be sour. The task was beyond anything he could have imagined: escorting over 100 prisoners who spoke two different languages to the Savinja Valley. Nothing like this had ever been attempted anywhere in Europe, never mind Slovenia, and he was responsible for the whole thing.

If he were to succeed, he'd have to get this rabble of Brits and French into line. 'When we move out, your men are under three orders,' said Švejk, through Franjo. 'Follow us. Do not talk except in a whisper. And no smoking.' The reason for no smoking stumped Ralph, but he soon understood when he learned they would mostly be marching by night.

Introductions complete, the column of escapees and Partisans together was near 150 strong. They set out from Ribniška Koča in the afternoon, on a thirteen-hour march through the night. Čolo went ahead; he was a natural scout. Scouting meant more running and isolation; the other Partisans lacked the experience for it and Čolo appreciated the quiet. Ralph thought well of him, for Čolo had reacted with amusement on seeing Ralph's slouch hat.

In eastern Pohorje, the Šercer Brigade were helping take the

Soviet POWs arriving at Stalag XVIIIA, late 1941; this was the photograph subsequently smuggled out of Maribor by Alexander M. Connor.

Italian 2nd Army burns Slovenian village, 1942.

Arbeitskommando 3GW, Šentilj, 1943.

Arbeitskommando 1046GW, Maribor, 1943–44. *Left to right:*
Phill Cullen, Unknown, George Hagan, Jock Hall, Donald Funston,
Jock Osgood, Kit Carson, 'Macgrath'.

Arbeitskommando 1046GW, Maribor, 1943–44.
Left to right: Walter Lacy, Jock Hill, 'Lloyd' (could be Ewart Floyd), Donald Funston, Ralph Churches, 'Macgrath', Noel Herman.

Arbeitskommando 1046GW, Maribor, 1943–44. Leslie Laws.

Arbeitskommando 1046GW, Maribor, 1943–44.
Back row, left to right: Ralph Churches, Henare Turangi, William G. Bunston.
Front row, left to right: 'Hank' Dale (possibly Leslie G. Dale), Eric Lane, Kit Carson.

4th Zone HQ with local women and Franklin Lindsay
(*front row, far right*), Gornji Grad, August 1944.

Escape march
leaving Gornji Grad,
6 September 1944.
Left to right: 'Čolo' Karl Čolnik,
'Švejk' Franc Gruden (*behind*),
'Franjo' Franj Vesenjak, Ralph
Churches, Leslie Laws.

Nadlesk Airport, 1944.

Ronte and Ralph Churches,
Adelaide, 1954.

Ralph with Partisans,
Maribor, 1977.
Left to right: 'Švejk' Franc
Gruden, Ralph Churches,
'Franjo' Franj Vesenjak.

Escape site from across the Drava River, Ožbalt, 1972.
Lisa Zavodnik's house is visible.

Ožbalt, escape site, 1985.

Lovrenc na Pohorju, 1985.
Left to right: Ralph Churches, Jože Boldan, Leslie Laws.

Ožbalt, 1985.
Left to right: Leslie Laws, Ivan Kovačič, Ralph Churches, Franc Črešnar.

heat off the escapees and providing more cover for Ratweek by attacking a German military school. It was well fortified, and an enemy patrol spotted the Partisans as they approached. Many Partisans fell in the assault. Kovačič sent in the 3rd Battalion to break the deadlock, but many were seeing their first combat, and were too inexperienced to hold the line. The Germans broke out and evaded them.[15] All the Partisans' efforts for Operation Ratweek: taking Lovrenc, freeing the POWs, and attacking the school, counted for little. Ratweek was a failure, thanks to the SOE's inability to get explosives to the Partisans. The 14th Division attacked the railways as ordered, resorting to tearing up sections of track by hand, but the damage was easily repaired by German engineers.[16]

The mass escape might be Ratweek's only success. Čolo turned them south and they began a 1,000-metre descent into the next valley. The ground covered by the forest had not turned to mud yet after yesterday's rain, but the first autumn leaves made the paths slippery and the going slow. It was well past nightfall when they reached the village of Dovže, at the bottom of the valley. Along the valley floor ran the busy road between the garrison towns of Slovenj Gradec and Velenje. Švejk knew from his time in the 14th how dangerous this crossing could be, but tonight was as good as could be hoped. Both flanks were covered by woods, which crept right up to the road. Švejk had Franjo pass on new orders: they'd pull the same trick as the Partisans had used on the way to Ožbalt – divide into groups of ten, and cross one group at a time. The Crow exercised his position as leader and picked out men he trusted to head each group. Among them were Les and Len and a large, burly Australian called Donald Funston.

Ralph looked over at the Frenchmen, who were giving him the evil eye. 'Les, mate. I'm sorry to ask such a crap job of you. Can you babysit the Frenchies? I don't trust them.' Les sighed, but there was no one else for the job; no one spoke the language well enough to be commandingly blunt.

Čolo led the way over the road and a small livestock bridge across the Mislinja river. Two Partisans headed down either end of the road to watch for enemy patrols while the column quietly passed.

Sunday 3 September 1944

The column reformed, heading straight south, up the other side of the valley wall. Ralph's objections to anything other than a summer escape were proving wise – in a different season, this late at night, they'd be frostbitten. The ground levelled, and the column turned west along a ridgeline before finally coming to rest in the early hours of the morning at a farmhouse some-where south of Podgorje. Čolo went to chat with the farmer, and another Partisan prepared žganci.

Though the sun was rising and the men eating dinner, the 'day' was not done with them yet. Two Partisans from another unit arrived with a stocky man tied up with rope, an informer who'd sold out members of the underground in Maribor. Švejk was ordered to deliver the spy to the Savinja Valley for interroga-tion and presumably execution.[17] Yet another responsibility . . . The farmhouse had a shed, and Švejk locked the informer inside. Everyone else found what straw they could and fell asleep. Švejk wanted everyone to have a good feed, so he purchased one of the farmer's sheep and, while they all slept, the farmer butchered and skinned the animal, and sawed it in half lengthways. The two halves were lashed to poles to be carried and eaten in the safety of the Savinja Valley.[18]

In the early afternoon the escapees woke to shouts: 'He's gone! He's gone!' Pandemonium.

Franjo had gone to check and found no prisoner, and two boards in the wall of the shed prised free.[19] Either the sentry had fallen asleep or Švejk hadn't posted one. 'Everyone up, now!' shouted Švejk – the informer could be in Slovenj Gradec by now and an SS battalion already en route. The farm was compromised. They had to get to the Savinja Valley as fast as possible.

Stomachs were growling. They'd skip breakfast, or whatever meals were called on this schedule. Four escapees were picked out to carry the mutton, and the column moved off along the ridge in a hurry. They had to stop and wait for nightfall to cross the road at Zavodnje, which, like the road they'd already crossed, led to an enemy garrison. Would the Germans secure all the roads? It was a nervous wait. They were due to arrive at a Partisan courier station – the Lackov Partisans had come beyond the limits of their local knowledge and a guide would be needed to lead them further.

When the sun finally set, the column crossed the narrow valley floor in groups as before. A full moon lit it well. They climbed out of the valley for an hour and halted below a farmhouse and secret Partisan courier station. Čolo flashed his torch. No reply. He flashed again. Codes were a finicky thing, after all – had he not got it right? A voice rang out from the house, speaking German.

'*Wer da?*' Who's there?

Čolo was silent. The Partisans unlatched their safety catches.

231

'*Wer da?*' Louder this time.

'*Partizani!*' Čolo replied. Everyone held their breath.

'*PARTISANEN!!!*' yelled the occupants of the house. German machine guns opened fire. The whole column except for Švejk hit the deck. He put his Sten to his shoulder and returned fire. Alojz dived, braced his Bren gun against the ground and sprayed the farmhouse. Franjo got down with Ralph and Les. 'Back! Go back!' he urged. The escapees didn't need telling twice.

Švejk didn't know if it was a single machine-gun crew or a bigger ambush. Either way, a direct assault would be suicidal – they had too many unarmed men and were too disorganized. But he had an old trick up his sleeve. If he could give the impression of having enough men – if the escapees could be brought up, and the Germans led to think they were fighting a whole brigade – they would believe they were being overrun. The night was well lit, but not enough to tell that most of his charges were unarmed. Švejk ceased firing so everyone, and especially the Germans, could hear better. '1st Battalion, left! 2nd Battalion, right! Advance!'[20]

The Partisans formed two columns and moved through the forest. Švejk scanned the treeline and saw Ralph and the others backing away. 'Churches! *Naprej!*' Švejk bellowed, gesturing at a path on the left flank.

The Crow took a deep breath. He needed to regroup his men. He mustn't let them down. 'Don't run! Don't scatter!' He learned a lesson in issuing positive orders. His men heard 'Run! Scatter!' and took flight as fast as their legs would carry them.[21]

Donald Funston did not flee. He came rushing to Ralph's side, slapping a hand on The Crow's shoulder. Ralph was shaking now, unable to speak.

'What the hell is wrong with you?' Donald asked. He got no response, so Donald took charge. He formed his hands into a cone and bellowed, 'Everyone! Get back here at the bloody double, or you'll get left behind! We're moving off in three minutes flat!'[22] As the escapees returned, so did Ralph's nerve.

Franjo came rolling down the hill. 'Ralph! It worked! The Germans fled. We have to go before reinforcements arrive.'

The Germans had gone, but the courier the Partisans were supposed to meet was probably dead. Without a guide, they'd be marching near blind. 'Čolo! Find us a guide!' ordered Švejk.

Čolo ran to another farmhouse and barged the door open, startling a lad a bit younger than Franjo. It wouldn't be long before he was old enough to be conscripted into the Wehrmacht, but for now he was recruited by the Partisans. Čolo grabbed the lad by the neck of his pyjamas. 'You're leading us out.' The presence of firearms and the sound of gunfire left no room for negotiation. The boy had enough time to slip on shoes and a jacket before being led out of the house and hustled over to Švejk.

'Take us through the forest to Bele Vode,' Švejk ordered. Bleary-eyed and alarmed, the lad complied; every teenager knew the tracks around their village well. With this local knowledge, he led the column through the forests for three hours. Ralph threw nervous glances, trying to count how many were still with them. Down two hills, up two hills, the column's reserves were ebbing by the minute. But the only choice was to keep going. If the prisoners were caught with Partisans, the SS might kill them all.

233

Monday 4 September 1944

An hour before sunrise, they reached the edge of the village of
Bele Vode. The lad was thanked for his services and let go.[23]
Švejk knew the way from here. If they could cross the village,
they could go south around the 1,500-metre peak of Mount
Golte and then head west, which would put them on the path
to Savinja, the same way Švejk had left the valley a month
previously.[24]

Bele Vode was a small village and thankfully didn't sit on a
major road, but Švejk wasn't taking any chances and ordered the
column to separate into groups of ten. It gave Ralph an opportunity for a headcount. They were six men down: four of his
own and two of the Frenchmen. Worst of all, his friend Kit was
among the missing.[25] Ralph felt the ground falling from under
him. He tried to explain the situation to Franjo and Švejk, but
the latter was in no mood for delays. 'I'm sorry, Ralph,' said
Franjo. 'There's nothing we can do. If they're lucky, they'll be
found by Partisans from another unit or sheltered by the villagers. We can't risk sending anyone back for them.'

Not willing to waste any more darkness, Švejk moved them
out. They were half a butchered sheep down too, but the second
pole of mutton had been dutifully retained.[26] The column
crossed to the side of the village unchallenged and walked on
for another hour. They had no food save the raw meat and
hadn't eaten since yesterday morning. Ralph still had a tin of
beef which he took a few mouthfuls from and passed to Leslie.
They drank from the rivers coming off the mountain. Finally
they came to a stop halfway up the south slope of Golte and lay

down on the forest floor for what remained of the night.[27] Some Partisans snapped leafy branches off the trees and used them as crude blankets.[28] Sleeping by day at least corrected the clothing shortage. As the forest warmed, the men in shorts could sleep.

Les awoke late in the afternoon to see Čolo sitting off in the distance, keeping watch. He could see that morale among the prisoners had taken a dark turn. Those escapees upset at the breakout now regarded Les and Ralph with contempt. Most were certain the six missing men had been cut to pieces during the ambush, and that it was Ralph and Leslie's fault. Though no one had seen it for themselves, some believed for the rest of their lives that the escape had led to the missing men's deaths.[29]

Švejk was also pondering the situation: he knew the way by road, not obscure forest trail, so Čolo, as exhausted as the rest of them, would have to lead and warn of any trouble. If there were Germans ahead, he'd have to move everyone deeper into the forests and pray they didn't get lost. But Švejk had a bigger problem. Though most escapees' morale had plummeted, they were still willing to continue. The Frenchmen were not, refusing to march any further and attempting to convince a few of the others to join the strike. What they hoped to achieve is unclear. Leslie's attempts to mediate went nowhere, and eventually the Partisans had to compel the Frenchmen to move at gunpoint.[30] That got them marching at least, and as night fell, the column moved out in silence, slowly, at a trudge. It made less noise, but in any case no one had the strength to go any faster. Soon they heard the gentle rushing of the Ljubnica river and turned south to follow it. The water was a welcome sound, obscuring their steps – though it could also cover any enemy lying in wait. Čolo was far ahead, scouring the forest for any sign of trouble.

Down they marched, passing little fields, isolated farms, and churches the size of cottages, the escapees growing hungrier, sleepier, angrier, and convinced they would never see home again. When the sun rose, it lit the edge of the valley. Escapee and Partisan alike collapsed at the vision before them: Ljubno and the Savinja Valley.[31] They had reached temporary safety.

36

Across the Sava

Tuesday 5 September 1944

They lay strewn across the hillside. The Savinja Valley was idyllic. Behind them was a stone cottage with chickens, a goat, and a few pigs milling about, the garden overflowing with beans and potatoes. Across the valley, grapevines and fruit trees were bursting with ripened fruit. The old couple who owned the cottage came out and exchanged greetings with the Partisans.[1] For the first time all week, the escapees ate more than žganci. In its place was a hearty potato and corn soup, with chunks of black bread and fresh fruit – and, of course, the half of mutton retained from the ambush. But despite the fruit and the landscape, the mood was bitter.

After a few hours of sleep, Ralph joined the Partisan officers inside the farmer's cottage, if only to escape the glares of his own comrades. On top of his immense task Švejk was now having to juggle propaganda duties: he was trying to 'educate' the farmers. The couple were regarding the lecture with polite indifference. Ralph looked at the walls full of religious icons. Despite their piety, the inhabitants seemed happy to cooperate with a Communist-led movement against the Germans.[2]

237

The Crow's mind was on his most pressing task: rallying the men. He wasn't sure if this was the end or if there was further to march. If the men weren't at least brought into line, the whole column might disintegrate. Franjo came in and provided the solution. 'Ralph, I've been told you'll be meeting British officers in the next town.'

Ralph rubbed his stubble. He feared the Frenchmen's mutinous sentiments were spreading; not to mention, the whole column was pretty lousy, and Ralph hated being unclean and untidy. He would try a carrot to get the men in line and, for those that didn't take the carrot, a stick. He went outside to find the men, many of whom were just waking from their slumber. Les was with Andy and Len. The Crow found a rock to stand on. 'Right, listen up! I know how tough this is, fellas, but pull yourselves together.' Most greeted this pep talk sullenly. 'We're British soldiers!' he went on. 'We must fight with everything at our disposal, not sit in our cosy billet waiting for others to fight on our behalf.' Some murmurs of approval; death glares from others. The Partisans watched on, curious. 'I can't stop anyone who wants to leave. But I know I would regard anyone who did as a deserter. Our Partisan friends have informed me we'll be meeting some of our officers in the next village.'[3]

The dissenters bristled. The Crow's threat of ratting them out was no longer idle. Most had not met one of their officers in over three years, let alone one who wielded actual authority. It didn't make The Crow popular, but for now it brought the dissenters into line. 'Now, you're all bloody filthy. That's no way to present to an officer. Everyone go get yourself cleaned up in the river!' The men dispersed and wandered down to the Savinja river.

Ralph had a point. They all stank, and the chilly waters proved a good substitute for tea in jolting the men awake.

Then Švejk gave the order to move out. He looked in far worse condition than his charges, who were still fat from The Combine. Švejk's last reserves seemed to have been sapped; he looked almost emaciated – pale, like the bodies Ralph had pulled from the railway shed.[4] Yet on he went, flanked by the Partisans of the Lackov Odred. Today they marched by daylight, but although they were in a 'safe' area the column took the vertical climb over the hills rather than the main road between the villages, and spent the next few hours winding through woods and meadows.[5]

On the descent, there, all of a sudden, was the shining white, red, and green of Gornji Grad, an elegant town with its large and imposing baroque church. Thriving, full of smiling people, and free. To the liberated prisoners it was the greatest sight in the world.

The column emerged on the east end of town. Remembering Franjo's information, The Crow formed his men up in marching order – for most of them the reality of returning to soldiering had not sunk in. Franjo dropped back: 'Hey, Ralph, could your men sing "Long Way to Tipperary"?'[6]

The Crow tried to keep up an orderly march, then, as they followed the road into town, he looked back over his shoulder:

> Up to mighty London came,
> An Irish man one day . . .

Les, Andy, Len, Donald, and Henare's voices led. Those with some fire left in their bellies joined in.

Map 10. The escape route

... all the streets were paved with gold
So everyone was gay!
Singing songs of Piccadilly,
Strand, and Leicester Square.
Till Paddy got excited and
He shouted to them there:
'It's a long way to Tipperary
It's a long way to go.
It's a long way to Tipperary
To the sweetest girl I know!'

Ahead of the column, by the grand white church, a reception committee had gathered. Partisans, officers, clerks, and curious locals watched the group march in. *That's* why Franjo wanted us singing, Ralph thought: the sight of 100 singing Allied soldiers was quite something. It proved beyond a shadow of a doubt that the Partisans were with the Allies. The Crow followed up with 'Pack Up Your Troubles in an Old Kit-Bag' – with both prisoner and Partisan living off not much else, it seemed an appropriate choice. Even a few of the men who'd been nothing but sour since escaping cracked a smile, basking in the affection of the crowd.

The Crow looked around for a British officer. Easier said than done – the Partisans had been given so many British uniforms by airdrop that several of the tunics matched his own. He gave up trying to distinguish by tunics and assessed hats, ruling out any that bore a red star. Finally, his eyes picked out a cap. It was not British: it bore a golden eagle. It was American.[7] 'Eyes right!' The Crow ordered. The column turned their heads. Major Franklin Lindsay beamed and saluted.

The pass-by complete, the column halted. The Partisans broke ranks to embrace old friends at 4th Zone HQ. Lindsay approached Ralph. 'You surprise me – I've always understood the Australians reserved saluting for special people and special occasions.'

'Believe me, sir,' replied Ralph, 'this measures up on both counts.'[8] He hadn't expected an American.

'Excellent,' said Lindsay. 'Fall your men out and have them give their details to our Partisan friends.' He gestured to a desk and typewriter with a female Partisan clerk. Ralph ordered the men to assemble and give their name, service number, and address. The clerk had a good grasp of English and bashed away on the keys, though with so many colourful accents among the group she had to make her best guesses. 'Hartlepool' became 'Hotlipool'.[9]

Once Leslie's name was down, Ralph beckoned him over. 'This is Leslie Laws, sir,' he told Lindsay. 'He's the one who got us in on this whole endeavour.'[10]

Lindsay congratulated Les and Ralph on a job well done. 'Thank you, sir.' Les was, like everyone else, exhausted but, despite the pageantry, his mind was on finishing the job. 'What's the plan, sir? Are we home safe?'

'I'm afraid not,' replied Lindsay. 'You'll be headed south to cross the Sava. I can't tell you anything more than that. But you'll be in safe hands. Trust me when I say the Partisans excel at pulling a fast one. There is something for which I need your help, though. We've got a flying officer with us, Melrose. His whole crew was killed, and he was beat up pretty bad. I'm sending him with you. Get him home.'[11]

'Of course, sir.'

That sorted, Lindsay waved for Ralph and Les to enjoy themselves. 'We've had plenty of food prepared for you. I even got a few English-speakers to mingle with you. Enjoy yourselves, and get a good night's rest.'

'Thank you, sir,' said Leslie and Ralph in unison.

With that, Franklin departed and left the men to bask in the afternoon sun and enjoy the picnic laid on for them. A few 'eternal Yank' Partisans chatted with them, warning them that the most dangerous roads lay ahead: territory controlled by the *Bela Guarda* (White Guards), the Partisans' name for the Domobranstvo.[12]

The Lackov Odred took a much-needed rest. There was no such luxury for Švejk, though, whose monumental task wasn't done yet: in the morning, he had been informed, the column would take on 150 new members – fresh recruits being sent south, along with some refugees and wounded for the hospitals or evacuation.*[13]

Wednesday 6 September 1944

During the night, reports came that another Ratweek effort to blow up the tunnel and cliff walls along the main Ljubljana–Zagreb railway line had done no long-term damage.[14] Lindsay's brief was primarily destruction, not rescue, and he was irritated that there had been no attempt by the Sava Navy to blow the railway bridge near Litija, thereby putting the line to Zagreb out

---

* One of these was probably Alma Karlin, the Austrian-Slovenian writer and one of the first women to solo circumnavigate the globe. She had been an early prisoner of the Slavic Section of Stalag XVIIID before later eluding the German authorities.

of action for the rest of the war. It had apparently been planned but, much to Lindsay's dismay, the Sava Navy had got cold feet during the night and called off the attack.[15]

The morning returned the escapees to a cracking pace, departing Gornji Grad at 08.15 while Lindsay watched from the hills.[16] In many ways, his jobs were incompatible. For MI9, he had to guarantee the safety of Allied personnel, pilots and prisoners. For SOE, he had to stir the hornets' nest.

The situation was far more fragile than anyone knew. The Partisans had escaped destruction many times, but it would take only one slip for the entire movement to be wiped out. In this tiny corner of Europe, the Slovenians had joined the war at a time when Europe stood on the brink, and though victory in much of Europe now seemed assured, in Slovenia it was perhaps not. There was still such a long way to go. How many of these young rebels flocking again to the Partisan banner would survive? Would the men Lindsay had helped free make it home?

On the group's way out, the 14th Division photographer Jože Petek snapped a photo of the column ascending a hill; it shows how everyone had had a chance to shave and clean up in Gornji Grad. Leading the way as usual was Čolo, the model scout. Behind him was Franjo, hatless and showing off his hair. Ralph was next, a look of determination in his eyes. Then Leslie, with his rucksack over his shoulder. Behind these four were the 250 members of the column, snaking along the track and into the forest. Švejk walked to the side, keeping watch.[17]

At least marching by night had kept a cap on the pace that could be set – by day the escapees could not keep up with the Partisans. Today's march covered thirty kilometres: 800 metres up, 750 metres down, and the men with inadequate clothing again hissed their dissent. Ralph put in more walking than anyone, going up and down the column doing headcounts and keeping the mood as good as he could. The group held together, blitzing their way south, and successfully crossing their first road in daylight. They bypassed two towns held by the enemy and had climbed above the next valley by sunset. They came to a rest on a hill above a river that ran alongside the main road from Ljubljana to Maribor. Night fell. Čolo scouted ahead, the men separated into tens again to get across, and the column reformed to storm up the side of the next valley, where they rested for the night at Hrastnik. The Crow joined Švejk in a farmhouse owned by a young couple, one of whose small children took a great interest in Ralph's hat and ran around the kitchen wearing it.[18]

Thursday 7 September 1944

A short morning march took them to Mala Sela, a wooded hill above the Sava, where a courier from the Sava Navy, the Kamnik-Zasavje Odred that had got Cuckold Mission across the Sava river, arrived to brief Švejk. Švejk then summoned Ralph, Leslie, and Franjo and laid a detailed map of the Sava across a fallen log. 'We'll be handing you over this evening to the Kamnik-Zasavje Odred,' Švejk declared. 'We'll wait until night, and you will cross here –' he pointed to a wooded area just west of the riverside village of Zgornji Hotič. 'A diversion has been planned to clear your way. The local farmers will move their work animals across the river tonight – they have permission from the Germans to do this. They'll do it as noisily as possible.' The column would wait in the forest to be handed over. For the

Lackov Odred, there would be a few days' rest in the Savinja Valley, then back to Pohorje.

Ralph took this moment to appraise their commander. He had been too hard on the man, he realized. Švejk's German jacket had become more ill-fitting by the day, and his face more sunken. More than anyone, the march had taken a toll on The Good Soldier Švejk. Ralph guessed the poor fellow had tuberculosis. Švejk may have been the night to the day of Franjo's charm and enthusiasm, but he had been a model officer: professional, relentless, inventive, and calm under pressure. Right now, though, he did not look as though he would survive the war.

Leslie and Ralph decided to keep the men in the dark about the plan, both to avoid worrying them and to protect the locals in case something went wrong.[19] It was only a little after midday, and time would pass more easily if they were ignorant of the task ahead. Everyone snatched what sleep they could. In the early evening, a Kamnik-Zasavje Odred officer, Tone Poljanšek, arrived to relieve Švejk.

Franjo came over. 'This is where we leave you, Ralph.'

Ralph found he couldn't speak. This man, still a boy in many ways, had risked his life to save them, making a dangerous diversion from his real mission: to save his own people and his homeland. 'Thank you, comrade.' Ralph embraced him. It was strange: with the Partisans of Štajerska Ralph found a camaraderie more profound than any other.

'Take this,' said Franjo, handing Ralph a small piece of paper. 'Write to me after the war.'

Ralph unfurled the paper to find Franjo's parents' names and address on it.[20] It was a shockingly risky act, testament to the strength of their bond. If Ralph were captured or killed by the

Germans or the Domobranstvo, then Franjo's family would be murdered. The young Partisan would have no home to return to.

With that dramatic gesture, the volunteers of the Lackov Odred departed, back north, back to the fight.

Ralph and Leslie scanned the way ahead. Were they destined to walk all the way to the Adriatic? Beyond lay not only the mighty Sava river, but also the main road from Ljubljana to Zagreb. It was one of the Ustaše regime's lifelines to the Reich, and one of the main routes to Belgrade.

Night fell, and at 22.00 the Sava Navy moved all 250 in the column to the riverbank. Upstream and downstream, the night was punctuated by a crashing of hooves in water. Beyond was the sound of distant gunfire – a diversionary attack.[21] Franklin was correct: the Partisans excelled at pulling a fast one. The column boarded small wooden boats, half a dozen at a time. The cacophony of cattle herding masked the sound of oars and punts as the boats battled against the current. Partisan scouts watched over the farmers, keeping an eye out for enemy patrols – an Axis garrison by the Litija railway bridge was less than 1,000 metres from the crossing site.[22] If the Sava Navy had attacked it, as Lindsay had wanted, the whole river would be swarming with Germans. The Sava Navy had most likely not got cold feet. Rather, it seems likely that they were trading the last chance of Ratweek success for the safety of the escapees and recruits and – most important to the Partisans – the safety of the only route south.

It took hours to complete the crossing, Ralph growing more nervous by the minute. Fearing recapture, he tore up Franjo's note and prayed he would remember the address.

Friday 8 September 1944

The crossing complete, the escapees were handed over to the care of the Dolenjska Odred, who had been given special orders to take the column south.[23] They marched through what was left of the night. These Partisans were far more nervous about the loyalty of the locals than in the north. The darkness faded at the edge of a treeline above a steep descent and the small village of Štangarske Poljane. Directly below was a meadow, a farmhouse, and a barn. The 250 men were divided into pairs. Each pair was directed to move in silence past the farm and into the barn – once one was in, the next would follow. When they'd all made it in, they lay down like sardines. The final Partisan closed the door on gloomy morning clouds.[24] Rain would pour down all day, but inside the barn they were warm and dry, though morale wavered as another serving of žganci was dolloped out. The Sava was crossed, and the column was less than thirty kilometres from Ljubljana.

At the isolated village of Nadlesk, MI9's Captain Jack Saggers had succeeded in his task. He and an Anglo-Partisan team had carved out a dirt airstrip (codenamed Piccadilly Club). Shielded by a large, hilly forest, the airfield received Allied aircraft from late July 1944.[25] Weapons, uniforms, and food were delivered by the box, while wounded Partisans and E&Es departed to southern Italy on the return journey. But the Domobranstvo were not far off. Gathering intelligence for the Germans, they had learned of the airfield but lacked the strength to strike alone. Thanks to Ratweek, some of their strongest units had been redeployed to guard key railway lines. Perhaps the Domobranstvo's only chance of victory was to isolate the Slovenian Partisans from the wider war: from the Yugoslav Partisans, and from the Allies. To achieve this, the airfield must be destroyed, and any escape lines with it. The Allied missions that ran them were to be killed or handed to the Germans.

To shore up their forces, the Domobranstvo called for German aid and were assigned battalions from the 14th SS-Police Regiment, and Wehrmacht mountain troops from the 188th Gebirgsjäger Division. Their combined force would attack the Allies in three prongs, the central objective being the airfield. The first prong, dubbed 'Schmitz', would attack from the north-east, pushing any Partisans towards the airfield. The second, 'Schumacher', would begin a drive from the north-west on 9 September and link up with Schmitz. The third column, 'Buchberger', would stalk the forests and move in from the west. Then the three prongs would launch a combined assault before dawn on 10 September. The operation began as the escapees slept through the day, with Schmitz moving out first.[26]

At the Štangarske Poljane, the rains had passed, so the escapees and Partisan recruits left the barn and moved out at 19.00. They now followed different paths, with the escapees heading south-east, almost parallel to the Sava, away from Ljubljana.[27]

37

The Chance to Become a Spy

Saturday 9 September 1944

The column had been marching near blind for five hours when midnight arrived. The moon had waned, and each man navigated by the sound of the footsteps in front. Ralph couldn't fathom how their Partisan guides knew where they were going. There was so little light that no one could see the column stop when the lead person halted, and everyone fell into each other like dominoes.[1] They reached a safe house past Gabrovka just after sunrise. That they walked in some daylight fuelled anxieties. Was it because they were late? Were they in slightly safer territory? Or were they trying to outrun someone?

Ralph got a few hours' sleep, rose early, and wandered into the farmhouse next to the barn, where the Partisan commander was conversing with the farmer and an RAF officer. All had glasses of *slivovica*. The officer noted Ralph's hat. 'Ah, you must be the Australian!' he said in German. Ralph took a seat, and a glass was poured. 'So, you speak German with an Austrian accent?'

'That's right, sir.'

'Capital! What a coincidence.'

'How's that, sir?'

'Well, we need a man to go into Austria for us. We'll sort you out with papers, funds, and send you over the border to meet some contacts. You'd be perfect!'[2]

Ralph was aware his mind wasn't in the best place, but he knew he wasn't completely crazy. Speaking as an Australian with an Austrian accent was one thing; passing himself off as Austrian would be quite another. 'There's one problem, sir. My nerves are shot. I'd crack if I was asked to show my train ticket, never mind questions by the Gestapo. Besides, I haven't seen my wife in four years. I need to get home.'

The officer looked disappointed; he seemed to have thought he'd found the answer to his prayers. 'Fair enough, old boy. It was pretty rough of me to put it on you. Though I still think you'd have done a fine job. You might have even foxed the *Gauleiter* (regional governor)!'[3]

The whole episode sounds outlandish, but Ralph was not the only escapee whom British intelligence tried to recruit.[4] The actual agency that made the offer remains a mystery. MI9 had an agreement with SOE to send joint teams into Austria.[5] Wolfsberg was a key target, and if Ralph had accepted, he might have helped to spring fellow prisoners. MI6 was another possibility: they had recently attempted to send agents over the border. One agent, a depressed young Austrian defector, let himself be captured and the attempt failed.[6] Reliable replacements were needed.

Either way, Ralph was wise to refuse. The Nazis helped create many resistance cells just to weed out potential enemies, and the following month an OSS mission saw its leader, Lieutenant Taylor, thrown in a Gestapo prison in Vienna. Taylor would survive to the end of the war in the Mauthausen concentration camp.[7]

Since crossing the Sava, much of the marching the escapees had done had been on hard dirt surfaces rather than soft forest trails. By now their tattered boots were falling to pieces. Most farmers had the equipment to make flying repairs, but only as a stopgap. Inside the shoes, blisters and wounds were worsening. The first rule of Partisan warfare was always to carry a spoon; the second was never to take your shoes off while you were resting within a day of the enemy: as a result, trapped within a sweaty prison, the soles of your feet had no chance to harden. Worse still, marching at night meant nothing to look at to distract from the pain. Sound and physical sensation were all they had. It was strange: here they were in a new part of the country, and they'd hardly seen an inch of Dolenjska by daylight.

Less than fifty kilometres away, the move against the airfield continued. While Ralph talked spies, Schumacher and Buchberger moved out. Taken by surprise, the Partisans near Schmitz and Schumacher slipped away, frustrating attempts to capture or kill them. Buchberger had more success. The combination of Wehrmacht mountain troops and Domobranstvo was ideal. In the forests west of the airstrip, Buchberger stumbled on three Partisan couriers. One was wounded, another escaped, but the third gave up the location of a camp of new Partisan recruits. Buchberger took a small detour to destroy the camp and capture or kill the occupants.[8] The Axis column finally encamped at 20.00. They were so close to the airstrip that sentries spotted three planes landing during the night. The aircraft were delivering supplies, and evacuating Partisan wounded and five New Zealander POWs who had escaped from northern Italy.[9] Come the morning, the three Axis columns would converge, destroying the airstrip. The escape line would perish with it.

Sunday 10 September 1944

Ralph and the column had again been marching for five hours when midnight arrived. Soon after, they passed the old fortress town of Žužemberk and had an unexpected encounter with the local press. A writer from the regional Partisan paper arrived with an English-speaking female assistant. There was no time to stop, so the interview was walk and talk. Ralph was first up. The questions were pretty standard: 'Are you from London?' was the last one. Ralph knew that the words for Australia, *Avstralija*, and Austria, *Avstrija*, were similar. 'No, dear, I'm from Australia. That's Australia, not Austria.' Ralph pointed north to the Alps and shook his head to illustrate the point. The reporter's assistant scribbled it down, then made her way along the column to get more quotes.[10] The party continued on, following the Krka river south-south-east. They halted at 06.00, and bunked down at a forest farmhouse near where the river turns east.

At 03.00 Buchberger should have established radio contact with the other columns and begun the assault. Portable radios were notoriously unreliable – mountains, rain, and forests could all interfere with the signal. Failing to establish contact, Buchberger's commander hesitated. Only after hearing gunfire in the far distance did Buchberger finally advance at 08.00, by which time most of the Partisans had had time to pack up and escape the encirclement. But Buchberger's vanguard could see the airfield's staff – a few Allied soldiers and Partisans – loading onto a jeep. A German took a shot at the car. The bullet smashed through the windscreen, but missed the driver, and the jeep took off, smashing its way out of town and joining the comrades fleeing east.[11] Nadlesk had fallen, but the men who ran it had escaped.

At 09.30 the escapees were rudely awoken. Normally given the whole day to rest, only a few hours of sleep had been snatched when the escapees were roused by the Dolenjska Partisans, given a dollop of žganci and urged on. A full daytime march was a shock. Bleary-eyed and tired, they saw the southern countryside clearly for the first time. It looked like a postcard of Štajerska in miniature. It had valleys, rivers, and windswept meadows, but the valleys were shallower, the rivers slower, and down south the sun beat harder on the grass. Near the river, apples ripened on the trees, but the fields that should have been overflowing with corn were covered in weeds: the war had not been kind to Dolenjska.

The column crossed the Krka river and continued south-south-east. [12] The Partisans were clearly spooked – not since the farmhouse ambush had the escapees been pushed this hard. At 13.00, having marched for fourteen of the last seventeen hours, the Partisans allowed a two-hour rest. The men were near collapse. Most were limping by now, either from huge blisters or ankles twisted during night marches. Anyone who hadn't already procured a sturdy branch-turned-walking stick soon did. The Partisans moved them on, trying again to set a terrifying pace. But the escapees' walk had slowed to a crawl. The Partisans, showing little patience, seemed to be leaving them behind. 'Get them to slow down,' pleaded Leslie. 'We'll never keep up.'

Ralph made several attempts, but the Partisans either didn't understand or pretended not to. Eventually they relented and slowed the pace, with one Partisan sent to the rear to make sure no one fell behind. Leslie and Ralph took Švejk's old position and watched from the flanks to do the same. All afternoon and into the evening the march went on, on dirt roads hardened by summer, the surface wrecking what was left of their boots and reflecting the sun's heat. They saw few signs of life save the occasional elderly villager, so thorough was the region's devastation. Eventually they came to a long steep hill covered with dense forest.

'Where are we going?' Ralph asked the lead Partisan. 'Why are we moving by day?'

'We're going to Semič. We arrive today.'

'And is that it? Are we going home from there?'

'I believe so.'

That'd have to do. Ralph needed something to rally the men. 'How far to Semič?' he asked.

'A few hours,' came the curt reply.

The men lay shattered and sprawled out in the shade of the trees. 'Listen up, lads!' barked The Crow. 'This is it. We're moving by day because it's the final stretch. One more push, and we'll be home free.' Ralph hoped his stirring words told a true story.

The news seemed not to elicit any emotion. Then one of the men piped up. 'We'll be with you, Crow, you slave-driving old bastard!'[13] Those still with a sense of humour burst out laughing. They gathered themselves up for one last push.

It took another two hours in the heat to climb the hill. Once at the top, they could see a broad plain with mountains in the distance. Below was what seemed to be a moderate-sized town. Please let this be Semič, Ralph thought. The path down was as steep as the climb up. It took another hour to reach the valley floor.

38

Base 212

'They have arrived at Base 212.' The Partisans' message was brief. Captain Saggers ought to have been feeling pleased – after all, getting escapees and aircrews home was his job. Now it was a problem. He had over 100 escapees in his care, more than anyone in the history of MI9, and, thanks to the Domobranstvo, no airfield to fly them from.

It would take a monumental effort to scout a new site, clear it, and flatten the ground. He didn't even want to think about the labour required for adequate drainage if it rained. Thanks to Britain's commitment to the exiled Greek government, he had no planes. Every RAF transport plane in the Mediterranean was flying non-stop helping the second British intervention in Greece.[1]

Jack Saggers donned a jacket and hopped in his car. He'd have to get on with it, and pray they were not discovered again.

The steep descent to Semič tested the escapees' will. The party shuffled down the hill, propping themselves up with sticks, sweat pouring off them. It was near 21.00 when they finally arrived. Then Leslie caught sight of something. 'Officer ahead! Form up!' The arms supporting each other dropped, and with his last strength every man held himself high. Again, they sang

'Long Way to Tipperary', shuffling forwards as the tune rang out.

'Eyes right!' shouted The Crow. The officer standing in front of a large building in the centre of town was Captain Jack Saggers. All turned to salute.

Saggers, a stickler for protocol, had had such a mess of a day he'd forgotten his cap. Blushing in embarrassment, he couldn't return the salute, but he could tell from the state the column was in that he should skip further formalities.[2]

Saggers turned to face Base 212. It was the old schoolhouse, now called the American School by the locals. Little more than a cleaned barn now, this was Saggers's safe house for E&Es. Semič was as safe as one could get in Partisan territory, which wasn't saying much. Saggers opened the doors to reveal the most beautiful sight: piles and piles of fresh hay. No more dusty barns, no more cold forest ground. The men stormed in like an invading horde and collapsed in the hay.

Saggers turned to Leslie and Ralph. 'Rather over-egging the pudding, aren't we?'

Leslie was too tired to be fazed by droll remarks on the scale of their success. 'Well, we're here, sir.'

'Quite so. Genuinely well done. Hell of a thing you've pulled off, and the Partisans, of course.'

'We owe them our lives, sir,' said Ralph. 'Are we safe now?'

'Yes, you should be. We just lost one of our airfields, but we're working on another. Should be getting you out within a few days. When the time comes, we'll fly you out.'

For the first time, there was a sense of hope among the party. Seeing the men relax, Saggers tried to hold their attention a moment longer. 'But I must stress, gentlemen: you may have to leave at the slightest notice. Never stray out of earshot during the day. And go nowhere at night. I'll leave you to it.'[3]

So that was it then: evacuation by air. By ship had been the most popular theory, though Ralph had hoped that wouldn't be the case; it was unlikely they had it in them to reach the Adriatic. A number had thought they'd be evacuated by submarine.[4] Planes had been on no one's mind. This was understandable: of the working crew, only a half dozen of the party had ever been airborne, and those that had, only on joyrides at country fairs. As his colleagues flopped in the hay, The Crow congratulated everyone on their achievement – 'We must have walked 500 miles!' The only reaction was a roll of the eyes.[5] Ralph knew they had travelled about 170 miles; he'd been checking his map often during the march. Obvious hyperbole was part of The Crow's management toolkit. The crew had marched for twenty-one of the last twenty-six hours, covering over sixty kilometres, and, hopefully, made it to safety.

Monday 11 September 1944

The sunny morning brought a reckoning for the escapees' feet. Since the escape no one had had more than a riverside sponge bath, and by now the soles of their feet had softened to a spongy, livid pulp, but Donald Luckett now found that pointing the soles towards the sun hardened them. Their new home had a lone toilet and water tap at the back that saw constant use.

Of Semič's inhabitants only the very young and old remained. For breakfast, the elderly women of the town had prepared a large soup. Their situation must have been awful: their sons were all dead or out fighting on opposite sides of this war and it had fallen to these women to do everything: tend the crops and the animals and raise the children. And now, on top of all that, they had to feed the guests of the Partisans. Yet all offers of help with cooking were refused. The soup was devoured with gratitude by the escapees.[6]

The following days were slow. Semič itself was pretty, if mournful. Pictures of 'the Big Four' – Churchill, Roosevelt, Stalin, and Tito – adorned the town. There was little in the way of recreation. Heeding Saggers's warning, no one left the town.

Wednesday 13 September 1944

With so much time on their hands, the inevitable rumours circulated. The reality of the civil war in Slovenia was not lost on the escapees, and many feared one of the townspeople would slip out and give up their position to the Domobranstvo. There was a welcome distraction when several American airmen arrived. Cigarettes were shared and stories exchanged. One of the newcomers said he was the sole survivor of a bomber and had had the most miraculous escape. He was a tailgunner, and under enemy fire the tail of his plane, with him still crouching in the rear turret, had been blown clean off. The detached tail had spun away with such ferocity that it had begun to act like a rotor, thereby slowing its descent. The tail had crashed into a pine forest, which had cushioned the fall. An astonished Partisan had come to check the wreckage, only to find the young man dazed but unharmed. The airmen were less than happy about the accommodation and hated the soup. They were amazed by the escapees' contentment.[7]

Ralph and Leslie were lounging outside and looked up to see an American sergeant blocking their sun. Accompanying him was another American with bags of camera equipment. He was a photographer for *Life* magazine by the name of John Phillips. He'd been further south, taking photos of Tito and the Yugoslav Partisans; now he was with the Slovenian Partisans. He asked the pair for a quick interview. 'Could I take a photo of your whole group?'[8]

'Sure, mate,' said Ralph. 'We'll see who we can rustle up. Oi! You buggers! Get here on the double. The world's press is calling!' Soon all those within earshot – around seventy of the ninety-nine – had assembled by Base 212. In the photo Ralph's slouch hat is visible in the background as he stands shoulder to shoulder with Leslie. The picture and story of the escape never made it to the pages of *Life* magazine; it gave away too much intelligence.

Thursday 14 September 1944

By now Axis forces had moved out of the vicinity to fight Partisan formations west of Ljubljana, and the most immediate threat to the escapees' safety had departed.[9] At Semič, the day brought more new arrivals: seven POWs, led by a Kiwi, Captain Walter Heslop.

Heslop's escape deserves its own book. He had been captured in North Africa in November 1941 and imprisoned in Italy. After Italy's surrender, Heslop was transferred to Germany, but he had broken out of his train before it had even left Italy. He stumbled upon and fought alongside Italian Partisans before his unit was forced to disperse after its commanders were killed. Heslop had spent another eight months on the run before leading six others east to the Slovenian Partisans.[10] Heslop was a modest man: seeing 100 other runaways, he had no desire to burnish his own legend, only to hear Ralph and Leslie's story. Not yet muzzled by intelligence officers, they told Heslop everything: how Leslie had established contact with the Partisans; how the original plan of a full rescue had not been fulfilled; how the Partisans had been happy to put the plan back on.[11] Ralph and Leslie now realized they were not the only escapees; they were part of a most successful escape line.

Sunday 17 September 1944

'Everyone up! Time to move!' The cry from the American Sergeant came at just past midnight, only a few minutes into 17 September. The shock jolted the escapees awake, and the American urged them out into the care of a small group of Partisans. There were only a few light sources in Semič, so the dazed men had trouble seeing their guides. The Partisans led the column out in double time: five minutes running, five minutes walking. The escapees were soon gasping for breath – no one could understand how the Partisans kept up this kind of pace. Once the light of the town faded, it was pitch black; tonight was a new moon, and the only light was from the stars. The more observant realized they were marching south-east – to an airfield, they hoped; to salvation.

An hour of running and marching passed, and the column was called to a halt. Several men dropped to the dirt, facedown, scraping their hands and knees. Ralph could hear the lead Partisan conferring with a courier. Then: 'Turn round! The evacuation is off!'

The men were in disbelief. They'd waited a week for this, bored out of their minds, with almost nothing but their dreams of freedom to pass the time. Back they trudged to Semič, and returned to bed.[12]

Many slept through the day. When the Sergeant burst in again in the evening, most of them were conscious this time. 'All right, we're giving it another go! We gotta be there by 23.30.' It was around 22.00: that meant practically running to reach their destination. Everyone just wanted it to be over. It was just as dark, and the Partisans set the same brutal speed. The horrible sensation of running blind was worse for the poor men at the rear: they had 200 boots' worth of dust thrown in their faces.

Just before midnight they arrived in a huge meadow near the village of Otok. They had arrived at the newly created airfield, codenamed Piccadilly Hope. The moment the men stopped, their perspiration seemed to freeze – at least the forest had retained some heat at night. The escapees stood milling about in the dark, too nervous to ask what was going on. Then the silence was broken by the sound of engines – the same engines they'd heard in Pohorje nearly three weeks earlier. Then more engines – a flock of droning motors approaching.

'Look!' Everyone's eyes were trained on the heavens. Against the stars could be made out the silhouettes of planes. The Partisans had built pyres around the meadow, and now they lit fires under them – beacons to mark the runway. Then Ralph spied a faint white shape drifting down. A parachute. The man hit the ground with a thud.

He got up and greeted the Partisans. '*Dober večer*' (Good evening). A conversation ensued. The parachutist switched on a torch and, pointing it at the sky, gave a sequence of flashes. Up above, the pilots would have seen the flashes, and now the roar of engines faded.

It returned as the planes made their approach. The lights of the oncoming plane blinded the onlooking crowd, the outline of the craft becoming clear, along with the khaki colour of its fuselage. It was a Dakota, a stubby, functional, twin-engine transport plane. It lowered itself onto the grassy runway and bumped to a halt, propellors drumming, and was guided to a parking spot by Saggers's staff. Then another was coming in, and another, and another – six Dakotas in all, each one laden with supplies that were unloaded eagerly by the Partisans.

Suddenly the voice of the parachutist was at Ralph's side. 'Lovely evening for it.'

The London accent took Ralph by surprise. 'You're British?'

'That's "sir", technically. But don't worry, I'm not one for formalities.'

Ralph's eyes were dazzled by the plane's lights and he couldn't make out the man's rank insignia. The parachutist, it turned out, was a lieutenant and, thanks to chance, he was having a strange war. He'd been safe from conscription as he was in a reserved occupation, and early in the war had taken in two Slovenians as lodgers. They had wanted to keep their language alive and had taught their landlord, whose middling Slovenian had subsequently been enough to land him an officer's commission in SOE.[13]

The planes had offloaded their cargos, and the escapees' eyes had now adjusted to the dark. Ralph watched some Partisan wounded being taken aboard the first plane. There was still room for more.

Ralph again became The Crow and took the lead. 'Right, original seven with me!' The words were bitter in Ralph's mouth. It was only six, really – Kit was gone. Ralph was holding onto the faintest hope that his friend was still alive, that he was being sheltered by some kindly family. Otherwise, the best to be hoped for was that Kit hadn't been killed upon recapture. Les, Andy, Bob, Len, and Griff formed up with Ralph.

'Can't wait to get away, Crow?' sneered one of the Australians. Ralph couldn't tell who it was, but he nearly lost it.

'I'm going first to make sure the guys at the other end know we're coming, you idiot! So you don't have to spend hours waiting around in the cold!'[14] Les put his hand on Ralph's shoulder and beckoned him to board. The wounded had the spots nearest the door, so the original six escapees took their seats by the cockpit. A grim-looking pilot emerged.

'If I don't get off this route, I'll be dead in six weeks!' he declared in a northern English accent.[15] Such charming optimism! Ralph was glad the Partisan wounded couldn't understand.

'Where are we going?' asked Len.

'Bari, Italy.'

Italy sounded nice. Behind them the other planes were being loaded. The pilot wasn't done with the pessimism. 'You best hold on tight when we take off,' he added. 'The runway's far too short, so it'll be a dicey do.'[16]

The engines groaned back into life. Ralph could feel his guts making the same noise. He'd never flown before, and a first time on a short runway in the dead of night wasn't ideal. The plane accelerated and began to lift. Ralph had a sudden sense of almost being able to touch freedom. A loud clang put paid to that feeling as the plane's undercarriage smacked the tops of the trees at the far end of the meadow. For a moment, all aboard thought the craft was poised to crash. But the Dakota continued to lumber into the sky and flew on to Italy.

39

The Journey Home

Monday 18 September 1944

The Dakota landed at an airfield outside Bari as dawn approached. Medical staff were waiting to unload the wounded and rush them to the hospital, but otherwise there was no one else to meet the escapees: once the ambulances were gone, they were alone apart from ground crew.[1] Ralph approached one of them to ask if anyone was coming.

'Haven't a bleeding clue, mate.'

They headed for the nearest compound and found a half-asleep duty sergeant, who woke a flying officer. He made some calls, leading to more calls, then more. While this military pantomime played out, Griff popped his head back out of the door. 'Two more planes have landed,' he announced. The transport hub for trucks wasn't far off, and by the time the fourth and fifth planes had landed there were lorries and even sandwiches to hand.

Leslie and Griff stayed behind to make sure the last plane arrived, and Ralph hopped up into the cab of one of the trucks. The convoy's sergeant insisted Ralph regale them with tales from behind the lines.

'Jesus, man!' said the Sergeant, when Ralph was done. 'You must have been desperate to get home.'[2]

The drive was short: the escapees were deposited in an empty barracks belonging to the British 8th Army. Ralph watched with pride as truckloads of passengers filtered in: his railway crew, the farm lads, the Frenchmen, the airman Melrose, Heslop and his escapees. They had made it. They were free.

But soon Leslie and Griffin turned up with bad tidings. The sixth plane had not arrived; it had suffered an engine failure on the ground. The stricken Dakota had been camouflaged, and the remaining escapees had returned to Semič. It could have been worse; better an engine failure on the ground than in the air. Still, the absence of twenty of their number weighed heavy as Ralph fell asleep.

'Wakey, wakey! Rise and shine!' an English lance corporal was shouting. 'Time for a wash-up and a brush-up!' It was strange to be returned to a proper barracks after so many years. Hot showers compensated for any culture shock. Oh, what a glorious feeling!

The first day outside Nazi territory went in a flash. Each man received a medical and was cautioned against excessive eating or drinking after the privations of the escape. An officer informed Leslie and Ralph that an engineer was being dropped to repair the last plane. The next day, new clothing and mess kits were issued.[3] Ralph retained his battered old hat, though, now well into its fifth year; there was no way he could lay his hands on a fresh one – the 8th Army didn't have any in its stores.

On parade, a stern officer warned against speaking to anyone about the escape: doing so could endanger the lives of the

Partisans and the many escapees and pilots still to come. The men took the point, while feeling a total vow of silence was a bit excessive. Each was then given a piece of paper to write a telegram home. It was lucky for Ralph that Ronte was living with his parents: he could let them all know at once. 'ESCAPED SAFE WELL', read his message.[4] A longer aerogram, which would take a week to reach home, was also issued.

That night Ralph and Leslie were woken to be told the sixth plane had landed; the last escapees were on their way. Total rescued as a result of their escape: ninety-nine prisoners of war. Fifteen minutes later, the latecomers entered the barracks. Ralph yelled with delight and ran to his friend: Kit Carson was among the passengers! Now it was 100.

The poor bloke had had an even longer road to here than his fellow captives. After the ambush at the farmhouse, Kit had run deep into the forest, most likely to the north. By good fortune, a few Partisans from a remote mountainous odred, the Koroška Odred, had been heading to the courier station and found Kit on their way. As the courier station was destroyed, they took him back to their HQ in the Kamnik-Savinja Alps.[5] From there he'd made his way south with more couriers, and finally reached Semič on 20 September – too late for the leading group, but in time to catch the sixth and final Dakota.[6]

The party complete, each man underwent an exhaustive interrogation from MI9.[7] All were sworn to the strictest secrecy. They could tell no one any detail of their escape: not their families, their spouses, not even their comrades. Each escapee signed the following document:

WARNING AGAINST GIVING INFORMATION WHICH MAY BE OF VALUE TO THE ENEMY

This applies to members of all British, American, Dominion, and all Imperial Services and continues even after discharge therefrom.

1. It is the duty of all persons to safeguard information which might be useful, directly or indirectly, to the enemy. Such information includes details of any attempted or premeditated escapes, and information of a secret nature of which a P/W may have obtained knowledge whilst in captivity.

2. It is an offence, punishable with imprisonment, to publish or communicate to any unauthorised person, any information or anything which purports to be information on any matter which would or might be directly or indirectly useful to the enemy.

3. Information regarding escapes by Prisoners of War, including attempted or premeditated escapes as well as any information of a secret nature of which you have obtained knowledge while in captivity, should be communicated only to an Intelligence Officer, or to such other persons as are officially authorised to interview you.

On no account will any such information be communicated to the Press or to representatives of any Red Cross Society.

I have read this warning, and understand that I shall be liable to disciplinary action if I disclose to anyone information of the kind mentioned above.[8]

Ralph and Leslie then underwent a second joint interrogation, this time by a posh colonel with a large, hoof-shaped moustache. Ralph wondered if he was the model for the cartoon character Colonel Blimp.

'There's been a lot of fuss made over this,' said the Colonel, 'but what you've done isn't very remarkable.' He unfurled a map of Slovenia. 'Look: you've covered barely 100 miles as the crow flies. Can't understand why more of our fellows aren't doing it.'

'Maybe, sir,' replied Ralph, 'it's because they're not bloody crows.'[9]

Ralph went back the following day and found a more sympathetic intelligence officer to tell the story to. The officer asked Ralph to write a detailed report. True to his word to Leslie, Ralph wrote a special testimonial. He noted everything Leslie had done to launch the escape and asked that he be considered for an award.[10]

Unbeknown to Ralph, Captain Heslop was doing the same on Ralph's behalf. There was no Australian presence in the Mediterranean any more – the AIF had gone home to fight Japan – so a special office of the New Zealand 2nd Division, still in the Mediterranean after all these years, was looking after any Australians who happened to pass by. Heslop sought them out and recounted everything, with a recommendation that Ralph be decorated.[11]

The escapees were separated and billeted by British and New Zealand forces. A fair sum of spending money was handed out, not that there was much to spend it on. Separated from the Brits, Ralph spent most of his time with Griff, Phil, and Bob; Kit was probably bedridden, having used every ounce of strength to catch up.

A few days later Anzacs and Brits alike were moved on to Naples, which proved far more agreeable. Though the city had been devastated by Allied, then Axis, bombing campaigns, the escapees were able to visit the opera and Pompeii. Once again Ralph found himself feeling more a tourist than a soldier, but this time he felt he'd earned it.

Saturday 30 September 1944

The feelings were bittersweet; the Anzacs were embarking. They were with a large contingent of prisoners exchanged with Germany via Switzerland, allowed because they had a medical exemption from fighting again. But for many of the escapees, today would mean leaving the best friends they'd ever had. Ralph almost wanted to stay behind and travel with Les, Len, and Andy to Britain. But that would be considered desertion, and besides, he needed to get back to Ronte. The Brits all came down from their barracks to give the Anzacs a send-off. Ralph looked across at Leslie standing on the wharf. He'd miss him: the loudmouth Australian bank clerk and the gentle English jazz pianist had been an unlikely duo. But they'd done all right. Without them, the greatest escape of the war would never have occurred.

'Three cheers for the bloody Crow!'[12] one of the Brits shouted. It made Ralph tear up. The horn sounded, and the ship pulled away.

The Brits were headed to Salerno, where they spent some time before finally departing on Friday 13 October. It was not an unlucky date for them: they made it safely to Liverpool a week later.[13] The Anzacs stopped off in Egypt, and in Cairo Ralph was finally able to get himself a new slouch hat, as well as a suitcase full of tourist trinkets and gifts for good measure.

On the first night back at sea, something wonderful occurred. 'Ralph?'

Ralph turned on the deck to see an Australian lieutenant looking at him in disbelief. 'Jim?'

On the same boat, they had attempted to flee Greece. Now, on the same ship, Ralph and James Forrest were heading home.[14] James had been one of the medical repatriations. The pair gazed out at the sea. They weren't sure what they'd imagined when they'd set out all starry-eyed and eager to fight the Führer. Whatever it had been, this was not it.

In Sri Lanka, the passengers were transferred to an American ship and made for Australia, finally arriving in Melbourne on 17 November.

Friday 17 November 1944

They were given a warm welcome. Ralph's former commander in Greece, General Blamey, hosted a glitzy 'Welcome Back' dinner reception for all the POWs.

The next morning, the remaining twenty-two escapees would scatter: the Kiwis would board a ship to Auckland; the Victorians would go to their homes; the Queenslanders and New South Welshmen would catch a train to Sydney; the South and Western Australians would board a train for Adelaide. Before all that, however, they needed to get drunk – now.

Following the dinner reception, Ralph asked a taxi driver to take them to where booze could be found. Alcohol was rationed, and the liquor laws meant the pubs were way past closing time.

Ralph pressed some cash into the driver's hand, which seemed to concentrate the mind, and soon the group found themselves at an establishment that had no regard for the law. The drinks flowed so long it was a miracle they got back to barracks.

Saturday 18 November 1944

They all made their respective transports that morning, though many cursed The Crow one last time. They all had to embark with hangovers. From Melbourne's railway station Ralph joined a train to Adelaide. At the station the platform was crammed with soldiers: a few returnees from Europe, but mostly soldiers from the Pacific travelling home on leave.

The train rattled through Melbourne's suburbs, with Ralph excited to be on a passenger train for the first time since returning from the Graz conference. They crawled across the country, stopping at every small station. Ralph watched the sun set on the bushland, parched golden by heat. It could not have been a more vivid contrast to the steep mountains, blue waters, and lush green forests of Slovenia.

Sunday 19 November 1944

Ralph woke at sunrise the next morning as they were going through Murray Bridge on the approach to Adelaide. He was unshaven, dishevelled, and nervous.

All military personnel had to disembark a station early, at Keswick, where the platform was a throng of weeping and rejoicing families. Ralph put his bags down and searched the platform up and down. No luck. Then, as the platform began to clear, Ralph saw a tall woman in a summer dress with red trim.

Could it be? He must have got a whole inch shorter in captivity.

'Are you waiting for someone?' asked Ralph.

'I was,' replied Ronte. 'But it really is you, isn't it?'[15]

40

Greater Escapes?

On returning home, Ralph was given ninety days' leave. It was interrupted twice. In early December he had a bout of the shakes that was not just malaria. The army sent him, with Ronte, to a field hospital near Strathalbyn, in the Adelaide Hills. The hospital specialized in 'shell-shock' cases. He was discharged after eight days of the 'talking cure'. It patched things over a little, but he would show signs of post-traumatic stress disorder for the rest of his life.

There had been a mention in the press about Ralph's escape before he returned to Australia; his family were probably the source. Then he and Ronte were the subject of a street fashion shot in *The Australian Women's Weekly*, where his escape was mentioned. Then Captain Heslop's recommendation and account of Ralph's exploits were received. The Australian Army did not believe it. In February 1945 he was arrested by military police at his parents' house and escorted under guard by train to Melbourne and Army HQ at Victoria Barracks. There he was accused of spreading false rumours. Two days of incarceration and interrogation followed. A Victorian escapee, Lance Corporal Arnold Woods, was brought back from leave on his farm in Seymour at Ralph's suggestion. Only then was Ralph's story believed. Before he returned to Adelaide he was personally interviewed by General Blamey and forcefully told to not even say he had escaped.*

Ralph's skills and experience saw him returned to military intelligence. Promoted to sergeant, he was posted to Murchison in rural Victoria to a POW camp housing German prisoners. Thanks to a superior's hare-brained idea, Ralph went undercover as a German soldier to gather intelligence. His colloquial German may have been good, but Ralph's decision during the escape not to become a spy proved a sound one: he had little knowledge of Wehrmacht procedure or training to enable him to keep his cover, and after only a few days he was pulled out and made a translator.

At the end of the war in Europe he was sent to a training camp for intelligence agents. All the others there were battle-hardened officers; Ralph was the only NCO. He was placed seventh in a class of forty, described as 'an enthusiastic and cheerful soldier, who was popular with his fellow students: possesses an alert and analytical mind, and proved capable of accurate work under strain: has ability to lead, and organises well'.[1]

In Slovenia and Yugoslavia, meanwhile, news of his party's escape spread. Even Tito's HQ celebrated, though it inflated the number of escapees sixfold, which caused some alarm in SOE.[2] For MI9, Losco, and Lindsay, it was proof of concept. Such ambitious escapes *were* possible. Losco had missed the trial run, but no matter: he had his mission and was furnished with contacts. Major Losco would cross the Kozjak Mountains into Austria and establish a network of safe houses, supply dumps, and escape lines. Stalag XVIIIA and its Arbeitskommandos still

---

* Unsurprisingly, Ralph never committed this detail to writing.

held 39,000 prisoners, 6,000 of them British Empire troops. They were Losco's prize.[3] The Partisans would guard this line. Hundreds of their fighters now roamed the mountainous border region, armed to the teeth with British weapons.[4] Construction on an airfield near Gornji Grad had also begun. Were it to become operational, escapees could bypass the Sava gauntlet, and fly direct to Italy. It'd be a godsend for 4th Zone wounded, and would mean that Lindsay could easily arm all new recruits.

But then came a hammer blow to MI9's plans. Under British pressure, on 12 September the exiled King Petar recognized Tito as the military leader of Yugoslavia. Tito had almost everything he needed to take power. The Red Army was nearing eastern Serbia, and he had the authority of Stalin, Churchill, and the King. So why should he risk anything to maintain good relations with Imperialist Britain, when the King had spoken and the Soviets arrived? Indeed, Tito and many senior Communists feared the British would support former collaborators and oppose Yugoslav territorial gains. Those gains were mostly for Slovenia, including southern Austria, Primorska, and above all the port city of Trieste.[5] On 18 September, even as he was celebrating the escape, Tito quietly ordered all Anglo-American missions confined to their relevant HQ.[6]

Unable to leave 4th Zone HQ in the Savinja Valley, for Lindsay and Losco hopes of more mass escapes were scuttled. The Partisans also handicapped themselves by halting construction of the northern airfield. Losco was reduced to providing supplies for E&Es who passed through. For their part, the Partisans continued to aid E&Es. Only a few Arbeitskommandos remained in Štajerska, many having been evacuated into the Reich after the Ožbalt raid. But downed aircrews were still common and were rescued and conveyed to Semič. For Jack Saggers, the air-field situation was still difficult. Otok, where Ralph had taken off from, had no drainage and was often unable to take planes because the ground was too soft, with would-be passengers sent on foot to Croatia. When planes could land, they could only take off again with a reduced load. Five or six E&Es or Partisan wounded could board, rather than the normal two dozen.[7]

Lindsay, meanwhile, continued to arm and supply the Partisans, despite being shut out and a Partisan agent being assigned to report his every move. Everyone knew a German counter-attack would come, so Lindsay asked SOE for a mass airlift with enough supplies to heavily arm 2,000 Partisans and provide ammunition, food, and clothes for another 3,000. SOE said this could be done, but the drop never took place.[8] Either SOE admin were at fault, or RAF Command were too busy to spare the planes and crews. With no weapons, the Partisans had no choice but to evacuate new recruits south, where weapons were more plentiful.[9]

Another botched delivery had fatal consequences. Commander Stane, now leading all Slovenian Partisan forces, whose actions were so key to the fate of Štajerska and the escape, was killed on 7 November. He was testing a British light mortar when the bomb exploded in the tube.* A week later, SOE messaged all its liaison missions: it had realized that using parachutes to deliver bombs which were armed by a sharp downward knock wasn't a great idea.[10]

Lindsay's time with Cuckold came to an end at the beginning of December 1944, when he was ordered to move to Croatia.

---

* According to some accounts Stane was killed by a PIAT spigot mortar bomb, but the principle remains the same.

Even though everyone knew the Germans were gathering, on 6 December 4th Zone took a grave risk and threw a farewell party in Gornji Grad tavern, and spirits flowed. The pub itself had been sacked a month ago in a ram-raid attack by the Germans. Only a few bottles of spirits remained, and the pub itself was a ruin. For many it was their last drink. Partisan obstructions to the Cuckold Mission had soured relations between Lindsay and Partisan commanders, but ultimately they were comrades who had fought together. Many senior officers confessed to Lindsay their unhappiness at the orders they had received to obstruct the mission, and their misgivings about the Partisan tilt towards the Soviets.[11]

Lindsay left early in the morning and made it out in time, but for the Partisans it was too late. German troops withdrawn from both Eastern and Western Fronts, with armour and artillery, arrived for the final assault.* 4th Zone was cut off from Pohorje and the Sava, the 14th Division and other Partisan units went in the only direction they could – up into the mountains[12] – and the Germans recaptured all the valley's villages and farms. They burned everything they could not hold. Štajerska's jails filled with Partisans and civilians alike.

Yet those Partisans who were still breathing never abandoned Allied escapees. On 17 December 1944, thirty-six prisoners escaped from the last camps in Maribor and, though the path through Pohorje and across the Sava was blocked, the Partisans found a way, smuggling them home via the same route the 14th had taken into Štajerska: the long way round through Croatia.[13]

---

* Forces included the 13th and 19th SS-Police Regiments and the 18th Reserve Gebirgsjäger Division.

During that last winter a handful of others would, against all odds, make it across the Alps and be conveyed home, but by now the escapes were all but over.

For the 14th Partisan Division up in the mountains, the situation only worsened. That winter saw catastrophic snowfall, and there were so many German troops that all the roads could be held in an iron grip. Short on food and bitterly cold, Major Losco collapsed on a snow march and had to be carried.[14] He could do nothing more. His stores and the safe zone were destroyed. He could not even be quartermaster to escapees. Four days before Christmas he radioed MI9 from the sole working radio, borrowed from the Partisans.

> Our radio contact broke down. Zone now being chased by Huns who probably intend to clear area north of Sava. Consequently there is no future for [MI9] work and what little may crop up can be handled by mission. Further . . . all our stores have been captured. Bearing in mind imperative to cut down mission personnel to minimum send instructions if I am to come or remain.[15]

Between Partisan obstruction, the weather, and the enemy, he could achieve nothing. MI9 had been receiving messages to that effect for months. Losco was now asking for his life. After three days, a response was sent.

> Appreciate your position. But in view of prisoners still in working camps south Austria essential you remain and do what is possible. Doing utmost to get stores to you.
> Best wishes for Christmas.[16]

Cold, starving, in metres of snow, and on the run, it was the last message Losco received. On Boxing Day he and an MI6 associate attempted a risky road crossing.* They were spotted by Germans, shot and wounded, and captured. The last heard of them was an unconfirmed Partisan intelligence report that they were taken under guard to the SS military hospital in Ljubljana.[17] Either they died of their wounds, or they recovered and were imprisoned, tortured, and shot.

---

* The associate was Lieutenant Edward Parks. The works of Austrian historian Peter Pirker have more information about the MI6 missions in the area.

41

The War's End

The 14th Division took many casualties and escaped total destruction several times that winter. Still they fought on. Meanwhile they and the other Slovenian Partisans were betrayed: in early 1945 the Slovenian Partisans were absorbed by their Yugoslav counterparts,[1] and Slovenian was abolished as a language of command (in favour of the Bosnian-Croatian-Serbian language), despite Tito promising he would not do this.[2] Many Slovenian Partisans became disgusted at their political leaders.[3] But a stronger hatred still burned for the enemy. Winter thawed, and both sides prepared for the final showdown.

On 9 April 1945, the Partisans began probing the defences around Ljubljana. In May they began their drives on major cities. Partisan forces seized Trieste, and the 14th Division moved into southern Austria. In Ljubljana, the Germans, the Domobranstvo, its leadership and their families, and what remained of the SLS, fled the city. Before leaving, the Germans and Domobranstvo murdered their last political prisoners, including a Domobranstvo secretary who was in reality a Partisan spy who had reported on Urbančič and other senior collaborators.[4] The fleeing German-Domobranstvo column of 20,000 cut a path north, broke through the 14th Division, and surrendered to the British Army in Austria on 8 May.

On 9 May the Partisans liberated Ljubljana. It had been a long and brutal four years for the city: first Italians, then collaborators, then Germans, then more collaborators. In the towns and cities that had changed hands between Italians and Germans and the Partisans, the reaction was muted, but here on this glorious spring day, the city was celebrating. The detested occupiers were gone and almost everyone who hated or feared the Partisans had fled the city. Thousands lined the streets, welcoming the Partisans as liberators and heroes. Families reunited with long-lost relatives. Flowers were gathered, and the city shone with colour. Couples took picnics in the sun, and fireworks sounded through the night.[5]

That should have been it. The war in Europe was finally over. But something simmered below the surface: a hatred that would not die with the war. When Britain, America, and the Soviet Union agreed on the new German borders, and that all Germans outside these new borders would be deported, across Europe the result was that over ten million ethnic Germans were driven from their homes, including those in Slovenia.[6] And what of the collaborators? That would depend on whose hands they fell into. Feeling unable to cope with the influx of refugees, and there still being a shred of goodwill towards their Partisan allies, the British in Austria loaded the Domobranstvo onto trains. The passengers were lied to and told they were going to Italy. Instead, 12,000 people, the bulk of them Domobranstvo, were sent not to Italy but back to Slovenia. There they were taken to the forests of Kočevski Rog – near where resistance headquarters had once been – an area littered with rocky caves and pits. What would become the Yugoslav secret police recruited those Partisans who still wanted vengeance on the Germans and, above all, on the collaborators.[7] Specially assembled death squads gunned down all 12,000. The corpses were tossed into the pits, and the entrances dynamited shut.[8] Those whose loved ones were murdered at Kočevski Rog never forgot. 'Their innocent blood, shed two months after the end of the war,' wrote one woman who had two brothers in the Domobranstvo to the leaders of the Slovenian Communist Party, 'will one day drown you as well.'[9]

As for Slovenia, a totalitarian dictatorship descended. Sham elections formalized one-party rule. The monarchy was abolished, new laws and a constitution were introduced. But the country's infrastructure and finances were in ruins. In Stalinist tradition, show trials persecuted anyone seen as a political threat, even their own comrades.*[10] For the first time Slovenia was a country: the People's Republic of Slovenia, a constituent republic of the Federal People's Republic of Yugoslavia. However, Slovenia was not autonomous but ruled by a centralized regime in Belgrade. The 14th Division was even transferred to Serbia. Its members left the army in droves and simply went home.[11] Perhaps the only thing holding Slovenia together were its territorial ambitions, which went mostly unrealized, causing widespread public anger among Slovenians. Most of Primorska was now within Slovenia's borders, but the Partisans had to withdraw from southern Austria in a move ordered by Stalin.[12]

---

* The most infamous were the 'Nagode' trials targeting resistance members who had left the OF over opposition to the Communists, and the 'Dachau' trials targeting Party members who survived concentration camps.

Neither did Slovenia gain Trieste; it was first an international city and later was given to Italy.

In terms of Slovenia and Yugoslavia's place in the Communist order, these would have just been bumps in the road, had it not been for Stalin. Tito's loyalty was such he declared to his generals, 'If the Red Army needs us to lead its march toward the English Channel, we'll be there tomorrow!'[13] Of the new Communist states in Europe, only Yugoslavia and Albania were not puppet regimes established in the Red Army's wake. They had taken power largely by their own efforts, and this should have awarded the Yugoslav Communists special prestige. But the fact that he was not directly responsible for creating those regimes seemed to irk Stalin; he delighted at subtle taunts at Yugoslav expense.[14] Stalin tried to subjugate Yugoslavia economically, and was infuriated that Tito pursued his own foreign policy in the Balkans without first consulting 'the Boss'.

Stalin condemned Tito in 1948, and Yugoslavia broke from the USSR. For a time, repression there worsened. Private farms were seized, as if to say to the world, 'it is Stalin who is soft'.[15] Karl 'Čolo' Čolnik, the Lackov Odred scout, had his market garden taken by the state. He fled Slovenia with his wife, Anica,[16] just two of some 20,000 people who escaped the country during this time.[17]

Eventually, liberalization and an international turn prevailed. Several leading Communists, foremost from Slovenia, discovered that European social democracies were achieving much of what Communist dogma was aiming for.[18] Though by no means embracing democracy, conditions improved. Slovenia was given greater autonomy. Cultural and artistic restrictions eased; the rights of smallholders and small businesses were reinstated;

and 'workers' self-management' was introduced. Profitable firms paid dividends to their workforce on top of regular salaries.[19] Rapid economic growth funded ambitious social programmes. Travel, too, was liberalized: Yugoslavs could now emigrate and travel freely.[20] Finally, a small measure of what so many Partisans fought and died for became a reality.

Epilogue

Ralph was offered a career as an agent with military intelligence following Japan's surrender and the end of the war. He chose civilian life (thank goodness), and returned to work at the State Bank. Later, he put his talents of persuasion to use as a life insurance salesman, a career he excelled at. He began by engaging with the German-speaking community of rural South Australia, religious refugees in the 1840s who were now unfairly viewed with hostility. In 1950 he and Ronte adopted a daughter, Beverly. They subsequently had two sons: Steven, born in 1950, and myself, born in 1958.

Ralph's two early fellow captives, Gerrard Pollock and Henry Walter Steilberg, both survived the war – the latter not by much. Pollock remained on an Arbeitskommando until 1945, while Steilberg became relentless in his own escape attempts. Between April 1943 and September 1944, he escaped seven times. Infuriated, his captors imprisoned him in the notorious Terezín prison in occupied Czechoslovakia. On 21 April 1945, Steilberg made his final escape from a forced march out of the prison, reaching American lines four days later.[1] His story is described in Paul Rea's *Voices from the Fortress*.

From Ralph's escape, of the six prisoners separated at

Zavodnje, only three can be accounted for. Kit Carson rejoined the escape party, and Albert Avis was recaptured and sent to Stalag XVIIIC, from where he was liberated in 1945.[2] In the same month Reginald Allan, who may be Reginald Allen, was reported as freed from Stalag VIIIB. The remaining three – one Imperial and two French prisoners – are also most likely to have been recaptured and sent to other camps, though many of the escapees continued to believe all save Kit had been killed.

Roy Courlander, Ralph's predecessor as camp translator, survived the war. As the tide turned against Germany, he had headed to Belgium, where he defected back to the Allies, claiming his earlier defection to the Nazis had always been intended to gather intelligence. The British did not believe him. At his trial both Ralph and Griffin Rendell testified in his defence[3] – not out of any love for him, but because the prosecution's case rested on the evidence of a former 3GW inmate who had failed to understand the satirical intent behind Courlander's ramblings about Ella Shields and the Hitler Youth, and because Roy had actually been fairly popular. What his fellows didn't know was Roy was almost certainly a dedicated fascist, volunteering to fight the Soviets even before the British Free Corps was founded.[4] In any case, Roy Courlander was arrogant enough to believe that, whatever the outcome of the war, he could end it better off than when he started. He was sentenced to fifteen years' imprisonment. He later migrated to Sydney, Australia, where he became a middle-management member of the local underworld. Early in 1966, driving a red E-Type Jaguar, he paid an unannounced visit to our house. His convertible was the envy of our quiet suburban street. Roy had come to try a shakedown. Ralph was now one of the leading insurance managers in Australia, with the discretion for the investment of large pension funds. Roy asked Ralph to invest in his proprietor's 'legitimate' business interests, threatening blackmail if Ralph did not agree. Unaware of Ralph's escape, Roy threatened to denounce him as a Nazi collaborator (based on Roy's memory of Ralph's compliant persona at Šentilj). Needless to say, Roy got short shrift and a flea in his ear. He died broke and alone in a dingy Sydney flat in 1979 aged sixty-four.

William Fagan, Ralph's predecessor as Vertrauensmann, had a happy ending. While in Edinburgh waiting to return to New Zealand, he fell in love. Soon after, he returned home with his wife Mamie and two stepdaughters, and later had two sons, and then grandchildren. Bill died in 1977, aged sixty-six.

The fate of many in this story remains unknown. Others, like Lisa Zavodnik, nearly paid with their lives for aiding the escape – it was only thanks to the intervention of a German officer whom her husband had befriended that the Zavodnik family were spared deportation to a concentration camp. It is unknown if Lisa's cousin Anton survived the war. The camp guards' fate is also a mystery. Either they were released, or there is a mass grave in Pohorje where the poor fellows rest. As for Johann Gross of Vienna, it is to be hoped he lived a long and comfortable life on the gains he made with Ralph.

Of the Stalag XVIIID Partisans who died, commemorations were scant. We were unable to learn more about Mehmed Junis or Abdul E. Krim, though the pair are commemorated in Celje as part of the Celje Company, and the writer Matej Bor wrote a poem titled 'Junis, Krim' in their honour. Colin Cargill was never truly recognized for his bravery or his efforts. His gravestone is in the Commonwealth War Cemetery, Belgrade. Australia still mistakenly lists him as killed in Italy, not Slovenia.

John Denvir, the only survivor, returned to his family in New Zealand and started a taxi company. His received a raft of commendations from three armies, including a British Distinguished Conduct Medal and, thanks to Soviet liaisons with the Partisans, a Soviet Medal of Valour. He returned often to Slovenia for Ljubo Šercer Brigade reunions and was given an honorary commission as a Yugoslav major. James Caffin wrote a biography of John's life, titled simply: *Partisan*.

Miraculously, almost all the Partisans involved in the escape survived. For those who could navigate the strange new world, they became the new elite of Slovenia. But many could not: after Čolo had his business seized, he moved first to a refugee camp in Austria before settling with his wife Anica in Melbourne, Australia, where they established a thriving market garden. The machine-gunner Alojz was given command of an Arbeitskommando of German POWs, helping rebuild Slovenia. But, as a former member of the Wehrmacht himself, he fell under suspicion in the post-war paranoia. He left the army and worked in an unassuming job in a timber mill. Švejk returned to Dolenjska and lived well as a Communist Party (now known as the League of Communists to distance them from the Soviets) man. Franjo entered the legal profession and rose to become Chief Justice of the Maribor Supreme Court. But, as with Ralph, the war had taken its toll, and he often resorted to heavy drinking.[5] Josefine, who had scouted the way at Rogla, ended the war lying low on a relative's farm in southern Austria that was also an Arbeitskommando. There she fell in love with a Kiwi POW, Bruce Murray. They married, and Josefine emigrated to New Zealand with Bruce. Their story is described by her son-in-law Doug Gold in his book, *The Note Through the Wire*.

Franklin Lindsay, the instigator of the rescue, ended the war a lieutenant-colonel, heading the US mission in Belgrade before going on to work for the CIA, where he would rue the failure of American policymakers to learn anything from Slovenia and Yugoslavia. It was a refusal to accept that those who joined Communist groups could be patriots first, and Communists second, Lindsay argued, that led America into Vietnam,[6] and to employ tactics that often resembled those used by Germany and Italy in Slovenia. He wrote a book concerning the (declassified) elements of his wartime career, *Beacons in the Night*. His later career is documented in *Spy Capitalism: ITEK and the CIA* by Jonathan E. Lewis. Franklin Lindsay died in 2011 at the age of ninety-five.

Captain Jack Hugh Saggers and most of the remaining Allied mission staff evacuated Slovenia in April 1945. He survived the war and returned home. His MI9 work has remained mostly secret. Officially, he was SOE.

Losco received nothing. He has never been recognized for his efforts, nor properly commemorated. MI6 and MI9 (the latter disbanded in 1945) remain notoriously tight-lipped about their operations, even from the Second World War. He has a place – oddly – in the Commonwealth War Graves Memorial in Athens, even though the Belgrade memorial is closer to where he died. This lack of recognition is partly because Lindsay and his comrades in Slovenia knew Losco only as 'Matthews'.

The leading escapees were quietly decorated. Probably owing to Ralph's testimony, Leslie Laws received the Distinguished Conduct Medal (DCM).[7] Ralph was commended too, once his story had been believed: he was awarded the British Empire Medal (BEM).[8] The Australian citation was for 'Devotion to duty'. Later, he discovered the British citation was quite different. 'For gallant and distinguished conduct in the field', the same citation as a DCM. He could only guess that his Australian superiors changed the award to maintain secrecy. Even after the war, Leslie and Ralph were sworn to silence; they had medals but could not speak even to their families of why they wore them. Such silence was particularly ironic because those in Slovenia were able to speak freely of the escape.

Ralph continued to be a wholehearted believer in God, King (now Queen), and Country; his experiences reinforced a deep hatred for fascism and all its collaborators. He, like Lindsay, was uncomfortable with the Vietnam War and believed that many who followed Communist movements, and many Communists themselves, were patriots. Ralph felt that fascism remained the great enemy of humanity.

Ralph became engaged with local veterans' associations, primarily the Returned Services League of Australia (RSL).[9] However, few – save the Partisans and his fellow POWs – could truly appreciate what he'd been through: the shame of being captured, the starvation of the cages in Greece and the dread train that followed, the horror of seeing thousands of Soviets butchered, spending much of his captivity in relative luxury; then seeing the destruction wrought on Slovenia. He could cope in the smaller RSL branches, because he could steer the organization. In large city branches things were different. In Sydney in particular, where he lived for much of the 1960s and 1970s, Ralph found the RSL intolerable. In 1962 the league had begun a huge anti-Communist campaign.[10] The RSL were looking in the wrong direction. Many Ustaše, the Croatian fascists who were Hitler's conduit for the Holocaust in the Balkans, fled to

Australia. Here they launched a terrorist campaign. Through the 1960s and 1970s they threatened, murdered, and bombed their way through Australian communities. Those who spoke against them, including Ralph, received death threats. Shaken but angry, he offered them nothing but contempt in response. Australian intelligence services and policymakers, meanwhile, ignored the threat. Only when the Ustaše bombed a Sydney high street, injuring sixteen people, was action taken. Even then, one MP suggested it was a Communist false-flag attack.[11]

Another Nazi collaborator who fled to Australia was Lyenko Urbančič. He endeared himself to the RSL during their anti-Communist campaign, launching his own political career in the meantime.*[12] Despite his senior position, as he was not a uniformed collaborator, the British did not send Urbančič back to Slovenia. Fleeing from Austria to Australia, he became a leading member of the conservative New South Wales Liberal Party, rebranding himself as a victim of Communism and a 'true, classical conservative'.[13] Urbančič steered New South Wales politics far to the far right before eventually being outed in 1979 as an SS propagandist. He was not expelled from the party following this revelation. Disgusted, Ralph conspired with other former POWs to have Urbančič prosecuted for his work with the Nazis.[14] These efforts were unsuccessful, and Lyenko Urbančič died in Sydney in 2006.

Shunned by many in the RSL, it was with other former POWs that Ralph found solace, frequently writing to his fellow

---

* NSW Police recorded an RSL representative attended meetings of Lyenko's '50 Club', which NSW Police described as an 'Antisemitic and extreme right' organization.

escapees, including Kit, Leslie, Andy, Len, Griff, and a few Partisans, though sadly he had not managed to remember Franjo's address.

In 1972, when I was fourteen, Ralph had three months' long-service leave. By now Yugoslavia was open for tourism. 'I must go and visit the people who looked after me during the war,' he told Ronte. 'Would you like to come?'

Ralph and Ronte flew first to Athens, where they retraced the steps of Lusterforce and even got that romantic stay beside Tolo beach. They travelled down the coast that Ralph had rowed past at night thirty-one years before. They threw thank-you parties at each village that had offered Ralph food and shelter. They travelled on to Croatia; here he was astonished to find a minor conference happening at his hotel in Dubrovnik. All the attendees were German Army officers. The sight of their uniforms, and hearing them speak, brought on a significant attack of the shakes that took a day to control. They took the bus to Slovenia, in first Semič, then Ljubliana, then Maribor, and Ralph was reunited with his old friends, most joyously Franjo. He was pleasantly surprised to see Švejk, now introduced as Franc Gruden: the Commissar had been in such poor shape in 1944 that Ralph had doubted he'd survived the war. In Slovenia the escape was public knowledge, and at last Ralph was able to reminisce freely.

He and Ronte visited again in 1977. Afterwards, they went on to London, where a reunion was had with Leslie, Len, and Andy. Sadly, Ralph never reconnected with his fellow prisoners from earlier in his captivity, above all Gerry Pollock, Walter Steilberg and Jim Forrest: the memories of Corinth, Thessaloniki, and the train were too much to bear. So loath was Ralph to recall or show any weakness that he kept his partial deafness, the result of the assault by a German guard, hidden from me his entire life.

In the early 1980s, the escape was partially declassified, but the involvement of intelligence services was still a secret. At my urging, Ralph wrote a short memoir, *A Hundred Miles as the Crow Flies*, but only through a slip-up or frustration did he ever reveal that the story he told from then on was not wholly true.[15] He did, though, leave several errors – breadcrumbs of sorts. He wrote they met the Newfoundlander Major Jones (who was more famous in Slovenia), and not Franklin Lindsay, during the escape. Jones wasn't even in the country at the time, so it appeared an honest mistake, an effect of the passing of time on his memory. But Ralph and Lindsay met and corresponded at the time that the memoir was written, so naming Jones was perhaps a deliberate attempt to hide Lindsay's involvement.

This secrecy and altering of the story created its own problem: in order to conceal the parts played by SOE and MI9, Ralph and Leslie ended up telling their families different stories, accounts that reflected their differing situations. Leslie had mellowed after the war, leading a quiet life of music, painting, and lawn bowls, and in his version, he had simply asked the Partisans to return for the working crew, and they'd agreed.[16] It was a straightforward explanation from a straightforward man. Ralph, on the other hand, had only grown more ornery and theatrical, and talked up the drunken salesman story, of how over drinks he had convinced Partisan commanders to return for the others, over the objections of his fellow escapees. That this was closer to the truth was corroborated by Leslie's best friend Andrew Hamilton.[17] Captain Heslop heard the story from both Ralph and Les at the time, and only recommended Ralph for a decoration.[18]

294

In 1985, Australian and Slovenian filmmakers produced a documentary on the escape, called *March to Freedom/Pot k Svobodi*. Ralph and Leslie both travelled to Slovenia for filming, Leslie primarily to see the Zavodniks again. Sadly, Lisa had died, but Les was tearfully reunited with Stanko and Mitsi.

The documentary would have been the perfect chance to set the story straight, had both men not sworn to carry the truth to their graves. Taking their vow of secrecy so seriously made little sense, but both believed it their duty. That truth was only discovered via a handful of declassified MI9 documents, and painstaking research across Australian, British, American, Slovenian, and New Zealander sources. The full report on the escape, it appears, was never declassified, and remains 'Top Secret'.

Hopes were raised when British archival file WO 208/3363 'Yugoslavia' came to light, containing MI9 escape reports from Yugoslav territory, but infuriatingly it contained only incomplete accounts of the Australian and New Zealander members of the escape, which had already been released by the Australian and New Zealand archives. The remaining details are contained within the file Dvr, Leslie Laws, CSDIC/CMF/SKP/3867, which is either in a different folder, has never been declassified, or has been lost.

Only in Slovenia was the escape remembered, let alone commemorated. There it was dubbed Vranov let (The Crow's Flight) and occupied a unique place in history. It was something all Partisans – both those who approved of the world they built, like Franjo and Švejk, and those who did not, like Alojz and Čolo – could be proud of. From 1944, when the Partisans began recording rescues, Slovenian Partisans rescued over 800 POWs and airmen.[19] Add in 1943, and the total number would be closer to 1,000. Even as relations between the Partisans and their allies deteriorated, the rescues had continued. Partisans risked their lives to save these men until the end, making theirs the most successful escape line in Europe.

Yet, in the many histories of escape, evasion, and espionage, these efforts rate hardly a mention. Perhaps this is because, aside from its daring and capable field agents, Allied intelligence in that part of Europe seemed characterized by ignorance, incompetence, and gross negligence. SOE had promised enough supplies to field entire armies yet couldn't manage a replacement radio. The deficiencies may not have been entirely their fault; perhaps blame also lay with RAF Command.

Perhaps Partisan efforts have been ignored because the war in Slovenia was considered too complicated and messy to navigate; it doesn't fit a tidy narrative of angelic Allied liberators. Perhaps it is that, by contrast with the impression of the war's end for the Western Allies elsewhere – largely celebration and relief, from the liberation of France to smiling Dutch girls in fields of flowers and the end of Nazism – the parallel events in Slovenia and Yugoslavia seem inherently barbarous, only affirming the enduring characterization of the Balkans as a place of savagery, and of the Partisans likewise, with Communism blamed for making them so. The terrifying reality, though, is that these murderous reprisals were mimicked across the continent. As Keith Lowe writes in his study of the aftermath of the war, *Savage Continent,*

Numbers aside . . . the violence that occurred in Yugoslavia at the end of the war was no crueller than that which occurred in other countries . . . Despite the stereotypes, therefore, the cruelty that took place in this unfortunate part of the Balkans should not be considered unique – rather it was symbolic of a dehumanisation that had taken place across the continent.[20]

And what of the Slovenian Partisans themselves? How to reconcile bravery with atrocity, men and women who fought for freedom and liberty but helped create a dictatorship? Their country's wartime losses were devastating: 6.5 per cent of all Slovenians were killed. Nearly 30,000 died as members of the Partisans, an astonishing number for a nation so small.[21] Everyone who survived experienced loss. But the effect the Slovenian Partisans had on the war was far out of proportion to their numbers. In the summer of 1942, when the critical battles were fought, they tied up over 80,000 troops. They played a great role in the defeat of Italy. Partisan resistance helped to halt, and then destroy, Hitler's plans to wipe out the Slavs. From 1943 to 1945, Partisans occupied the attention of entire German divisions that would otherwise have been on the front lines. Had Partisan organization, and Allied supplies, been greater, they could have crippled much of Germany's transport links. Without the resistance, Slovenia might not exist today.

Ralph lived to see a livestream of me honoured as his proxy at Ožbalt and Lovcrenc na Pohorju in 2014. At ninety-seven he was too frail to travel to the seventieth anniversary of his escape. He was the only POW still alive, but we met Partisans who remembered him with great affection. The Partisans gave my father his freedom. To his dying day, he was grateful.

Appendix: The Escapees

The authors have attempted to contact the families of all the escapees, and all those who assisted the escape – however, this was not always possible. If your relatives were involved, or you have further information on the escape, please email crowtalk@thecrowsflight.com.

Australians:

1. Stanley Broad, 2/15th Battalion, QX8000.
2. Leslie Bullard, 2/6th Battalion, VX3549.
3. William G. Bunston, 1st Australian Army Postal Corps, VX36694.
4. Kenneth G. Carson, 2/4th Battalion, NX9186.
5. Ralph F. Churches, 2/48th Battalion, SX5286.
6. John E. Douglas, 2/4th Battalion NX26868.
7. Donald Funston, 2/32nd Battalion VX29769.
8. Walter Gossner, 2/15th Battalion, PX10.
9. Alan H. Mills, 6th Australian Divisional Supply Column, NX1499.
10. Kenneth B. Rubie, 2/4th Battalion, NX5373.
11. Arthur D. Shields, 2/8th Battalion, VX29281.
12. Arnold E. Woods, 2/8th Battalion, VX6534.

British:

13. Leonard F. Austin, Royal Army Service Corps, VX41137.
14. Robert F. Barrs, Royal Engineers, 2013646.
15. Winston G. Belcher, Royal Engineers, 2003566.
16. Frank Brooker, Royal Artillery, 788115.
17. Joseph Caddick, Royal Artillery, 845921.
18. Leonard Caulfield, Royal Artillery, 830622.
19. Reginald Church, Royal Pioneer Corps, 2112047.
20. Samuel J. Copestick, Royal Engineers, 2093306.
21. Leslie G. Dale, Royal Corps of Signals, 2594702.
22. Percy Dean, Royal Corps of Signals, 2332410.
23. Kenneth Dutt, Royal Corps of Signals, 2333306.
24. Patrick Egan, Royal Engineers, 1942752.
25. Joseph Ferrznolo, 4th Hussars, 7910104.
26. Ewart A. Floyd, Royal Engineers, 1876919.
27. George E. French, Royal Army Service Corps, S/149447.
28. Ernest Gillbanks, Royal Horse Artillery, 832756.
29. William Greenslade, Royal Army Ordnance Corps, 1054772.
30. Daniel Griffin, Royal Engineers, 1894609.
31. Francis Gunn, Royal Horse Artillery, 902867.
32. Denis Haggerty, Royal Horse Artillery, 936966.
33. Andrew P. Hamilton, Royal Engineers, 1899026.
34. Leonard Hague, Royal Engineers, 1990171.
35. Robert Healey, Royal Artillery, 890192.
36. Harry Hughes, Royal Army Service Corps, T/111077.
37. Allen Hurden, Royal Engineers, 1879228.
38. Bertie D. Hutcheon, Royal Engineers, 2068083.
39. Robert Inglis, Royal Engineers, 1989155.
40. Walter Lacy, Royal Engineers, 1987390.
41. Leslie A. R. Laws, Royal Engineers, 2195978.
42. William E. G. Lloyd, Royal Army Service Corps, T/67908.
43. Donald W. Luckett, Royal Engineers, 1870492.
44. Frederick Maltby, Royal Engineers, 2002697.

45. Francis Marshall, Royal Engineers, 2005125.
46. Walter Martin, Royal Horse Artillery, 890656.
47. Frederick Mazingham, Royal Artillery, 1605015.
48. James McNally, Royal Horse Artillery, 877182.
49. John H. Mooney, Royal Horse Artillery, 898620.
50. Thomas Oddie, Royal Artillery, 1463570.
51. Clifford J. Orange, Royal Engineers, 2119798.
52. Ronald Pattinson, Middlesex Yeomanry, 2344137.
53. Richard Pennels, Royal Engineers, 1874271.
54. Joseph Perry, Royal Engineers, 2114485.
55. Edward Pool, Royal Horse Artillery, 1559608.
56. Stanley Reed, Duke of Cornwall's Light Infantry, 5436591.
57. James Robson, Royal Engineers, 2077642.
58. Harry Rotherham, Royal Horse Artillery, 908045.
59. Frederick Russell, Royal Artillery, 1533418.
60. Allan Salisbury, Special Air Service, 3604977.
61. Robert Scoon, Royal Engineers, 1989052.
62. Clifford O. Smith, Royal Army Service Corps, S/126379.
63. Robert Swan, 4th Battalion Green Howards, 4752024.
64. John Thompson, Northumberland Hussars, 558139.
65. John Thomson, Royal Horse Artillery, 937049.
66. Alfred Valentine, Royal Engineers, 1905696.
67. Cyril Vickers, Royal Corps of Signals, 2331677.
68. Harold Warwick, Northumberland Hussars, 324627.
69. George Williams, Royal Artillery, 1568921.
70. Alwyne Wilson, Northumberland Hussars, 1557854.
71. Ronald V. Wollaston, Royal Artillery, 904582.

French:

72. Joseph Barre, forced labourer from Angers, Main-et-Loire.
73. André Bayol, forced labourer from Maillane, Bouches-du-Rhône.
74. Pierre Belin, POW status unknown, from Dijon, Côte-d'Or.

75. Orlando Businelli, forced labourer from Biganos, Gironde.
76. Marcel Chabaud, forced labourer from Saint-Raphaël, Var.
77. Albert Conseil, 100th Infantry Regiment, from Calais, 2945.
78. Marcel Duval, forced labourer from Terrasson-Lavilledieu, Dordogne.
79. Marcel Erre, POW status unknown, hometown unknown.
80. André Hirondelle, forced labourer from Châtillon-sur-Seine, Côte-d'Or.
81. Etienne Karne, forced labourer from Pfaffenheim, Haut-Rhin.
82. Paul Lafargue, forced labourer from Monclar-de-Quercy, Tarn-et-Garonne.
83. Jacques Leretour, forced labourer from Rouen, Normandy.
84. Fortuné Lillamande, POW status unknown, from Maillane, Bouches-du-Rhône.
85. François Marquier, POW status unknown, from Alzon, Gard.
86. Jean Pasquelin, POW status unknown, from Montreuil, Paris.
87. Charles Rouges, forced labourer from Cazes-Mondenard, Tarn-et-Garonne.
88. Jean Aroman Saint, forced labourer from Montauban, Tarn-et-Garrone.
89. Georges Sanz, 407th Pioneer Regiment, from Rue Guénot, Paris.
90. Jean Verleau, 70th Engineer Regiment, from Saint Dénis de Gilles.
91. Adelson Waroux, 33rd Infantry Regiment, from Ancône, Drôme.

New Zealanders:

92. Lindsay W. C. Anderson, 24th Battalion, 24990.
93. James Hoffman, 7th Anti-Tank Regiment, 29086.
94. Philip Hoffman, 18th Battalion, 29673.
95. Alfred G. Lloyd, 25th Battalion, 33528.
96. Robert C. McKenzie, 26th Battalion, 15569.

97. Colin J. Ratcliffe, 19th Battalion, 4785.
98. Griffin M. Rendell, 24th Battalion, 24255.
99. Phillip G. Tapping, 25th Battalion, 31727.
100. Henare Turangi, 28th Battalion, 26072.

Notes

1: Setting the Stage

1 Ralph Frederick Churches, Australians at War Film Archive, No. 1094, interview, 1 December 2003, part 1/10
2 Peter Morton, 'Adelaide', SA History Hub, History Trust of South Australia, 13 January 2015, https://sahistoryhub.history.sa.gov.au/places/adelaide
3 Wendy Lowenstein, *Weevils in the Flour: An Oral Record of the 1930s Depression in Australia*, Hyland House: South Yarra, 1978, p. 14
4 Colin Steel in ibid., p. 35
5 Churches, Australians at War Film Archive, part 2/10

2: Becoming a Soldier

1 Churches, Australians at War Film Archive, part 2/10
2 Ronte Churches, interview, 21 July 2021
3 Churches, Australians at War Film Archive, part 3/10

3: Greece

1 Craig Stockings and Elanor Hancock, *Swastika Over the Acropolis: Re-interpreting the Nazi Invasion of Greece in World War II*, Brill: Leiden, 2013, p. 37

2 Ibid., p. 62
3 '335 Secretary of State for Dominion Affairs to the Prime Minister of New Zealand, 25 February 1941', in *Documents Relating to New Zealand's Participation in the Second World War 1939–45: Volume 1*, Historical Publications Branch: Wellington, 1949
4 Michael Tyquin, *Greece: February to April 1941, Australian Army Campaign Series 13*, Big Sky Publishing: Sydney, 2014, p. 45
5 Stockings and Hancock, *Swastika Over the Acropolis*, p. 51
6 Alexandros Papagos, *The Battle of Greece, 1940–1941*, trans. Pat Eliascos, J. M. Sczacikis 'Alpha' Editions: Athens, 1949, p. 309
7 Andrew Cunningham in James Goldrick, 'Cunningham: Matapan, 1941', in *Great Battles of the Royal Navy as Commemorated in the Gunroom, Britannia Royal Naval College, Dartmouth*, eds. Eric Grove, Arms and Armour: London, 1994, p. 203
8 'Yugoslavia Joins the Axis Powers. And Then They Don't', *World War Two*, directed by Astrid Deinhard and Spartacus Olsson, Bernried am Starnberger See: Onlion Entertainment GmbH, Germany, 2020
9 Maria Hill, 'The Australians in Greece and Crete: A Study of an Intimate Wartime Relationship', thesis for PhD in History, Australian Defence Force Academy, University of New South Wales, Canberra, 2008, p. 124
10 Ibid., p. 116
11 Howard Greville, *Prison Camp Spies: Intelligence Gathering Behind the Wire*, Australian Military History Publications: Loftus, 1998, p. vi
12 Sydney Fairbain Rowell, *Full Circle*, Melbourne University Press: Carlton, 1974, p. 68

4: Debacle

1 Stockings and Hancock, *Swastika Over the Acropolis*, p. 159
2 Thomas Blamey in Ivan D. Chapman, *Iven G. Mackay: Citizen and Soldier*, Melway Publishing: Melbourne, 1975, p. 222

3 Keith Stewart in ibid.
4 Rowell, *Full Circle*, p. 72
5 David Horner, *General Vasey's War*, Melbourne University Press: Carlton, 1992, p. 101
6 Norman D. Carlyon, *I Remember Blamey*, Macmillan Co. of Australia: Melbourne, 1980, p. 43
7 Rowell, *Full Circle*, p. 76
8 David Horner, 'Britain and the Campaign in Greece and Crete in 1941', *National Institute for Defence Studies 2013 International Forum of War History: Proceedings* (2013), p. 40.
9 Stockings and Hancock, *Swastika Over the Acropolis*, p. 402
10 W. G. McClymont, *To Greece*, Official History of New Zealand in the Second World War 1939–1945, Historical Publications Branch: Wellington, 1945, p. 400
11 AWM54 534/3/4, 'Anzac Corps, Operation Order No. 2 – The Withdrawal from Greece of Anzac Corps (April 1941)'
12 Horner, *General Vasey's War*, p. 104
13 Maitland Wilson in Carlyon, *I Remember Blamey*, p. 46
14 Ibid., p. 47

5: Stragglers

1 McClymont, *To Greece*, p. 401
2 A. W. Beasley, *Zeal and Honour: The Life and Times of Bernard Freyberg*, Winter Productions: Wellington, 2015, p. 6
3 Gavin Long, *Greece, Crete, and Syria*, Australian War Memorial: Canberra, 1953, p. 152
4 Ibid.
5 B883-QX4141, 'Gaston Renard Charles Service Record'
6 McClymont, *To Greece*, p. 417
7 Peter Ewer, *Forgotten Anzacs: The Campaign in Greece 1941*, Scribe Publications: Brunswick, 2016, p. 278
8 Churches, Australians at War Film Archive, part 2/10

9 Ibid., part 3/10
10 AWM52-1/5/13/17, 'Reports on Evacs from S and T Beaches During Period 24–28 April, 1941', p. 1
11 Robert Kimber, *Walking Under Fire: The 1941 Greek Campaign of Major Bernard O'Loughlin, AIF*, Avonmore Books: Kent Town, 2018, p. 109
12 Long, *Greece*, p. 170
13 Kimber, *Walking Under Fire*, p. 175
14 McClymont, *To Greece*, p. 423
15 AWM52-1/5/13/17, p. 3

6: Rowing to Crete

1 Ralph Churches, unpublished manuscripts, 1945
2 McClymont, *To Greece*, p. 443
3 Hill, 'Australians in Greece and Crete', p. 235
4 Ibid., p. 144
5 Carlyon, *I Remember Blamey*, p. 45
6 J. B. Stuart in McClymont, *To Greece*, p. 121
7 Churches, unpublished manuscripts, 1945

7: Captive

1 AWM254-123, 'Interrogation Report on Seven Prisoners of War who Escaped from German Hands in 1046 G. W. Maribor'
2 Churches, Australians at War Film Archive, part 3/10
3 Ibid.
4 Paul Rea, *Voices from the Fortress: The Extraordinary Stories of Australia's Forgotten Prisoners of War*, ABC Books: Sydney, 2007, p. 36
5 Churches, unpublished manuscripts, 1945
6 Ewer, *Forgotten Anzacs*, p. 295

7   Long, *Greece*, p. 180
8   Mike Carlton, *Cruiser*, Random House Australia: Sydney, 2010, p. 255
9   Long, *Greece*, p. 180
10 Ewer, *Forgotten Anzacs*, p. 296
11 Carlton, *Cruiser*, p. 260
12 Ibid., p. 298

8: The Corinth Cage

1   Francina Flemming, *A P.O.W.'s Letters: Life, Love, and Resilience*, Francina Flemming: Banora Point, 2019, p. 41
2   Churches, unpublished manuscripts, 1945
3   James Crossland, *Britain and the International Committee of the Red Cross*, Palgrave Macmillan: Basingstoke, 2014, p. 113
4   George Morley, *Escape from Stalag 18a*, Meni Publishing and Binding: Cranbourne, 2006, p. 11
5   Peter Monteath, *P.O.W.: Australian Prisoners of War in Hitler's Reich*, Pan Macmillan Australia: Sydney, 2011, p. 102
6   Churches, unpublished manuscripts, 1945
7   Thomas Stout, *Medical Services in New Zealand and the Pacific*, Official History of New Zealand in the Second World War 1939–1945, War History Branch: Wellington, 1956, p. 105
8   Barney Roberts, *A Kind of Cattle*, Australian War Memorial and William Collins Pty: Sydney, 1985, p. 35
9   Roberts, *Cattle*, p. 105
10 Greville, *Prison Camp Spies*, p. 9
11 Churches, unpublished manuscripts, 1945
12 Greville, *Prison Camp Spies*, p. 17
13 Churches, unpublished manuscripts, 1945
14 Ibid.
15 Time Ghost, *091: Invasion of Crete: A Bloody Mess – WW2 – May 23rd 1941*, www.youtube.com/watch?v=wqv3IILkIqQ

16 Churches, unpublished manuscripts, 1945
17 Time Ghost, *091: Invasion of Crete*
18 Crossland, *Red Cross*, p. 82

9: Surviving to Thessaloniki

1 Monteath, *P.O.W.*, p. 16
2 Churches, unpublished manuscripts, 1945
3 Stout, *Medical Services*, p. 117
4 Roberts, *Cattle*, p. 42
5 Churches, unpublished manuscripts, 1945
6 Stout, *Medical Services*, p. 117
7 Primo Levi, *If This is a Man*, Horwitz: London, 1963, p. 60
8 Crossland, *Red Cross*, p. 107
9 Monteath, *P.O.W.*, p. 109
10 Charles Granquist, *A Long Way Home: One POW's Story of Escape and Evasion During WWII*, Big Sky Publishing, Newport: 2010, p. 74
11 Monteath, *P.O.W.*, p. 108
12 Stout, *Medical Services*, p. 110
13 Churches, unpublished manuscripts, 1945
14 Granquist, *Long Way Home*, p. 76
15 Churches, unpublished manuscripts, 1945

10: The Train to Maribor

1 Churches, unpublished manuscripts, 1945
2 Monteath, *P.O.W.*, p. 109
3 Roberts, *Cattle*, p. 45
4 Churches, unpublished manuscripts, 1945
5 Ibid.
6 Ibid.
7 Granquist, *Long Way Home*, p. 75

8 Monteath, *P.O.W.*, p. 110
9 Henry Steilberg in Churches, unpublished manuscripts, 1945

11: Occupation

1 Ernst L. Presseisen, 'Prelude to Barbarossa: Germany and the Balkans 1940–41', *Journal of Modern History*, 32 (1960), p. 369
2 Biljana Radivojević and Goran Penev, 'Demographic Losses on Serbia in the First World War and their Long Term Consequences', *Economic Annals*, 59: 203 (2014), p. 42
3 R. L. Knéjévitch, 'Prince Paul, Hitler, and Salonika', *Royal Institute of International Affairs*, 27: 1 (1951), p. 40
4 Michael R. Barefield, 'Overwhelming Force, Indecisive Victory: The German Invasion of Yugoslavia 1941', *United States Army Command and General Staff College Monograph*, 1993, p. 22
5 Ladislav Bevc, *Liberal Forces in Twentieth Century Yugoslavia: Memoirs of Ladislav Bevc*, Peter Lang: New York, 2007, p. 133
6 Gerhart Feine in Helga Horiak Harriman, 'Slovenia as an Outpost of the Third Reich', MA dissertation, Wells College, Aurora, 1969, p. 23
7 Ibid., p. 43
8 Adolf Hitler in Gregor Joseph Kranjc, *To Walk with the Devil: Slovene Collaboration and the Axis Occupation, 1941–1945*, University of Toronto Press: Toronto, 2013, p. 54
9 FO 536/6/3159/42, Miha Krek to George Rendel, p. 5
10 Erhard Wetzel, Dokument No. 2 (NG-2325), 27 April 1942, reprinted in 'Generalplan Ost', *Vierteljahrshefte für Zeitgeschichte*, 6: 3 (1958), pp. 297–9
11 Harriman, 'Outpost', p. 13
12 Tone Kregar and Aleksander Žižek, *Okupacija v 133 Slikah: Celje 1941–1945*. Muzej novojše zgodovine: Celje, 2006, p. 70
13 Tomaž Teropšič, *Štajerska vplamenih: Taktika, orožje in oprema štirih vojsk na Štajerskem v drugi svetovni vojni*, Posavski Musej: Brežice, 2012, p. 42

14 Zorica Petrović, 'The Roman Catholic Church and Clergy in the Nazi Fascist Era on Slovenian Soil', *Athens Journal of History*, 4: 3 (2018), p. 238

15 Harriman, 'Outpost', p. 52

16 Galeazzo Ciano, *The Ciano Diaries 1939–1943: The Complete Unabridged Diaries of Count Galeazzo Ciano, the Italian Minister for Foreign Affairs, 1936–1943*, ed. Hugh Gibson, Doubleday & Company Inc: Garden City, 1946, p. 344

17 Božo Repe, 'The Liberation Front of the Slovene Nation', in Jože Pirjevec and Božo Repe (eds.), *Resistance, Suffering, Hope: The Slovene Partisan Movement 1941–1945*, trans. Breda Biščk and Manca Gašperšišč, National Committee of Union of Societies of Combatants of the Slovene National Liberation Struggle: Ljubljana, 2008, p. 37

18 *Slovenski Poročevalec*, 20 September 1941

12: All-You-Can-Eat Potatoes

1 Churches, unpublished manuscripts, 1945

2 Roberts, *Cattle*, p. 53

3 Ibid.

4 Rea, *Voices from the Fortress*, p. 55

5 FO 916/25, Stalag XVIIID 1941, Red Cross Report, 21 July 1941, p. 1

6 Geneva Convention 1929, Section II, Chapter 1, Article 27

7 Churches, unpublished manuscripts, 1945

8 Ibid.

9 Kregar and Žižek, *Okupacija v 133 Slikah*, p. 70

10 Roberts, *Cattle*, p. 61

11 Ibid., p. 67

12 Ibid., p. 68

13 Churches, unpublished manuscripts, 1945

14 Ibid. and Roberts, *Cattle*, p. 56

15 Churches, unpublished manuscripts, 1945

16 E. Stephenson, 'Experiences of a Prisoner of War: World War 2 in Germany', *Australian Military Medicine*, 9: 1 (2000), p. 30
17 John S. Bratton, 'One Man's War: Letters 1939–1945', letter of 6 August 1941, from www.stalag-xviii-a.com
18 Churches, unpublished manuscripts, 1945
19 Donald William Luckett, private papers, E. M. Thornton to Donald Luckett, 7 April 1944

13: Farmhand

1 Churches, unpublished manuscripts, 1945
2 Daniela Münkel, *Nationalsozialistiche Agrarpolitik und Bauernalltag*, Campus: Frankfurt am Main, 1996, p. 170
3 Walter Steilberg in Ralph Churches, unpublished manuscripts, 1986
4 Churches, unpublished manuscripts, 1945
5 Frau Barta in Churches, unpublished manuscripts, 1986
6 Ibid.
7 Piter Troch, 'Education and Yugoslav Nationhood in Interwar Yugoslavia – Possibilities, Limitations, and Interactions with Other National Ideas', PhD thesis, University of Gent, 2012, p. 92
8 Churches, unpublished manuscripts, 1986
9 Churches, Australians at War Film Archive, part 5/10
10 FO 916/25, Stalag XVIIID 1941, Red Cross Report, 26 December 1941, p. 4
11 Churches, unpublished manuscripts, 1986

14: Resistance

1 Tone Ferenc, 'Wehrmannschaft: v Boju Proti Narodnoosvobodilni Vojski na Stajerskem', *Contributions to Contemporary History*, 2 (1958), pp. 83, 86

2 Teropšič, *Štajerska vplamenih*, p. 154

3 Ferenc, 'Wehmannschaft', p. 89

4 Damijan Guštin, 'The Partisan Army – Armed Resistance in Slovenia During World War II', in Jože Pirjevec and Božo Repe (eds.), *Resistance, Suffering, Hope: The Slovene Partisan Movement 1941–1945*, trans. Breda BišČk and Manca Gašperšišč, National Committee of Union of Societies of Combatants of the Slovene National Liberation Struggle: Ljubljana, 2008, p. 51

5 Friedrich Rainer – Gauleiter von Kärnten, 'Wandzeitung: Eine wichtige Feststellung', 1942. With thanks to Luka Kolbl and his private collection

6 Amedeo Osti Guerrazzi, *The Italian Army in Slovenia: Strategies of Antipartisan Repression, 1941–1943*, trans. Elizabeth Burke and Anthony Mahanlahti, Palgrave Macmillan: New York, 2013, p. 37

7 Ibid., pp. 27, 37

8 Peter Starič, *My Life in Totalitarianism 1941–1991: The Unusual Career of an Electronics Engineer*, Xlibris Publishers: Bloomington, 2012, p. 57

9 Vida Deželak Barič, 'Participation, Role and Position of Slovenian Women in World War II Resistance Movement', *Qualestoria. Rivista di Storia Contemporanea*, 43: 2 (2015), p. 151

10 James Caffin, *Partisan – John Denvir New Zealand Corporal Yugoslav Brigadier*, Harper Collins: Auckland, 1945, pp. 76, 86

11 Teodora Just, 'Partizanska Intendantska Služba Na Štajerskem Med NOB', thesis, University of Ljubljana, 2008, p. 4

12 Vittorio Ambrosio in Guerrazzi, *Italian Army*, p. 39

13 Ibid., p. 53

14 Caffin, *Partisan*, p. 97

15 Guerrazzi, *Italian Army*, p. 54

15: Thoughts of Escape

1 Churches, Australians at War Film Archive, part 5/10
2 Ibid.
3 Churches, unpublished manuscripts, 1945
4 Ibid.

16: The Extermination Camp

1 Lara Iva Dreu, 'Stalag XVIIID (306) – Nacistično Taborišče Za
  Sovjetske Vojne Ujetnike v Mariboru', *Retrospektive*, 3: 1 (2020),
  p. 38
2 Alan Slocombe, 'A Prisoner's Tale Retold: Chapter 1', BBC WW2
  People's War, www.bbc.co.uk/history/ww2peopleswar/stories/81/
  a6955581.shtml
3 Alexander M. Connor, photograph collection, Australian War
  Memorial, '1941. Russians Captured by German Army in 1941',
  item no. P00092.094
4 Dreu, 'Stalag XVIIID', p. 38
5 Janez Ujčič in STA, 'Russian Ambassador Lays Wreath at Former
  Nazi Camp in Maribor', *Total Slovenia News*, 9 May 2020, www.
  total-slovenia-news.com/politics/6202-russian-ambassador-lays-
  wreath-at-former-nazi-camp-in-maribor
6 Greville, *Prison Camp Spies*, p. 23
7 Captain Walter John Heslop in AWM119-A86, 1944
8 Christin Streit, 'The German Army and the Policies of
  Genocide', in Gerhard Hirschfeld (ed.), *The Policies of Genocide:
  Jews and Soviet Prisoners of War in Nazi Germany*, German
  Historical Institute/Allen & Unwin: London, 1986, p. 12
9 Ibid.
10 Valentina Oreh in Dreu, 'Stalag XVIIID', p. 39
11 Churches, Australians at War Film Archive, part 5/10

17: Vengeance

1 Peter Štih, Vasko Simoniti, and Peter Vodopivec, *A Slovene History: Society, Politics, Culture*, trans. Paul Townend, Inštitut za novejšo zgodovino: Ljubljana, 2008, p. 426

2 Taddeo Orlando in Guerrazzi, *Italian Army*, p. 65

3 General Mario Robotti in ibid., p. 44

4 Ibid., p. 56

5 Edvard Kocbek in Kranjc, *To Walk with the Devil*, p. 72

6 Caffin, *Partisan*, p. 121

7 Ibid., p. 126

8 Guerazzi, *Italian Army*, p. 68

9 Vanja Martinčič, *Slovene Partisan: Weapons, Clothings and Equipment of Slovene Partisans*, Muzej ljudske revolucije Slovenije: Ljubljana, 1990, p. 9

10 Jozo Tomasevich, *War and Revolution in Yugoslavia, 1941–1945: Occupation and Collaboration*, Stanford University Press: Stanford, 2011, p. 103

11 Guerazzi, *Italian Army*, p. 70

12 Stanko Petelin, *Krajevna Skupnost Podpeč-Preserje v NOB*, SZDL: Ljubljana, 1983, p. 200

13 Metod Milač, *Resistance, Imprisonment, and Forced Labor: A Slovene Student in World War II*, Peter Lang: New York, 2002, p. 233

14 In Uroš Košir, 'When Violins Fell Silent: Archaeological Traces of Mass Executions of Romani People in Slovenia', *European Journal of Archaeology*, 23: 2 (2019), p. 3

15 Robert Frank, 'Formacija Brigad NOV in PO Slovenije', thesis, University of Ljubljana, 2003, p. 13

16 Ferenc, 'Wehrmannschaft', p. 97

17 Erich Hribernik in Jim Paterson, *Partisans, Peasants, and P.O.W.s: A Soldier's Story of Escape in WWII*, J. Paterson: Cottesloe, 2008, p. 176

18 Karl Čolnik in *March to Freedom/Pot k Svobodi*, directed by Tomaž Kralj, SBS and TV Ljubljana – Jugoslavija: Sydney and Ljubljana, 1985

18: The Crow

1 Eric Edwards, 'For You the War is Over', unpublished manuscript, 1995, p. 138
2 J. E. F. Stuckey, *Sometimes Free: My Escapes from German P.O.W. Camps*, J. E. F. Stuckey: Ashurst, 1977, p. 25
3 Luckett, private papers, British Red Cross Society Personal Parcels Centre to Donald Luckett, 11 February 1942
4 MP727/1-GO3/738, Harvey Harold Pepper to Australian General Staff (Intelligence), 24 September 1945
5 Roberts, *Cattle*, p. 75
6 Helen Fry, *MI9: A History of the Secret Service for Escape and Evasion in World War Two*, Yale University Press: New Haven and London, 2020, p. 11
7 Ibid., p. 15
8 L. B. Inch to Willian Fagan, Robert McKenzie, and James Arrol, 'Re: L/Cpl Roy Nicholas Courlander', 28 June 1949. With thanks to Geoff and Spencer Rendell for this letter
9 Ralph Churches in Bill Rudd, 'Anzac Freemen in Europe', 2017, www.anzacpow.com/welcome_letter, 'Part 5, Chapter 8, The British Free Corps'
10 Stuckey, *Sometimes Free*, p. 35
11 Churches in Rudd, 'Anzac Freemen', Part 5, Chapter 8
12 Ralph Churches to ZZB NOB Maribor, 1972, in Letters and Diaries

19: El-Alamein, Stalingrad, and Slovenia

1 Guerrazzi, *Italian Army*, pp. 67, 91
2 Ibid., p. 92
3 In ibid., p. 84
4 Pietro Brignoli, *Santa Messa Per i Miei Fucilati: Le Spietate Rappresaglie Italiane Contro i Partigiani in Croazia dal Diario di un Cappellano*, Longanesi: Milan, 1973, entries 5 and 21 August 1942

5 Ibid., entry 20 August 1942

6 Štih, Simoniti, and Vodopivec, *Slovene History*, p. 429

7 Brignoli, *Santa Messa*, entry 25 August 1942

8 Bojan Godeša, 'Introduction: Slovenian Resistance Movement and Yugoslavia 1941–1945', in Jurij Perovšek and Bojan Godeša (eds.), *Between the House of Hapsburg and Tito: A Look at the Slovenian Past 1861–1980*, Institute of Contemporary History: Ljubljana, 2016, p. 104

9 Damijan Guštin, 'Armed Resistance: Relationship Between the Yugoslav (NOPOJ) and Slovenian Partisan Army 1941–1945', in Perovšek and Godeša (eds.), *Between the House of Hapsburg and Tito*, p. 127

10 Ferdo Gestin, *Svet Pod Krimom*, SAZU: Ljubljana, 1993, pp. 70–1

11 Caffin, *Partisan*, p. 142

12 Guerazzi, *Italian Army*, p. 108

13 France Filipič, *Pohorski Bataljon*, Državna Založba Slovenije: Ljubljana, 1979, p. 565

14 Ferenc, 'Wehrmannschaft', p. 104

20: In the Papers

1 Fry, *MI9*, p. 20

2 Hubert Speckner, *In der Gewalt des Feindes: Kriegsgefangenenlager in der 'Ostmark' 1939 bis 1945*, R. Oldenbourg Verlag: Vienna, 2003, p. 318

3 Leonard Frederick Austin, private papers, 1985

4 Connor, photograph collection, item no. P00092.082

5 Harriman, 'Outpost', p. 43

6 Kurt Pauli, 'Alamein-Front zwischen Angriff und Abwehr', *Marbuger Zeitung*, 2 November 1942, p. 1

7 'Der Italienische Wehrmachtbericht', *Marburger Zeitung*, 7/8 November 1942, p. 1

8 Churches, unpublished manuscripts, 1945

9 Ralph Churches to Edvard Vedernjak, 3 January 2010, in Letters and diaries

10 'Für Deutschland Gefallen', *Marburger Zeitung*, 14 January 1943, p. 5

11 Ralph Churches to ZZB NOB Maribor, 1972, in Letters and diaries

21: The First Spies

1 Kranjc, *To Walk with the Devil*, p. 100

2 FO 536-6/42/3165, Report from German Occupied Territory, 28 October 1942

3 FO 536-6/43/3144C, E 3/44A/41/43, 'Zavesa Report 12 July 1943'

4 Liberation Front of Slovenia, *Dolomitska Izjava*, 1 March 1943

5 In Guerrazzi, *Italian Army*, p. 116

6 Frank, 'Formacija Brigad', p. 29

7 Kranjc, *To Walk with the Devil*, p. 120

8 Milovan Đilas, *Wartime*, Harcourt Brace Jovanovich: New York, 1977, p. 338

9 Frank, 'Formacija Brigad', p. 31

10 Tone Ferenc, Dare Jeršek, Miroslav Luštek, and Lozje Požun, 'Pregled pomembnejših dogodkov v letu 1943', *Prispevki za novejšo zgodovino*, 4: 1–2 (1963), p. 157

11 'Political and Economic Intelligence Reports: Slovenia', WO 204/9672A, YS/266/3, 1944, p. 4

12 Franc Miklavčič, in Janez Stanovnik (ed.), *Narodnoosvobdilni Boj v Slovenskem Narodnem Spominu: Slovenski Zbornik 2007*, ZZB NOB: Ljubljana, 2007, p. 243

13 WO 202/520, 'Escaped British Prisoners of War'

14 In Matilda Maučec, 'Lackov Odred', *Kronika*, 8: 3 (1960), p. 141

22: The Combine

1 Dick Huston, 'Memoirs', year unknown, www.stalag18a.org/dickhuston.html#Markt_Pongau
2 Churches, Australians at War Film Archive, part 5/10
3 Len Austin, private papers, 1985
4 Churches, Australians at War Film Archive, part 6/10
5 PR86-103, papers of Alexander M. Connor, year unknown, p. 23
6 Churches, Australians at War Film Archive, part 6/10
7 PR86-103, p. 23
8 Edwards, 'For You the War is Over', p. 139
9 Ralph Churches, *A Hundred Miles as the Crow Flies*, Estate of R. F. Churches: Kensington Victoria, 2017, p. 26
10 Malte Zierenberg, *Berlin's Black Market: 1939–1950*, Palgrave Macmillan: New York, 2015, p. 43

23: The Greatest Show in Maribor

1 PR86-103, pp. 16, 25
2 Churches, *Crow*, p. 26
3 Connor, photograph collection, item no. P00092.094
4 Eric Edwards, Australians at War Film Archive, No. 1538, 4 March 2004, part 7/9
5 CSDIC CMF/SKP/3805-3811 in AWM54 781/6/7
6 Edwards, 'For You the War is Over', p. 141
7 Austin, private papers
8 PR86-103, p. 26
9 Churches, Australians at War Film Archive, part 7/10
10 Connor, photograph collection, item nos. P00092.082 and P00092.085
11 Connor, photograph collection, item no. P00092.079

12 Mojca Šorn, 'Life in Occupied Slovenia During World War II', in Perovšek and Godeša (eds.), *Between the House of Hapsburg and Tito*, p. 160
13 Connor, photograph collection
14 Ralph Churches to Andrew Hamilton, 11 January 1980, in Letters and Diaries
15 Edwards, 'For You the War is Over', p. 148
16 PR86-103, p. 25

24: The March of the 14th Division

1 In Franklin Lindsay, *Beacons in the Night: With the OSS and Tito's Partisans in Wartime Yugoslavia*, Stanford University Press: Stanford, 1993, p. 91
2 Caffin, *Partisan*, p. 175
3 Tina Toman, '14. Divizija: Pohod Oskrba', dissertation, University of Ljubljana, 2007, p. 43
4 David Greentree, *Gebirgsjäger vs Soviet Sailor: Arctic Circle 1942–1944*, Bloomsbury: London, 2018, p. 36
5 Marjan Žnidarič, *Na Krilih Junaštva in Tovarištva*, Društvo piscev zgodovine, NOB Slovenije: Ljubljana, 2009, p. 118
6 Teropšič, *Štajerska vplamenih*, p. 375
7 Ibid., p. 72
8 Kranjc, *To Walk with the Devil*, p. 131
9 Ibid., p. 195
10 Mark Aarons, *War Criminals Welcome: Australia, a Sanctuary for Fugitive War Criminals Since 1945*, Black Inc: Melbourne, 2001, p. 347
11 Gregor Joseph Kranjc, 'On the Periphery: Jews, Slovenes, and the Memory of the Holocaust', in John-Paul Himka and Joanna Beata Michlic (eds.), *Bringing the Dark Past to Light: The Reception of the Holocaust in Postcommunist Europe*, University of Nebraska Press: Nebraska, 2019, p. 602

12 Lyenko Urbančič, 'Sam ena pot – pot generala Rupnik', *Jutro*, 29 June 1944
13 Kranjc, *To Walk with the Devil*, p. 154
14 Starič, *My Life in Totalitarianism*, p. 130
15 Teropšič, *Štajerska vplamenih*, p. 75
16 Žnidarič, *Na Krilih*, p. 158
17 Frank, 'Formacija Brigad', p. 44
18 Ibid., p. 150
19 Maučec, 'Lackov Odred', p. 143
20 Žnidarič, *Na Krilih*, pp. 168, 181

25: Bombs and Recreation

1 Kenneth Carson in Edwards, 'For You the War is Over', p. 144
2 Ibid.
3 PR86-103, p. 26
4 Paterson, *Partisans, Peasants, and P.O.W.s*, p. 182
5 J. Abel and J. W. Jack (eds.), 'Prisoners of War Pamphlet', *Joint Council of the Order of St. John and the New Zealand Red Cross Society*, No. 8, January 1943
6 Connor, photograph collection
7 Churches, Australians at War Film Archive, part 7/10
8 AWM254-123, Report 1944, p. 5
9 Edwards, 'For You the War is Over', p. 149
10 Zierenberg, *Berlin's Black Market*, p. 41
11 Edwards, Australians at War Film Archive, part 7/9
12 Edwards, 'For You the War is Over', p. 141
13 *Die Deutsche Wochenschau*, No. 703, 10 February 1944
14 Franz Steindl, 'Sie wollten die Untersteiermark "befreien" – Das Ender einer Bandendivision', *Marburger Zeitung*, 7 March 1944, p. 1
15 Ralph Churches, *A Hundred Miles as the Crow Flies*, Estate of R. F. Churches: Kensington Victoria: 2017, p. 17

26: Thieves and Traitors

1 Churches, *Crow*, p. 22
2 Luckett, private papers, p. 67
3 Edwards, Australians at War Film Archive, part 7/9
4 Luckett, private papers, p. 69
5 PR86-103, p. 24
6 Ibid., p. 25
7 Churches, *Crow*, p. 17
8 *March to Freedom/Pot k Svobodi*
9 Ibid.
10 Captain Walter Heslop in AWM119-A86
11 John H. Waller, *The Unseen War: Espionage and Conspiracy in the Second World War*, Random House: New York, 1996, p. 318
12 Churches, *Crow*, p. 26
13 Edwards, 'For You the War is Over', p. 156
14 CSDIC 3805-3811 Appendix C in New Zealand Archives, file unknown
15 Ralph Churches in Rudd, 'Anzac Freemen in Europe', Part 5, Chapter 8
16 MP742/1-336/1/1277, report of death of Pte E. R. Black at Stalag XVIIIA
17 P3/66, statement of Ernst Stevenson in AWM54 781/6/7
18 CSDIC 3805-3811 Appendix C in New Zealand Archives, File Unknown
19 Ibid.
20 Adrian Weale, *Renegades: Hitler's Englishmen*, Pimlico: London, 2002, p. 110

27: Looking for the Connection

1 Churches, *Crow*, p. 6
2 Edwards, Australians at War Film Archive, part 7/9

3 Austin, private papers
4 Churches, *Crow*, p. 37
5 Austin, private papers
6 'Angriff auf die französische Küste', *Marburger Zeitung*, 7 June 1944, p. 1
7 Directive No. 22, 14 February 1942 in Charles Messenger, *'Bomber' Harris and the Strategic Bombing Offensive, 1939–1945*, Arms and Armour Press: London, 1984
8 W. Hagemann in E. K. Bramsted, *Goebbels and National Socialist Propaganda 1925–1945*, Crescent Press: Michigan, 1965, p. 322
9 Ralph Churches to Pat Palmer, 24 August 1993, in Letters and diaries
10 Churches, *Crow*, p. 21
11 PR86-103, p. 24
12 Leslie Laws, 'I Was There – Memoir Extract', *Escape Lines Memorial Society Newsletter*, 46 (2018), p. 4
13 Luckett, private papers, p. 69
14 Huston, 'Memoirs'
15 Seán Damer and Ian Frazer, *On the Run: Anzac Escape and Evasion in Enemy Occupied Crete*, Penguin Books: Auckland, 2006, p. 199

28: The Escape Network

1 WO 208/3250, 'History of IS9: Central Mediterranean Forces', p. 128
2 Lindsay, *Beacons*, p. 27
3 Ibid., p. 15
4 Matija Žganjar, *Zomljena Krila: Reševanje Zavezniških Letalcev na Slovenskem Med Drugo Svetovno Vojno*, Zveza Združenj Borcev za Vrednote NOB Slovenije: Ljubljana, 2012, p. 217
5 Lindsay, *Beacons*, p. 8
6 Michael R. D. Foot and J. M. Langley, *MI9: Escape and Evasion*, Biteback Publishing: London, 2020, p. 205

7 Lindsay, *Beacons*, p. 56

8 Ibid., p. 82

9 Ibid., p. 34

10 WO 202/457, Cuckold to Bari, 26 June 1944

11 Lindsay, *Beacons*, p. 89

12 AMW54 779/3/128, CSDIC/CMF(East)/SKP/5

13 WO 208/3250, 'History of IS9: Central Mediterranean Forces', p. 133

14 WO 373/46/226, Recommendation for Award, Losco, Andrew Anthony

15 Žganjar, *Zomljena Krila*, p. 431

29: A Partisan Agent

1 Leslie Laws in *March to Freedom/Pot k Svobodi*

2 Churches, *Crow*, p. 21

3 CSDIC 3805-3811 in AWM54 781/6/7

4 Laws, 'I Was There – Memoir Extract', p. 4

5 AWM119-A86, R. F. Churches Awarded BEM – Escaped POW

6 Johann Gross in Churches, *Crow*, p. 28

7 Ibid.

8 Leslie Bullard, Private Papers, 1940–45

9 Churches, Australians at War Film Archive, part 6/10

10 Churches, *Crow*, p. 29

11 Austin, private papers

12 In Churches, Australians at War Film Archive, part 6/10

13 Churches, *Crow*, p. 30

14 Edwards, 'For You the War is Over', p. 165

15 Arieh J. Kochavi, *Confronting Captivity: Britain and the United States and the PoWs in Nazi Germany*, University of North Carolina Press: Chapel Hill and London, 2005, pp. 186, 212

16 Luckett, private papers, p. 69

17 Anton in Churches, *Crow*, p. 34

30: The Battle of Savinja Valley

1 Žnidarič, *Na Krilih Junaštva*, p. 190
2 Lindsay, *Beacons*, p. 132
3 Vili Kos in Ralph Churches, Lado Pohar, Tone Kropušek, Franc Črešnar, and Vili Kos, *Vranov Let v Svobodo*, Društvo piscev zgodovine NOB Slovenije: Ljubljana, 2000, p. 151
4 Lindsay, *Beacons*, p. 135
5 Franklin Lindsay in WO 202/309, in Thomas M. Barker, *Social Revolutionaries and Secret Agents: The Carinthian Slovene Partisans and Britain's Special Operations Executive*, Columbia University Press: Boulder, 1990, p. 123
6 Žganjar, *Zomljena Krila*, p. 431

31: Getting Away

1 Churches, *Crow*, p. 35
2 Churches, Australians at War Film Archive, part 6/10
3 Austin, private papers
4 Churches, *Crow*, p. 38

32: Meeting the Partisans

1 Ibid.
2 Churches et al., *Vranov Let v Svobodo*, p. 144
3 CSDIC 3805-3811 in AWM54 781/6/7
4 Lindsay Rogers, *Guerrilla Surgeon*, Collins: London, 1957, pp. 171–2
5 In Churches, Australians at War Film Archive, part 6/10
6 Slovenian National Archive, file no. unknown, Štabu IV. Operativne zone NOV in POJ Operacijski Odsek. Vojaško poročilo – štab XVI. Divizije NOB in POJ Operacijski Odsek. 2 September 1944

33: Dutch Courage

1 Churches, *Crow*, p. 43
2 Ibid., p. 45
3 Captain Walter Heslop in AWM119-A86
4 Austin, private papers
5 Churches, Australians at War Film Archive, part 6/10
6 Andrew Hamilton to Ralph Churches, 21 January 1980, in Letters and diaries
7 Austin, private papers
8 Churches, Australians at War Film Archive, part 6/10
9 Jože Boldan in Churches, *Crow*, p. 46
10 Ibid., p. 47
11 Štab XVI. Divizije NOB in POJ Operacijski Odsek. Vojaško poročilo – štab XVI. Divizije NOB in POJ Operacijski Odsek. 2 September 1944

34: The Mass Escape

1 Churches, *Crow*, p. 48
2 Ivan Kovačič in *March to Freedom/Pot k Svobodi*
3 Ralph Churches in Luckett, private papers, p. 70
4 Churches, *Crow*, p. 53
5 Ronald Wollaston, 'Gunner Ronald Victor Wollaston', year unknown, www.pegasusarchive.org/pow/ronald_wollaston
6 Karel Vranjek in *March to Freedom/Pot k Svobodi*
7 Churches, *Crow*, p. 53
8 WO 208/3325/55 and WO 208/3325/56
9 Laws, 'I Was There – Memoir Extract', p. 5
10 Edwards, 'For You the War is Over', p. 168
11 Edwards, Australians at War Film Archive, part 7/9
12 In Edwards, 'For You the War is Over', p. 168
13 Edwards, Australians at War Film Archive, part 7/9

14 In Luckett, private papers, p. 73
15 Doug Gold, *The Note Through the Wire*, Allen & Unwin: Auckland, 2019, p. 236
16 In Edwards, 'For You the War is Over', p. 169
17 Štab XVI. Divizije NOB in POJ Operacijski Odsek. 2 September, 1944
18 Gold, *Through the Wire*, p. 239
19 Štab XVI. Divizije NOB in POJ Operacijski Odsek, 2 September 1944
20 Churches, *Crow*, p. 57

35: Into the Mountains

1 Laws, 'I Was There – Memoir Extract', p. 5
2 Kenneth Dutt, unpublished diary, 1944
3 Luckett, private papers, p. 74
4 Laws, 'I Was There – Memoir Extract', p. 5
5 Luckett, private papers, p. 72
6 PR86-103, p. 27
7 Cuckold to Force 399, 3 September 1944, in WO 202/457
8 WO 208/3250, 'History of IS9, Central Mediterranean Forces', p. 133
9 Franc Gruden in *March to Freedom/Pot k Svobodi*
10 Ibid.
11 Alojz Volern, 'Memories of Alojz Volern: The Years Leading up to Joining and Serving with the Partisans, and the Years After the War', Robert Posl: 2017, p. 47
12 Karel Čolnik in *March to Freedom/Pot k Svobodi*
13 In *March to Freedom/Pot k Svobodi*
14 Luckett, private papers, p. 75
15 Žnidarič, *Na Krilih Junaštva in Tovarištva*, p. 218
16 WO 202/224, 'Operation Ratweek Results, Slovenia, September 1944'

17 *March to Freedom/Pot k Svobodi*
18 Wollaston, 'Gunner Ronald Victor Wollaston'
19 Luckett, private papers, p. 76
20 Franc Gruden in *March to Freedom/Pot k Svobodi*
21 Churches, *Crow*, p. 69
22 Donald Funston in Churches, Australians at War Film Archive, part 8/10
23 Churches, *Crow*, p. 71
24 Vili Kos, maps and notes, 1985
25 AWM54 781/6/7, CSDIC/CMF/SKP/3880, Kenneth Carson interrogation report
26 Churches, *Crow*, p. 69
27 Dutt, unpublished diary
28 Luckett, private papers, p. 74
29 B883-NX5373, Kenneth Burke Rubie service record
30 Conversations with Aljoz Volern, April 2017
31 Ivan Nemanič in Churches et al., *Vrano Let v Slobodo*, p. 146

36: Across the Sava

1 Luckett, private papers, p. 72
2 Churches, *Crow*, p. 66
3 Ibid, p. 86
4 Ibid., p. 93
5 Kos, maps and notes
6 Churches, Australians at War Film Archive, part 8/10
7 Dutt, unpublished diary
8 Churches, *Crow*, p. 90
9 Research Institute Ljubljana, *Allied Airmen and Prisoners of War Rescued by the Slovene Partisans*, Research Institute Ljubljana: Ljubljana, 1946, p. 60
10 Churches, *Crow*, p. 91
11 Žganjar, *Zomljena Krila*, p. 295

12 Luckett, private papers, p. 74
13 Alma M. Karlin and Jerneja Jezernik (ed.), *Dann geh ich in den grünen Wald: Meine Reise zu den Partisanen*, Drava: Klagenfurt, 2021, with special thanks to Jerneja Jezernik
14 WO 202/224, 'Operation Ratweek Results Slovenia, September 1944'
15 Lindsay, *Beacons*, p. 141
16 Dutt, unpublished diary
17 Petek, Jože, photographs of the 14th Division, 6 September 1944
18 Churches, Australians at War Film Archive, part 8/10
19 Churches, *Crow*, p. 97
20 Ibid., p. 95
21 Laws, 'I Was There – Memoir Extract', p. 6
22 PR85/371 – AWM419/19/42, Citations and Map of Sgt R. F. Churches
23 *March to Freedom/Pot k Svobodi*
24 Luckett, private papers, p. 75
25 Žganjar, *Zomljena Krila*, p. 13
26 Miha Svete, 'Bojna pot 2: Domobranskega udarnega bataljona "Vuka Rupnika"', dissertation, University of Ljubljana, 2016, p. 40
27 Kos, maps and notes

37: The Chance to Become a Spy

1 Luckett, private papers, p. 76
2 Churches, *Crow*, p. 100
3 Ibid.
4 Morley, *Escape from Stalag 18a*, p. 77
5 WO 208/3259, 'History of IS9: Central Mediterranean Forces 1943 November–1945 May'
6 Peter Pirker, *Subversion deutscher Herrschaft: Der britische Kriegsgeheimdienst SOE und Österreich*, Vienna University Press: Vienna, 2012, p. 324

7   Jack H. Taylor, 'Dupont Mission', OSS
    Archives, 1945, www.jewishvirtuallibrary.org/
    the-dupont-mission-october-1944-may-1945
8   Svete, 'Bojna pot', p. 40
9   Research Institute Ljubljana, *Allied Airmen and Prisoners of War*,
    p. 42
10 Churches, *Crow*, p. 133
11 Svete, 'Bojna pot', p. 41
12 Dutt, unpublished diary
13 Churches, *Crow*, p. 112

38: Base 212

1   WO 208/3259, 'History of IS9: Central Mediterranean Forces
    1943 November–1945 May'
2   *March to Freedom/Pot k Svobodi*
3   Luckett, private papers, p. 78
4   Churches, Australians at War Film Archive, part 9/10
5   Luckett, private papers, p. 78
6   Ibid.
7   Ibid., p. 79
8   Churches, *Crow*, p. 122
9   Svete, 'Bojna pot', p. 41
10 WO 373/64/647, 'Recommendation for Award for Heslop,
    Walter John'
11 AWM119-A86, R. F. Churches Awarded BEM – Escaped POW
12 Dutt, unpublished diary
13 Churches, *Crow*, p. 105
14 Ralph Churches, 'Escape Memories', *Transcontinental*, May 1985
15 Churches, Australians at War Film Archive, part 9/10
16 Churches, 'Escape', *Transcontinental*

39: The Journey Home

1 Laws, 'I Was There – Memoir Extract', p. 6
2 Churches, *Crow*, p. 132
3 B883-NX5373, Kenneth Burke Rubie service record
4 Churches, *Crow*, p. 133
5 Žganjar, *Zomljena Krila*, p. 306
6 AWM54 781/6/7, CSDIC/CMF/SKP/3880, Kenneth Carson interrogation report
7 B883-NX5373, Kenneth Burke Rubie service record
8 In R20107912 NZ Interrogation Section – Unit Historical Records
9 Ralph Churches in *March to Freedom/Pot k Svobodi*
10 Ralph Churches to Andrew Hamilton, 10 January 1980, in Letters and Diaries
11 AWM119-A86, R. F. Churches Awarded BEM – Escaped POW
12 Churches, *Crow*, p. 146
13 Luckett, private papers, p. 82
14 Ralph Churches, unpublished manuscripts, 1945
15 Ronte Churches in Churches, *Crow*, p. 155

40: Greater Escapes?

1 In B883-SX5285, Ralph Churches service record
2 WO 202/456, Bari to Cuckold, 15 September 1944
3 WO 208/3259, 'History of IS9: Central Mediterranean Forces 1943 November–1945 May', p. 160
4 WO202/457, Cuckold to Bari, 18 September 1944
5 Sebastian Ritchie, *Our Man in Yugoslavia: The Story of a Secret Service Operative*, Routledge: London, 2005, p. 80
6 Blaž Torkar, *Mission Yugoslavia: The OSS and the Chetnik and Partisan Resistance Movements, 1943–1945*, McFarland & Company Inc.: Jefferson, 2020, p. 62

7 Žganjar, *Zomljena Krila*, p. 469

8 WO 202/457, Force 399 to Cuckold, 17 November 1944

9 Teropšič, *Štajerska vplamenih*, p. 79

10 WO 202/457, Force 399 to Cuckold, 15 November 1944

11 Lindsay, *Beacons*, p. 206

12 Cuckold to Force 399, December 9th, WO202/457

13 AMW54 781/6/7, CSDIC AIS/CMF/SKP/4678

14 Lindsay, *Beacons*, p. 321

15 WO 202/457, Matthews [Losco] to MI9, 21 December 1944

16 WO 202/456, MI9 to Matthews [Losco], 24 December 1944

17 Ritchie, *Our Man in Yugoslavia*, p. 123; Žganjar, *Zomljena Krila*, p. 304

41: The War's End

1 Štih, Simoniti, and Vodopivec, *Slovene History*, p. 436

2 Jože Pirjevec, *Tito and His Comrades*, University of Wisconsin Press: Madison, 2018, p. 114

3 PRO FO 371/48811, R57176/92 in Barker, *Social Revolutionaries*, p. 155

4 Marica Malahovsky in Bojan Godeša, *Kdor Ni z Nami, Je Proti Nam: Slovenski Izobraženi Med Okupatrji, Osvobodilno Fronto in Protierolucionarnim Taborom*, Cankarjeva Založba: Ljubljana, 1994, p. 317

5 Starič, *My Life in Totalitarianism*, pp. 139–40

6 Keith Lowe, *Savage Continent: Europe in the Aftermath of World War II*, Viking: London, 2012, pp. 234, 243

7 Volern, 'Memories of Alojz Volern', p. 89

8 Božo Repe, 'Changes in Life Style and Social and National Structures in Slovenia after World War Two', in Zdenko Čepič (ed.), *1945 – A Break with the Past: A History of Central European Countries at the End of World War Two*, Institute for Contemporary History: Ljubljana, 2008, p. 200

9 Velimira to Boris Kidrič in Aleš Gabrič, 'Opposition in Slovenia 1945', in Čepič (ed.), *1945 – A Break with the Past*, p. 183
10 Ibid., p. 151
11 Ales Gabrič, 'Slovenian Language and the Yugoslav People's Army', in Perovšek and Godeša (eds.), *Between the House of Hapsburg and Tito*, p. 217
12 Tomasevich, *War and Revolution in Yugoslavia*, p. 759
13 Josip Broz Tito in Pirjevec, *Tito and His Comrades*, p. 167
14 Ibid., p. 166
15 Tomasevich, *War and Revolution in Yugoslavia*, p. 759
16 A12091, R95-96, Colnik Karol, Australian Immigration File
17 Repe, 'Changes to Life Style', p. 200
18 Pirjevec, *Tito and His Comrades*, pp. 232, 237
19 Štih, Simoniti, and Vodopivec, *Slovene History*, p. 402
20 Igor Tchoukarina, 'Yugoslavia's Open-Door Policy and Global Tourism in the 1950s and 1960s', *European Politics and Societies and Cultures*, 20: 10 (2014), p. 13

Epilogue

1 WO 373/103/444, 'Recommendation for Award for Steilberg, Walter Henry Chrestense'
2 WO 417/96/2, 'Army Casualty Lists 17 August – 8 September 1945'
3 Ronald Corson to Griffin Rendell, 15 June 1949
4 Weale, *Renegades*, p. 120
5 Ralph Churches, diary, 1985, in Letters and diaries
6 Lindsay, *Beacons*, p. 345
7 WO 373/63/54, 'Recommendation for Award for Laws, Leslie Arthur Robert'
8 AWM88-AMF19, 'Citation SX5286 Private Ralph Frederick Churches'
9 Ronte Churches, interview, 9 August 2021

10 G. L. Kristianson, *The Patriotism of Politics: The Pressure Group Activities of the Returned Services League*, ANU Press: Canberra, 1966, p. 103

11 Kristy Campion, 'The Ustaša in Australia: A Review of Right-Wing Ustaša Terrorism from 1963–1973, and Factors that Enabled their Endurance', *Salus Journal*, 6: 2 (2018), pp. 48–9

12 NSW Special Branch, 'Australian Action Co-Ordinating Committee "The 50 Club"', 7 September 1966, in A6119-2332

13 'A Zealot Fights the Communist Conspiracy', *Sydney Morning Herald*, 29 September 1984

14 A. J. Kliner to Ralph Churches, 1 June 1986, in Letters and diaries

15 Ralph Churches to Uroš Zavodnik, January 2001, in Letters and diaries

16 Laws, 'I Was There – Memoir Extract', p. 5

17 Andrew Hamilton to Ralph Churches, 21 January 1980, in Letters and diaries

18 AWM119-86 and Andrew Hamilton to Ralph Churches, 21 January 1980, in Letters and diaries

19 Research Institute Ljubljana, *Allied Airmen and Prisoners of War*

20 Lowe, *Savage Continent*, p. 263

21 Vida Deželak Barič, 'Pregled mrliških matičnih knjig za ugotovitev števila ter strukturežrtev druge svetovne vojne in neposredno po njej', Inštitut za novejšo zgodovino, 2012, p. 12

Bibliography

Journal Articles, Theses, and Academic Papers

Anastasakis, Othan Evangelos. 'Authoritarianism in 20th Century Greece: Ideology and Education Under the Dictatorships of 1936 and 1967'. Thesis for PhD in Economics and Political Science, University of London, 2014.

Barefield, Michael R. 'Overwhelming Force, Indecisive Victory: The German Invasion of Yugoslavia 1941'. United States Army Command and General Staff College Monograph, 1993.

Barič, Vida Deželak. 'Participation, Role and Position of Slovenian Women in World War II Resistance Movement', *Qualestoria. Rivista di Storia Contemporanea*, 43: 2 (2015), pp139–62.

Barič, Vida Deželak. 'Pregled mrliških matičnih knjig za ugotovitev števila ter structure žrtev druge svetovne vojne in neposredno po njej'. *Inštitut za novejšo zgodovino*, 2012.

Barker, Thomas M. 'Partisan Warfare in the Bilingual Region of Carinthia', *Slovene Studies*, 11: 1–2 (1989), pp193–210.

Božič, Brane, Ludvik Čarni, Milica Kacin, Slavka Kajba, Marija Oblak, and Matija Žgajnar. 'Kronološki pregled dogodkov v Ljubljani v prvi polovici 1942. Leta', *Contributions to Contemporary History*, 2 (1958), pp205–74.

Campion, Kristy. 'The Ustaša in Australia: A Review of Right-Wing Ustaša Terrorism from 1963–1973, and Factors that Enabled their Endurance', *Salus Journal*, 6: 2 (2018), pp37–58.

Close, D. H. 'The Police in the 4th August Regime', *Journal of the Hellenic Diaspora*, 13: 1–2 (1986), pp91–105.

Črnič, Aleš, Mirt Komel, Marjan Smrke, Ksenija Šabec, and Tina Vovk. 'Religious Pluralism in Slovenia', *Teorije in Praska*, 50: 1 (2013), pp205–32.

Delivanis, D. J. 'Greek Economic and Financial Efforts 1940–1941', *Balkan Studies*, 23: 1 (1982), pp219–24.

Dreu, Lara Iva, 'Stalag XVIIID (306) – Nacistično taborišče za Sovjetske vojne ujetnike v Mariboru', *Retrospektive*, 3: 1 (2020), pp30–57.

Ferenc, Tone, Dare Jeršek, Miroslav Luštek, and Lozje Požun. 'Pregled pomembnejših dogodkov v letu 1943', *Prispevki za novejšo zgodovino*, 4: 1–2 (1963), pp113–80.

Ferenc, Tone. 'Wehrmannschaft: v Boju Proti Narodnoosvobodilni Vojski na Srajerskem', *Contributions to Contemporary History*, 2 (1958), pp81–156.

Frank, Robert. 'Formacija Brigad NOV in PO Slovenije'. Thesis, University of Ljubljana, 2003.

'Generalplan Ost', *Vierteljahrshefte für Zeitgeschichte*, 6: 3 (1958), pp281–325.

Harriman, Helga Horiak. 'Slovenia as an Outpost of the Third Reich'. MA dissertation, Wells College, Aurora, 1969.

Harriman, Helga Horiak. 'The German Minority in Yugoslavia, 1941–1945'. PhD dissertation, Oklahoma State University, 1975.

Hassiotis, Loukianos. 'Veterans' Stories of the British Campaign in Greece (1941)', *Byzantine and Modern Greek Studies*, 42: 2 (2018), pp287–302.

Hill, Maria. 'The Australians in Greece and Crete: A Study of an Intimate Wartime Relationship'. Thesis for PhD in History, Australian Defence Force Academy, University of New South Wales, 2008.

Horner, David. 'Britain and the Campaign in Greece and Crete in 1941', *National Institute for Defence Studies 2013 International Forum of War History: Proceedings* (2013), pp35–45.

Humar, Dushan Valentine. 'The Slovenian Minority in Italy 1918–1943: A Study of the Policy of the Italian Government'. MA dissertation, Loyola University, Chicago, 1951.

Just, Teodora. 'Partizanska Intendantska Služba na Štajerskem med NOB'. Thesis, University of Ljubljana, 2008.

Kaltenbrunner, Mattias. 'K-Häftlinge im KZ Mauthausen und die Mültviertler Hasenjagd'. MA dissertation, University of Vienna, 2011.

Knéjévitch, R. L. 'Prince Paul, Hitler, and Salonika', *Royal Institute of International Affairs*, 27: 1 (1951), pp38–44.

Kojančič, Klemen. 'Between Vlasov and Himmler, Russian SS-Sonder Regiment I "Waräger" in Slovenia, 1944–45', *Journal of Slavic Military Studies*, 30: 1 (2017), pp50–60.

Kolar, Bogdan. 'Consequences of the Communist Revolutionary Ideology for the Catholic Community in Slovenia', *The Person and the Challenges*, 3: 2 (2013), pp93–111.

Koliopoulos, John S. 'General Papagos and the Anglo-Greek Talks of February 1941', *Journal of the Hellenic Diaspora*, 8: 3–4 (1980), pp27–46.

Koliopoulos, John S. 'Unwanted Ally: Greece and the Great Powers, 1939–1941', *Balkan Studies*, 23: 1 (1988), pp89–98.

Košir, Uroš. 'When Violins Fell Silent: Archaeological Traces of Mass Executions of Romani People in Slovenia', *European Journal of Archaeology*, 23: 2 (2019), pp1–22.

Krzak, Andzey. 'Operation "Marita": The Attack Against Yugoslavia', *Journal of Slavic Military Studies*, 19: 3 (2011), pp543–600.

Laws, Leslie. 'I Was There – Memoir Extract', *Escape Lines Memorial Society Newsletter*, 46 (2018), pp4–7.

Maučec, Matilda. 'Lackov Odred', *Kronika*, 8: 3 (1960), pp141–9.

Pavletič, Gašper Šenica. '1. Brigad VDV – Enota za Borbo Proti Peti Koloni'. Dissertation, University of Ljubljana, 2020.

Petrović, Zorica. 'The Roman Catholic Church and Clergy in Nazi-Fascist Era on Slovenian Soil', *Athens Journal of History*, 4: 3 (2018), pp227–52.

Pirker, Peter. 'Partisans and Agents: Myths of the SOE Clowder Mission', Zeitgeschichte, 1: 38 (2011), pp21–55.

Pokrivač, Sandra. 'Britanski Misije pri Slovenskih Partizanih 1943–1945'. Dissertation, University of Maribor, 2011.

Presseisen, Ernst L. 'Prelude to Barbarossa: Germany and the Balkans 1940–41', *Journal of Modern History*, 32 (1960), pp359–70.

Radivojević, Biljana, and Goran Peñev. 'Demographic Losses on Serbia in the First World War and Their Long Term Consequences', *Economic Annals*, 59: 203 (2014), pp29–54.

Reinhard, Maria Isabella. '"An Isolated Case": The Slovene Carinthians and the 1920 Plebiscite', *Nationalities Affairs*, New Series 48 (2016), pp85–105.

Repe, Božo. 'Slovenia During the Second World War', International Scientific Conference 'The Second World War in the XX Century', Moscow, 5–9 September 1994.

Stephenson, E. 'Experiences of a Prisoner of War: World War 2 in Germany', *Australian Military Medicine*, 9: 1 (2000), pp42–50.

Svete, Miha. 'Bojna pot 2. Domobranskega udarnega bataljona "Vuka Rupnika"'. Dissertation, University of Ljubljana, 2016.

Tchoukarina, Igor. 'Yugoslavia's Open-Door Policy and Global Tourism in the 1950s and 1960s', *European Politics and Societies and Cultures*, 20: 10 (2014), pp1–22.

Toman, Tina. '14. Divizija: Pohod Oskrba'. Dissertation, University of Ljubljana, 2007.

Troch, Piter. 'Education and Yugoslav Nationhood in Interwar Yugoslavia – Possibilities, Limitations, and Interactions with Other National Ideas'. PhD thesis, University of Gent, 2012.

Vidovič-Miklavčič, Anka. 'Idejnopolitični značaj SLS od leta 1935 do začetka vojne leta 1941', *Prispevki za novejšo zgodovino*, 2 (2001), pp43–57.

Williams, Heather. 'The Special Operations Executive and Yugoslavia, 1941–1945'. PhD dissertation, University of Southampton, 1994.

Zalaznik, Mira Miladinović. 'The Origins and Impact of State Force: The Cases of Angela Vode and Igor Šenturjc', *Act Neophilologica*, 46: 1–2 (2013), pp13–24.

Ževart, Milan. 'Elaborat Štabu Treeckove Bojne Skupina o Narodnoosvobodilnem Boju na Štajerskem', *Časopis za Zgodovino in Narodopisje*, 56: 21 (1985), pp18–38.

Ževart, Milan. 'Nemška Ofenzica Proti Lackovema Odredu v Drugi Polovici Novembra in Preureditev Odreda v Začetku Decembra 1944', *Časopis za Zgodovino in Narodopisje*, 56: 21 (1985), pp18–38.

Ževart, Milan. 'Svobodna Partizanska Ozmelija na Slovenskem Štajerskem v Casu Narodnoosvobodilnega Boja', *Časopis za Zgodovino in Narodopisje*, 59: 24 (1988), pp167–99.

Books

Aarons, Mark. *War Criminals Welcome: Australia, a Sanctuary for Fugitive War Criminals Since 1945*. Black Inc: Melbourne, 2001.

Barker, Thomas M. *Social Revolutionaries and Secret Agents: The Carinthian Slovene Partisans and Britain's Special Operations Executive*. Columbia University Press: Boulder, 1990.

Beasley, A. W. *Zeal and Honour: The Life and Times of Bernard Freyberg*. Winter Productions: Wellington, 2015.

Bevc, Ladislav. *Liberal Forces in Twentieth-Century Yugoslavia: Memoirs of Ladislav Bevc*. Peter Lang: New York, 2007.

Bramsted, E. K. *Goebbels and National Socialist Propaganda 1925-1945*. Crescent Press: Michigan, 1965.

Brignoli, Pietro. *Santa Messa per i Miei Fucilati: Le Spietate Rappresaglie Italiane Contro i Partigiani in Croazia dal Diario di un Cappellano*. Longanesi: Milan, 1973.

Caffin, James. *Partisan – John Denvir New Zealand Corporal Yugoslav Brigadier*. Harper Collins: Auckland, 1945.

Carlton, Mike. *Cruiser*. Random House Australia: Sydney, 2010.

Carlyon, Norman D. *I Remember Blamey*. Macmillan Co. of Australia: Melbourne, 1980.

Catherwood, Christopher. *The Balkans in World War II: Britain's Balkan Dilemma*. Palgrave Macmillan: Basingstoke, 2005.

Čepič, Zdenko (ed.), *1945 – A Break with the Past: A History of Central European Countries at the End of World War Two*. Institute of Contemporary History: Ljubljana, 2008.

Chapman, Ivan D. *Iven G. Mackay: Citizen and Soldier*. Melway Publishing: Melbourne, 1975.

Churches, Ralph. *A Hundred Miles as the Crow Flies*. Estate of R. F. Churches: Kensington Victoria, 2017.

Churches, Ralph, Lado Pohar, Tone Kropušek, Franc Črešnar, and Vili Kos. *Vranov Let v Svobodo*. Društvo piscev zgodovine NOB Slovenije: Ljubljana, 2000.

Ciano, Galeazzo. *The Ciano Diaries 1939–1943: The Complete Unabridged Diaries of Count Galeazzo Ciano, the Italian Minister for Foreign Affairs, 1936–1943*, ed. Hugh Gibson. Doubleday & Company Inc: Garden City, 1946.

Corsellis, John, and Marcus Ferrar. *Slovenia 1945: Memories of Death and Survival After WWII*. Bloomsbury: London, 2020.

Crossland, James. *Britain and the International Committee of the Red Cross*. Palgrave Macmillan: Basingstoke, 2014.

Damer, Seán, and Ian Frazer. *On the Run: Anzac Escape and Evasion in Enemy Occupied Crete*. Penguin Books: Auckland, 2006.

Đilas Milovan. *Wartime*. Harcourt Bruce Jovanovich: New York, 1977.

Documents Relating to New Zealand's Participation in the Second World War 1939–45: Volume 1. Historical Publications Branch: Wellington, 1949.

Ewer, Peter. *Forgotten Anzacs: The Campaign in Greece 1941*. Scribe Publications: Brunswick, 2016.

Filipič, France. *Pohorski Bataljon*. Državna Založba Slovenije: Ljubljana, 1979.

Flemming, Francina. *A P.O.W.'s Letters: Life, Love, and Resilience*. Francina Flemming: Banora Point, 2019.

Foot, Michael R. D., and J. M. Langley. *MI9: Escape and Evasion*. Biteback Publishing: London, 2020.

Fry, Helen. *MI9: A History of the Secret Service for Escape and Evasion in World War Two*. Yale University Press: New Haven and London, 2020.

Gestin, Ferdo. *Svet Pod Krimom*. SAZU: Ljubljana, 1993.

Godeša, Bojan. *Kdor Ni z Nami, Je Proti Nam: Slovenski Izobraženi Med Okupatrji, Osvobodilno Fronto in Protierolucionarnim Taborom*. Cankarjeva Založba: Ljubljana, 1994.

Gold, Doug. *The Note Through the Wire*. Allen & Unwin: Auckland, 2019.

Granquist, Charles. *A Long Way Home: One POW's Story of Escape and Evasion During WWII*. Big Sky Publishing: Newport, 2010.

Greentree, David. *Gebirgsjäger vs Soviet Sailor: Arctic Circle 1942–1944*. Bloomsbury: London, 2018.

Greville, Howard. *Prison Camp Spies: Intelligence Gathering Behind the Wire*. Australian Military History Publications: Loftus, 1998.

Grove, Eric (ed.). *Great Battles of the Royal Navy as Commemorated in the Gunroom, Britannia Royal Naval College, Dartmouth*. Arms and Armour: London, 1994.

Gryzmala-Busse, Anna. *Nations Under God: How Churches Use Moral Authority to Influence Policy*. Princeton University Press: Princeton, 2015.

Guerrazzi, Amedeo Osti. *The Italian Army in Slovenia: Strategies of Antipartisan Repression, 1941–1943*, trans. Elizabeth Burke and Anthony Mahanlahti. Palgrave Macmillan: New York, 2013.

Himka, John-Paul and Joanna Beata Michlic (eds.). *Bringing the Dark Past to Light: The Reception of the Holocaust in Postcommunist Europe*. University of Nebraska Press: Nebraska, 2019.

Hirschfelt, Gerhard (ed.). *The Policies of Genocide: Jews and Soviet Prisoners of War in Nazi Germany*. German Historical Institute/ Allen & Unwin: London, 1986.

Horner, David. *General Vasey's War*. Melbourne University Press: Carlton, 1992.

Jambrek, Peter. *Crimes Committed by Totalitarian Regimes*. Slovenian Presidency of the Council of the European Union: Ljubljana, 2008.

Karlin, Alma M. Jezernik, Jerneja (ed.). *Dann geh ich in den grünen Wald: Meine Reise zu den Partisanen*. Drava: Klagenfurt, 2021.

Klanjšček, Zdravko, Tone Ferenc, Ivan Ferlež, Metod Mikuž, Alenka Nedog, Jože Novak, Miroslav Stepančič, and Miroslav Stipovšek. *Narodno Osvobodilna Voljna na Sloveneskem 1941–1945*. Vojaški Zgodovinski Inštitut Jugoslovanske Ljudske Armade in Inštitut za Zgdovino Delavskega Gibanja v Ljubljani: Ljubljana, 1976.

Kimber, Robert. *Walking Under Fire: The 1941 Greek Campaign of Major Bernard O'Loughlin, AIF*. Avonmore Books: Kent Town, 2018.

Kochavi, Arieh J. *Confronting Captivity: Britain and the United States and the PoWs in Nazi Germany*. University of North Carolina Press: Chapel Hill and London, 2005.

Kositch, Lazo M. *The Holocaust in the 'Independent State of Croatia' – An Account Based on German, Italian, and Other Sources*. Liberty: Chicago, 1981.

Kranjc, Gregor Joseph. *To Walk with the Devil, Slovene Collaboration and the Axis Occupation, 1941–1945*. University of Toronto Press: Toronto, 2013.

Kregar, Tone. *Vigred Se Pvrne: Druga Svetovna Voljna na Celjskem*. Muzej novojše zgodovine: Celje, 2009.

Kregar, Tone and Aleksander Žižek. *Okupacija v 133 Slikah: Celje 1941–1945*. Muzej novojše zgodovine: Celje, 2006.

Kristianson, G. L. *The Patriotism of Politics: The Pressure Group Activities of the Returned Services League*. ANU Press: Canberra, 1966.

Lilly, Carol S. *Power and Persuasion: Ideology and Rhetoric in Communist Yugoslavia 1944–1953*. Westview Press: Boulder, 2001.

Lindsay, Franklin. *Beacons in the Night: With the OSS and Tito's Partisans in Wartime Yugoslavia*. Stanford University Press: Stanford, 1993.

Levi, Primo. *If This is a Man*. Horwitz: London, 1963.

Long, Gavin. *Greece, Crete, and Syria*. Australian War Memorial: Canberra, 1953.

Lowe, Keith. *Savage Continent: Europe in the Aftermath of World War II*. Viking: London, 2012.

Lowenstein, Wendy. *Weevils in the Flour: An Oral Record of the 1930s Depression in Australia*. Hyland House: South Yarra, 1978.

Lušteke, Miroslav (ed.). *Dokumenti Ljudske Revolucije v Sloveniji: Knjiga 1 Marec 1941–Marec 1942*. Inštitut za Zgodovino Delavskega Gibanja v Ljubljana: Ljubljana, 1962.

Luthar, Oto. *Margins of Memory: Anti-Semitism and the Destruction of the Jewish Community in Prekmurje*. ZRC Publishing House: Ljubljana, 2012.

Martin, Allan William. *Robert Menzies: A Life, Volume 1*. Melbourne University Press: Carlton, 1993.

Martinčič, Vanja. *Slovene Partisan: Weapons, Clothings and Equipment of Slovene Partisans*. Muzej ljudske revolucije Slovenije: Ljubljana 1990.

McClymont, W. G. *To Greece*. Official History of New Zealand in the Second World War 1939–1945. Historical Publications Branch: Wellington, 1945.

Messenger, Charles. *'Bomber' Harris and the Strategic Bombing Offensive, 1939–1945*. Arms and Armour Press: London, 1984.

Melnyk, Michael James. *The History of the Galician Division of the Waffen-SS: Volume Two, Stalin's Nemesis*. Fonthill Media: Stroud, 2016.

Milač, Metod. *Resistance, Imprisonment, and Forced Labor: A Slovene Student in World War II*. Peter Lang: New York, 2002.

Monteath, Peter. *P.O.W.: Australian Prisoners of War in Hitler's Reich*. Pan Macmillan Australia: Sydney, 2011.

Morley, George. *Escape from Stalag 18a*. Meni Publishing and Binding: Cranbourne, 2006.

Mučeniška Pot k Svobodi. Slovenski Knjižni v Ljubljani: Ljubljana, 1946.

Münkel, Daniela. *Nationalsozialistische Agrarpolitik und Bauernalltag*. Campus: Frankfurt am Main, 1996.

Papagos, Alexandros. *The Battle of Greece 1940–1941*, trans. Pat Eliascos. J. M. Sczacikis 'Alpha' Editions: Athens, 1949.

Paterson, Jim. *Partisans, Peasants, and P.O.W.s: A Soldier's Story of Escape in WWII*. J. Paterson: Cottesloe, 2008.

Perovšek, Jurij, and Bojan Godeša (eds.). *Between the House of Hapsburg and Tito: A Look at the Slovenian Past 1861–1980*. Institute of Contemporary History: Ljubljana, 2016.

Petelin, Stanko. *Krajevna Skupnost Podpeč-Preserje v NOB*. SZDL: Ljubljana, 1983.

Pirjevec, Jože. *Tito and His Comrades*. University of Wisconsin Press: Madison, 2018.

Pirjevec, Jože, and Božo Repe (eds.). *Resistance, Suffering, Hope: The Slovene Partisan Movement 1941–1945*, trans. Breda Biščk and Manca Gašperšič. National Committee of Union of Societies of Combatants of the Slovene National Liberation Struggle: Ljubljana, 2008.

Pirker, Peter. *Subversion deutscher Herrschaft: Der britische Kriegsgeheimdienst SOE und Österreich*. Vienna University Press: Vienna, 2012.

Poljšak, Tone. *Nebo in Zemlja za Svobodo*. Sodelovanje NOB Slovenije Z Zavezvniki: Ljubljana, 1998.

Prusin, Alexander. *Serbia Under the Swastika*. University of Illinois Press: Champaign, 2017.

Rea, Paul. *Voices from the Fortress: The Extraordinary Stories of Australia's Forgotten Prisoners of War*. ABC Books: Sydney, 2007.

Research Institute Ljubljana. *Allied Airmen and Prisoners of War Rescued by the Slovene Partisans*. Research Institute Ljubljana: Ljubljana, 1946.

Ritchie, Sebastian. *Our Man in Yugoslavia: The Story of a Secret Service Operative*. Routledge: London, 2005.

Roberts, Barney. *A Kind of Cattle*. Australian War Memorial and William Collins Pty: Sydney, 1985.

Rogers, Lindsay. *Guerrilla Surgeon*. Collins: London, 1957.

Rowell, Sydney Fairbain. *Full Circle*. Melbourne University Press: Carlton, 1974.

Schweinickle, O. U. *The Book of a Thousand Laughs*. Wheeling: West Virginia, 1928.

Sirc, Ljubo. *Between Hitler and Tito: Nazi Occupation and Communist Oppresion*. A. Deutsch: London, 1989.

Speckner, Hubert. *In der Gewalt des Feindes: Kriegsgefangenenlager in der 'Ostmark' 1939 bis 1945*. R. Oldenbourg Verlag: Vienna, 2003.

Stanovnik, Janez, Grčar, Slavko, and Pirnovar Hardvik (eds.). *Narodnoosvobdilni Boj v Slovenskem Narodnem Spominu: Slovenski Zbornik 2007*. ZZB NOB: Ljubljana, 2007.

Starič, Peter. *My Life in Totalitarianism 1941–1991: The Unusual Career of an Electronics Engineer*. Xlibris Publishers: Bloomington, 2012.

Steinberg, Jonathan. *All or Nothing: The Axis and the Holocaust, 1941–1943*. Routledge: London, 1990.

Štih, Peter, Vasko Simoniti, and Peter Vodopivec. *A Slovene History: Society, Politics, Culture*, trans. Paul Townend. Inštitut za novejšo zgodovino: Ljubljana, 2008.

Stockings, Craig, and Elanor Hancock. *Swastika Over the Acropolis: Re-interpreting the Nazi Invasion of Greece in World War II*. Brill: Leiden, 2013.

Stout, Thomas. *Medical Services in New Zealand and the Pacific*. Official History of New Zealand in the Second World War 1939–1945. War History Branch: Wellington, 1956.

Stuckey, J. E. F. *Sometimes Free: My Escapes From German P.O.W. Camps*. J. E. F. Stuckey: Ashurst, 1977.

Teropšič, Tomaž. *Štajerska vplamenih: Taktika, orožje in oprema štirih vojsk na Štajerskem v drugi svetovni vojni*. Posavski Musej: Brežice, 2012.

Tomasevich, Jozo. *War and Revolution in Yugoslavia, 1941–1945: Occupation and Collaboration*. Stanford University Press: Stanford, 2011.

Torkar, Blaž. *Mission Yugoslavia: The OSS and the Chetnik and Partisan Resistance Movements, 1943–1945*. Macfarland & Company Inc.: Jefferson, 2020.

Trew, Simon. *Britain, Mihailović, and the Chetniks, 1941–1942*. Palgrave Macmillan: Basingstoke, 1998.

Tyquin, Michael. *Greece: February to April 1941, Australian Army Campaign Series 13*. Big Sky Publishing: Sydney, 2014.

Waller, John H. *The Unseen War: Espionage and Conspiracy in the Second World War*. Random House: New York, 1996.

Weale, Adrian. *Renegades: Hitler's Englishmen*. Pimlico: London, 2002.

Ževart, Milan. *Styriaca: Izbrana Dela*. Muzej Velenje: Velenje, 2005.

Žganjar, Matija. *Zomljena Krila: Reševanje Zavezniških Letalcev na Slovenskem Med Drugo Svetovno Vojno*. Zveza Združenj Borcev za Vrednote NOB Slovenije: Ljubljana, 2012.

Zierenberg, Malte. *Berlin's Black Market: 1939–1950*. Palgrave Macmillan: New York, 2015.

Žnidarič, Marjan. *Na Krilih Junaštva in Tovarištva*. Društvo piscev zgodovine NOB Slovenije: Ljubljana, 2009.

Unpublished Private Papers

Austin, Leonard Frederick. Private papers. 1985.

Bullard, Leslie. Private papers. 1940–45.

Churches, Ralph. Letters and diaries. 1947–2011.

Churches, Ralph. Unpublished manuscripts. 1945.

Churches, Ralph. Unpublished manuscripts. 1986.

Churches, Ronte. Interview. 21 July 2021.

Churches, Ronte. Interview. 9 August 2021.

Dutt, Kenneth. Unpublished diary. 1944.

Edwards, Eric. 'For You the War Is Over'. Unpublished manuscript. 1995.

Inch, L. B. to Willian Fagan, Robert McKenzie, and James Arrol. 'Re: L/Cpl Roy Nicholas Courlander'. 28 June 1949.

Kos, Vili. Maps and notes. 1985.

Luckett, Donald William. Private papers of D. W. Luckett, held by Imperial War Museum, London. 1989.

Volern, Alojz. 'Memories of Alojz Volern: The Years Leading up to Joining and Serving With the Partisans, and the Years After the War'. Robert Posl. 2017.

Newspapers

Edinost, The Guardian, Jutro, Marburger Zeitung, The New York Times, Slovensko Domobranstvo, Slovenec, Slovenski Poročevalec, The Sydney Morning Herald, The Transcontinental.

Archive Files

Australian National Archive:
A12091-R95-96, A6119-2332, AWM119-A86, AWM254-123, AWM419/19/42, AWM52-1/5/13/17, AWM52-8/2/17/27, AMW52-8/2/17, AWM54 534/3/4 , AWM54 779/3/128, AWM54 781/6/7, B883-NX5373, B883-QX1679, B883-QX4141, B883-SX5285, MP727/1-GO3/738, PR85/371, PR86-103.

New Zealand National Archives:
R20107912.

Slovenian National Archive:
File No. Unknown, Štabu IV. Operativne zone NOV in POJ Operacijski Odsek. Vojaško poročilo – štab XVI. Divizije NOB in POJ Operacijski Odsek. 2 September 1944.
SI AS 1757, Varnostna policija in varnostna služba na zasedenih ozemljih Gorenjske in slovenske Koroške, šk. 2.

UK National Archive:
FO 371/44255 R98160, FO 536/6/3159/42, FO 536/6/43/3144C/E, FO 916/25, FO 916/240, HS 5/896, WO 202/224, WO 202/456, WO 202/457, WO 204/9672A, WO 202/520, WO 202/309, WO 208/3250, WO 208/3259, WO 371/44255, WO 373/46/202, WO 373/46/226, WO 373/63/54, WO 373/63/183, WO 373/64/647, WO 373/103/444, WO 417/96/2.

United States National Archive:
CIA 25X1A2g.

Other Documents

Abel, J. and J. W. Jack (eds.). 'Prisoners of War Pamphlet'. *Joint Council of the Order of St. John and the New Zealand Red Cross Society*. No. 8, January 1943.

Australian Government Department of Foreign Affairs. 'Historical Documents Volume 4: 1940 June–1941 July'. Extracted from www.dfat.gov.au/about-us/publications/historical-documents/Pages/volume-04/1940-july-1941-june-volume-4, 11 January 2021.

Bratton, John S. 'One Man's War: Letters 1939–1945'. Extracted from www.stalag-xviii-a.com, 17 June 2021.

Catholic Bishops of Yugoslavia. 'Patirsko Pismo, katoličkih biskupa Jugoslavije, izdravo s općih Biskupskih Konferencija Zagreb, dne 20, rujna 1945'. 20 September 1945.

Huston, Dick. 'Memoirs'. Year unknown. Extracted from www.stalag18a.org/dickhuston.html/Markt_Pongau, 30 June 2021.

Liberation Front of Slovenia. 'Dolomitska Izjava'. 1 March 1943.

Rainer, Friedrich – Gauleiter von Kärnten, 'Wandzeitung: Eine wichtige Feststellung', 1942.

Slocombe, Alan. 'A Prisoner's Tale Retold: Chapter 1', BBC WW2 People's War. Extracted from www.bbc.co.uk/history/ww2peopleswar/stories/81/a6955581.shtml.

Taylor, Jack H. 'Dupont Mission'. OSS Archives. 1945. Extracted from Jewish Virtual Library, www.jewishvirtuallibrary.org/the-dupont-mission-october-1944-may-1945, 27 April 2021.

Wollaston, Ronald. 'Gunner Ronald Victor Wollaston'. Year unknown. Extracted from www.pegasusarchive.org/pow/ronald_wollaston, 6 September 2021.

TV and Film

Churches, Ralph Frederick. Australians at War Film Archive, No. 1094, interview 1 December 2003.

Die Deutsche Wochenschau, No. 703. 10 February 1944.

Edwards, Eric. Australians at War Film Archive, No. 1538, 4 March 2004.

March to Freedom/Pot k Svobodi. Directed by Tomaž Kralj. Sydney and Ljubljana: SBS and TV Ljubljana – Jugoslavija: Sydney and Ljubljana, 1985.

World War Two. Directed by Astrid Deinhard and Spartacus Olsson. Bernried am Starnberger See: Onlion Entertainment GmbH, Germany, 2018–22.

Online Articles

Association of Slovene Officers. 'Celjska Partizanska Četa'. 2016. Extracted from www.zsc.si/wp-content/uploads/2016/06/Celjska-partizanska-%C4%8Det1.pdf, 28 December 2020.

Cirman, Primož. Interview with Ivan Grobelnik, 'Noč, ko so iz nacističnega zapora rešili 129 ljudi interview'. Necenzurirano. 27 April 2021. Extracted from https://necenzurirano.si/clanek/mnenja/noc-ko-so-iz-nacisticnega-zapora-resili-129-ljudi-intervju-868748, 14 June, 2021.

Horvat, Marjan. 'Komandant Stane (spet) med Slovenci: Čigava podoba kroži po Evropi na kovancu za dva evra?' Mladina. 31 March 2011. Extracted from https://www.mladina.si/53641/komandant-stane-spet-med-slovenci/, 7 May 2021.

Morton, Peter. 'Adelaide'. SA History Hub, History Trust of South Australia. 15 January 2015. Extracted from https://sahistoryhub.history.sa.gov.au/places/adelaide, 14 November 2021.

Rudd, Bill. 'Anzac Freemen in Europe', 2017. Extracted from www.anzacpow.com/welcome_letter, 22 June 2021.

STA, 'Russian Ambassador Lays Wreath at Former Nazi Camp in Maribor', *Total Slovenia News*, 9 May 2020. Extracted from www.total-slovenia-news.com/politics/6202-russian-ambassador-lays-wreath-at-former-nazi-camp-in-maribor, 20 October 2020.

Vranetić, Ivan. 'The Righteous Among Nations Database', Yad Vashem – The World Holocaust Remembrance Centre.

Vidmar, Bogdan. 'Ob 76 – letnici strmš ke tragedije: Dražgoše
so sie opomogle, strmec pa ne'. Časnik, 14 September 2019.
Extracted from http://novice.najdi.si/predogled/novica/377e9
4ad6d2138e4a61340e8d9afa282/%C4%8Casnik/Slovenija/Ob-
76-letnici-strm%C5%A1ke-tragedije-Dra%C5%BEgo%C5%
A1e-so-si-opomogle-Strmec-pa-ne, December 10, 2020.

Photos

Connor, Alexander M. Photograph Collection. Australian War
Memorial. Catalogue numbers P00092.050–P00092.120.
Petek, Jože. Photographs of the 14th Division. 6 September 1944.
Current location of collection unknown.

Acknowledgements

I would like to thank the patient indulgence of many friends who have heard me tell versions of this story for too many years. Jamie Bradbeer for suggesting I begin to write the details down. Helen Garner for challenging me to find more of the story's heart. Heather Morris for assuring me that the story needed a wide readership. Jurij Rifelj for being a tireless promoter of Slovenian–Australian friendship. Jana Grilc for opening so many doors in Slovenia. Herman Novak for being my first Slovenian trail guide (and mushroom hunter). Špela Strasser and Matej Pistor for mapping The Crow's Flight trail and being such excellent company, day after day. Dare Alič for bringing Partisan history to life in stories along the escape route. All the Slovenians I have met anywhere in the world who have encouraged me with generous hospitality, kindness and pride in this story. Monty Halls who invited me to Slovenia to talk about my father on film. Liberty Smith who found so much archival material. Edmund Goldrick who was a gift from heaven, the perfect researcher, historian, critic and enthusiast, the story would not be grounded by documentation without him. My brother Steven who gave endless practical suggestions and highly amusing critiques, as well as proofreading. My mother Ronte for her recollections and her patience with questions and opinions as to my father's motives. Lisa Charter for her delighted interest and feedback, particularly in the early draft stage. Mary Smith for being a disinterested reader, seeking clarification and more direct structure, as well as for just keeping my feet on the ground. My daughter Lucy for travelling to Slovenia with me, walking in Ralph's footsteps and wanting to know the story. To my father for his outrageous character, his way of making his own crazy luck and for finding his way home.

Edmund Goldrick would like to thank Diane and Phil Sullivan, without whose love and kindness his participation would not have been possible. Špela Gašperšič and Jaka Kolbl Krokar for their endless generosity and kindness. Luka Kolbl for inadvertently setting up this adventure, and providing invaluable materials and translation assistance. Ahmad Elmouniery for going above and beyond to extract material from the UK National Archives. Rebecca Banović for her wise counsel. Živa Jahr for further translation help. Dare Alič, Gregor Joseph Kranjc, Deidre Mussen, Roger Stanton, Blaž Torkar, and Eduard Vedernjak, for their historical expertise. The late Brian Sims and his friend Dennis Hill for providing Brian's research. That research led to the 'eureka' moment that confirmed the involvement of Allied intelligence in the escape. The staff of the Australian National Archives, the Australian War Memorial Archives, the Manildra Library, the National Museum of Contemporary History of Slovenia, and the UK National Archives, for their tireless assistance. The families of escapees for personal insights and materials, foremost Shirley Jorritsma, Steve Luckett, and Geoff Rendell. My godfather, Eric Grove, for his historical inspiration. Sadly, Eric did not live to see this published. Lastly, my parents, James and Ruth, for their constant love and support.

Image Credits

All photos are from the personal collection of Ralph Churches, with the exception of the following:

p. 1   *bottom* courtesy of State Library of South Australia (SLSA): SRG 168/1/58/20

p. 3   *top* courtesy of SLSA: B 9359/2

p. 4   *bottom* Australian War Memorial (AWM), reference number P09366.001

p. 5   *bottom* courtesy of *The Adelaide Advertiser*

p. 6   *top* AWM, photo by Bruce Brock, reference number P02038.043

p. 7   *top* '2nd NZEF troops on retreat in Greece. Taken by an unidentified photographer in 1941.' From the Collection: New Zealand. Department of Internal Affairs. Reference number: DA-01603-F. Permission to use kindly granted by the Alexander Turnbull Library at the National Library of New Zealand (NLNZ); *bottom* AWM, photo by George Silk, reference number 007617

p. 8   *top* Muzej Novejše Zgodovine Slovenije (MNZS); *bottom* 'Prisoners of war being questioned by the International Red Cross, Wolfsberg, Austria.' From the Collection: New Zealand. Department of Internal Affairs. Reference number: DA-11730-F. Permission to use kindly granted by the Alexander Turnbull Library at the NLNZ

p. 9   *top* AWM, reference number P00092.094; *bottom* MNZS
p. 10 *top* from the collection of Shirley Jorritsma
p. 12 *bottom* MNZS
p. 13 *bottom* MNZS